Courting the People

The Indian higher judiciary has acquired an increasingly important role in India's public discourse in the last few decades. The Supreme Court and the state High Courts have emerged as enormously powerful judicial institutions in the aftermath of the Internal Emergency of 1975-77. The principal means through which these judicial powers have been enacted is the jurisdiction of Public Interest Litigation (PIL). This book studies the political role that PIL has come to play in contemporary India. It revisits the circumstances and manoeuvres that led to the rise of PIL and traces its political journey since then, arguing that the enormous powers that PIL confers upon the appellate judiciary stems from its populist character.

Based on empirical research, it shows how PIL grants the appellate courts enormous flexibility in procedure allowing them to manoeuvre themselves into positions of overweening authority. It focuses on the most intensive laboratory of PIL in recent times, the city of Delhi, and foregrounds the role that PIL has played in the radical reconfiguration of the city in the 21st century. While PIL cases are usually politically analyzed solely in terms of their effects, whether beneficial or disastrous, this book locates the political challenges that PIL poses in its very process: arguing that its fundamentally protean nature stems from its mimicry of ideas of popular justice.

This book examines PIL as part of a larger trend towards legal informalism in post-Emergency India. Casting a critical eye at these institutional reforms that aimed to adapt the colonial legal inheritance to 'Indian realities', this book looks at the challenges posed by self-consciously culturalist juridical innovations like PIL to ideas of fairness in adjudication as well as democratic politics.

Anuj Bhuwania is assistant professor in the Department of Sociology at South Asian University, New Delhi. He studied law in National Law School of India University, Bangalore and School of Oriental and African Studies, London before doing his PhD in Anthropology at Columbia University in New York. He has held visiting positions at the Centre for Modern Indian Studies, University of Goettingen, the Centre for the Study of Developing Societies (CSDS), New Delhi and the Centre for the Study of Law and Governance (CSLG) in Jawaharlal Nehru University.

SOUTH ASIA IN THE SOCIAL SCIENCES

South Asia has become a laboratory for devising new institutions and practices of modern social life. Forms of capitalist enterprise, providing welfare and social services, the public role of religion, the management of ethnic conflict, popular culture and mass democracy in the countries of the region have shown a marked divergence from known patterns in other parts of the world. South Asia is now being studied for its relevance to the general theoretical understanding of modernity itself.

South Asia in the Social Sciences will feature books that offer innovative research on contemporary South Asia. It will focus on the place of the region in the various global disciplines of the social sciences and highlight research that uses unconventional sources of information and novel research methods. While recognizing that most current research is focused on the larger countries, the series will attempt to showcase research on the smaller countries of the region.

Published titles:
Government as Practice: Democratic Left in a Transforming India
by Dwaipayan Bhattacharya

Courting the People

Public Interest Litigation in Post-Emergency India

Anuj Bhuwania

CAMBRIDGE
UNIVERSITY PRESS

CAMBRIDGE
UNIVERSITY PRESS

University Printing House, Cambridge CB2 8BS, United Kingdom
One Liberty Plaza, 20th Floor, New York, NY 10006, USA
477 Williamstown Road, Port Melbourne, vic 3207, Australia
4843/24, 2nd Floor, Ansari Road, Daryaganj, Delhi – 110002, India
79 Anson Road, #06–04/06, Singapore 079906

Cambridge Univerisity Press is part of the University of Cambridge.

It furthers the University's mission by disseminating knowledge in the pursuit of education, learning and research at the highest international levels of excellence.

www.cambridge.org

Information on this title: www.cambridge.org/9781107147454

First published 2017

Printed in India

Library of Congress Cataloging-in-Publication Data
Names: Bhuwania, Anuj, author.
Title: Public interest litigation and political society in post-emergency India / Anuj Bhuwania.
Description: New York : Cambridge University Press, 2016. | Includes bibliographical references and index.
Identifiers: LCCN 2016013219 | ISBN 9781107147454 (hardback)
Subjects: LCSH: Public interest law—India. | India—Politics and government—21st century. | BISAC: SOCIAL SCIENCE / Sociology / General.
Classification: LCC KNS80.P78 .B48 2016 | DDC 344.54—dc23 LC record available at https://lccn.loc.gov/2016013219

ISBN 978-1-107-14745-4 Hardback

Contents

Acknowledgements

This book has come into being because of the support of a large number of people over a period of many years, and I have incurred more than my share of intellectual and personal debts in this process. The book is a reworked version of my PhD dissertation at the Anthropology Department in Columbia University. Brinkley Messick was a remarkably patient and supportive advisor, showing faith in this project right from its conception to the final phase. His sense of excitement about this project was infectious and reinvigorating just when my self-belief was flagging. Partha Chatterjee's works were the inspiration that led me to graduate school in the first place, and it has been a privilege to work with him. I am also grateful to the other faculty members of my doctoral committee — Brian Larkin, Ritty Lukose and Sudipta Kaviraj — who have all contributed to this project in crucial ways and stayed enthusiastic throughout, always ready for critical engagement. The fieldwork for this book was funded by a National Science Foundation Doctoral Dissertation Research Fellowship for Law and Social Sciences and a Junior Research Fellowship from the American Institute for Indian Studies.

This book was incubated over a hot Delhi summer due to the personal legal predicament faced by Jean Drèze, Bela Bhatia and other residents of Sanjay Basti. The short but memorable experience of working closely with them on their case was the point of entry for me into this project. The interminable discussions of the short-lived 'Working Group on Delhi Land Laws' that Jawahar Raja, Shrimoyee Nandini Ghosh, Malavika Vartak and I collectively set up as a result of this case (with Lawrence Liang joining in later) first set the ball rolling. All of these partners in crime have remained valuable interlocutors throughout the project.

Pratiksha Baxi's camaraderie has been crucial in keeping my interest alive in social science work on law, and in legal anthropology in particular. The Centre for the Study of Law and Governance at Jawaharlal Nehru University provided an academic home in Delhi just when I was feeling snowed under by fieldwork and the enormity of my research agenda. Thanks in particular are due to Jaivir Singh and Niraja Gopal Jayal. Much of the writing was done while teaching at Jindal Global University (JGU) and I want to thank all my colleagues there for their support. I particularly want to thank my students who opted for the optional seminar on 'Public Interest Litigation' that I taught at JGU. I am grateful to my colleagues and students in the Sociology department at South Asian University, whose cooperation has made the completion of this book possible.

I want to thank all the people who agreed to be interviewed for this research, in particular Anita Shenoy, Aparna Bhat, Bhure Lal, Colin Gonsalves, Gyanant Singh, Harish Nair, Prashant Bhushan, Pushkar Sood, Dr Rajeev Dhavan, Sanjay Parikh, Shiv Sagar Tiwari, Justice Vijender Jain and Justice J.S. Verma. Conversations with Arun Thiruvengadam, Upendra Baxi and Usha Ramanathan over the years have greatly influenced my understanding of PIL. Many friends have, sometimes unwittingly, been my informal interlocutors during these years –Aniruddha Jairam, Arkaja Singh, Arudra Burra, Bipin Aspatwar, Diya Mehra, Jinee Lokaneeta, Jules Naudet, Lalit Batra, Mathew John, Rehan Abeyratne, Rohini Mohan, Sandipto Dasgupta, Shahrukh Alam, Shivprasad Swaminathan and Siddharth Narrain have all been subjected to multiple exchanges, dialogues and diatribes on PIL.

Niraja Gopal Jayal, Lawrence Liang, Arudra Burra, Gautam Bhatia and Jawahar Raja read the manuscript with a critical eye and their feedback was most useful. Karthik Rao Cavale's insightful inputs on Chapter 3 and Shivprasad Swaminathan's on Chapter 4 have helped tremendously. I am grateful to Srirupa Roy for her enthusiasm for this book project and for organizing a special event to discuss the manuscript at Gottingen. Narendra Subramanium, Lekha Sridhar and Prashant Iyengar provided excellent food for thought with their careful engagement with sections of the manuscript at this event.

The editors at Cambridge University Press, Delhi, in particular Debjani Majumder, Qudsiya Ahmed, Anwesha Rana and Aditya Majumdar, have been a pleasure to work with and I am grateful for their remarkable patience and unwavering support throughout this process. I want to thank the three anonymous peer reviewers for their constructive feedback, and to the Series Editors for including this book in the 'South Asia in the Social Sciences' series. Earlier versions of the first three chapters have been published in the following journals: Comparative Studies of South Asia, Africa and the Middle East (CSSAAME), South Asia Multidisciplinary Academic Journal (SAMAJ) and Projections: MIT Journal of Planning. I am grateful to Duke University Press and the other publishers for permission to republish the earlier material.

My parents, Om Prakash and Sumitra Bhuwania, have always had an abiding faith in the power of education in spite of a family milieu in which very little of it existed, but even they could have hardly anticipated that it would carry me this far afield. They have remained rock-solid in their support all these years. My brothers, Ashim and Achal Bhuwania, and parents-in-law Ujjwal and Sushma Gupta, though all eventually quite bemused by my prolonged student life, managed to remain understanding through it all.

Finally, the reason my academic interest in anthropology first got initiated was because of Trisha Gupta. She came to believe in this book project even more than I did, in spite of being forced to live with it for so long. Her indefatigable support, just when all seemed lost, is really why this book got written at all. Most tangibly it was her editing that untangled my knotty prose into some shape, improving it considerably at ridiculously short notice. My gratitude to her is immeasurable.

Introduction

In recent years, 'PIL' has made an appearance in many a Hindi film. Two examples come to mind. In the somewhat ungrammatically titled *Sahib, Biwi aur Gangster Returns*, the mention of PIL comes when a state legislator – the eponymous *Biwi*, whose official position has come to her by dint of being married to a small-time prince in the North Indian state of Uttar Pradesh – decides to take some interest in what's going on in her constituency. The first important piece of information her office assistant provides her with is that a PIL has been filed against land acquisition for a development project in her area. Her baffled response is, 'Yeh PIL kya hota hai?' ('What is PIL?') She is clearly ill-informed. But that the film chooses to invoke PIL to show her complete political cluelessness, and that the astounding nature of this fact will be immediately apparent to the audience watching popular cinema, the lowest common denominator in India if there is one, gives us some clue perhaps to the omnipresence of PIL in contemporary Indian life. The second film, a satirical comedy called *Jolly LLB*, is much more directly concerned with the operation of the judiciary. It centres around a small-town lawyer who is trying to make it big in Delhi's law courts and decides that filing a PIL might be the quickest way to get media attention. In a scene that made it into the film's promotional trailer, a judge is shown angrily throwing away Jolly's legal brief, saying, 'What kind of PIL have you filed? You have spelt Prosecution as Prostitution and appeal as apple!' Clearly, PIL is one kind of legal process everybody understands. As much as 'appeal' and 'prosecution', it has entered the Indian demotic lexicon.

So widespread is its reach that PIL has become a sort of metonym for the greatness of the Indian judiciary. No area of Indian law has been written about as extensively (and almost entirely hagiographically) as PIL. There are more American law review articles on PIL than on any other area of Indian law. Indeed, Indian judges routinely cite these approving articles to hail their own achievements. PIL has by now been successfully transplanted in other neighbouring South Asian countries as well[1]. PIL is celebrated by all and sundry as India's unique contribution to contemporary jurisprudence. Lest it appear that I subscribe to this culturalist understanding linking PIL to its Indian-ness, I hope it will soon be apparent that my aim is precisely to question such a move. The remarkable thing, as we will see, is that such a self-consciously culturalist manoeuvre was exactly what enabled and accompanied the rise of PIL.

This book will study the history and politics of Public Interest Litigation, or PIL as it is popularly known, a jurisdiction unique to the Indian higher judiciary that arose in the late 1970s in the aftermath of the political emergency of 1975–77. It has been hailed as the most dramatic democratizing move that the Indian judiciary had made in the post-independence period. For example, according to legal scholar Usha Ramanathan, PIL led to an explosive 'jurisprudence of constitutional relevance and the rejection of redundancy of peoples'.[2] She argues that it enabled the court to extend a unique invitation to journalists, activists, academics and anyone else who may be a witness to constitutional neglect and lawlessness to participate in the judicial process.

A PIL is pursued by filing a writ petition either in one of the various State High Courts or the Supreme Court. This avenue was already available under the Indian Constitution but PIL makes recourse to it significantly easier. PIL is primarily a revolution in procedure, and its innovative features that emerged in its early years have been usefully summarised by a commentator Wouter Vandenhole:

a. The rules of *locus standi* were relaxed.
b. The formal requirements regarding the lodging of a petition were simplified.
c. Evidence could be gathered by a commission appointed by the court.
d. The procedure adopted was claimed not to be of an adversarial nature.
e. The court could order far-reaching remedial measures.
f. The execution of the remedial orders was supervised and followed up.

As Vandenhole summed them up: 'The first two innovations concern the start of the procedure, the next two have to do with its course, and the last two with its outcome.'[3]

Legal scholar Lavanya Rajamani explains the effect of these innovations:

> The power of public interest litigation (PIL) in India lies in its freedom from the constraints of traditional judicial proceedings. PILs in India have come to be characterized by a collaborative approach, procedural flexibility, judicially supervised interim orders and forward-looking relief. Judges in their activist avatar reach out to numerous parties and stake-holders, form fact-finding, monitoring or policy-evolution committees, and arrive at constructive solutions to the problems flagged for their attention by public-spirited citizens. Judges have tremendous power, in particular in PILs, to design innovative solutions, direct policy changes, catalyse law-making, reprimand officials and enforce orders. And, they are not hesitant to exercise this power in what they perceive as the public interest. Where there is a perceived 'vacuum in governance, the Court rushes to fill it'.[4]

In order to begin to make sense of such celebratory clamour, a brief introduction to the structure of the Indian judicial system is necessary. Robert Moog, an eminent sociologist of Indian law, provides this useful summary:

> India's judiciary is a three-tiered, integrated system. The Supreme Court, which sits in New Delhi, is the only all-India forum. High Courts stand at the head of the judiciary in each state. These are the intermediate appellate courts in the system, but they also have writ jurisdiction. The third tier is the district-level courts. Despite India's federal system of government, the court system is integrated in the sense that there is no bifurcation between state and federal judiciaries. These three tiers form a single hierarchy and administer both state and federal laws.[5]

It is important to keep in mind that the heroic persona of the Indian judiciary – made possible by PIL – is reserved only for the State High Courts and the Supreme Court. Indeed, thanks to PIL, the higher judiciary is often viewed as the panacea for the various endemic social and political problems that plague India. The lower judiciary, the system of civil and criminal courts at the district level, on the other hand, is perceived as purely pathological – inefficient, corrupt and overly embedded in the Indian social milieu – while the appellate courts of course apparently transcend it. A remarkable paradox about studying India's judiciary is the simultaneously held diametrically opposite view of the two wings of the same integrated system. This schizophrenia has been sustained for a long time and is only getting worse. One clue to the management of such an unsullied image by the higher judiciary, in the face of the impression of such extreme pathology below it, is the distancing tactic that the members of the higher judiciary have perfected: to intermittently express despair at the condition of the lower courts. Robert Moog gives a good example of this when he quotes a Supreme Court judge declaring from the bench in 1995, 'It is common knowledge that currently in our country criminal courts excel in slow motion.'[6] The higher judiciary has successfully evaded any responsibility for the problems of the lower judiciary, although strictly speaking, they have direct vertical oversight over the latter.

Moog has analyzed such appellate treatment of lower courts in India in some detail. One effect of such despair is a constant 'search for alternatives, which range from versions of the more traditional *panchayats* (village or caste), such state-run forums as *lok adalats* (people's courts) or the widening array of tribunals…'[7] Another result of this skewed judicial system is, as Moog demonstrates, 'an increased flow of cases to High Courts and the Supreme Court in the form of appeals, revisions, reviews, or the use of the upper courts' writ jurisdiction to avoid the district courts entirely.'[8] Thanks particularly to the proliferation of writ petitions as convenient shortcuts to the High Court, the judicial system has gradually become so top heavy that by the early 1990s, Moog estimated that 'the High Court has become the single most active trial court in the state of Kerala'. Article 226 of the Indian Constitution empowers the High Courts to issue writs for the enforcement of Fundamental Rights and for any other purpose, allowing its use against a breach of any legal right by the state. The Supreme Court has an analogous provision under Article 32, enabling writ petitions to be filed directly before it. Such relative ease of access to the higher judiciary, Moog has argued, has further undermined:

> the public's perception of the quality of justice they receive from the subordinate courts. These very liberal appeals and writ policies encourage the impression that justice ultimately flows from the High Courts and/or the Supreme Court. They also feed the image that what the lower courts produce is a lower quality of justice, compounding the credibility problems these courts already have. These courts therefore become hurdles to get over, or avoid altogether (for example, through the writ jurisdiction), rather than forums from which final resolution of disputes is expected.[9]

Another symptom of this Indian version of 'appellate-court-itis',[10] is the common habit of lawyers describing themselves as 'Supreme Court advocate' or 'High Court advocate'. The premium put on these appellate courts means that associating with them quickly became a status symbol as if some of the charisma of these institutions would rub off on the lawyers practicing there. This practice, implying a higher status for a lawyer of a higher court, continues despite India having a rationalized legal profession since 1961 where there is no strict forum-based limitation on a lawyer and any lawyer is free to practice in a forum of her choice. This convention takes a particularly bizarre form when it comes to criminal lawyers because this is one field where the trial court is by definition the most important arena where evidence is recorded and where most of the real action actually occurs. But even then, in contemporary India's endless mediatized debates on criminal law reform, one will rarely find lawyers who regularly appear in trial courts. Invariably, it will be the appellate lawyers basking in the reflected glory of their higher location in the food chain of India's judiciary.

In this Indian malaise, the exalted status of appellate courts is also physically marked by their entry barriers, enhanced security set-up and monumental architecture. On the other hand, trial courts are easily accessible and are often compared derisively to railway stations, those most democratic and unruly of modern Indian public spaces. Indian appellate-court-itis has been compounded manifold by the political vanguardism of these courts in the post-emergency era through PIL. It is important to note that PIL has not only conferred a new conspicuousness and higher political status to India's appellate judiciary, but to its dramatis personae as well, the charisma of heroic PIL judges often matched by those of PIL lawyers, Amicus Curiae and PIL petitioners, even if the latter are increasingly vestigial, as we shall see. Playing to the gallery is par for the course and can bring rich dividends. The theatricality of PIL also lends it a devoted audience of legal journalists, hanging on to every word, who impart to these performances the publicity implicitly demanded from them. All of these are important constituencies of India's appellate courts whose self-perception gets progressively accentuated, thanks to PIL.

***

Returning to live in Delhi in 2006, after being away for nearly four years, I found that PIL had become ubiquitous in everyday discourses around the city. The urban fabric seemed torn asunder by PIL cases intervening in almost every part of the administration. The courts gave the impression of governing the city through the instrument of PIL. Newspaper headlines routinely quoted statements by the Delhi High Court threatening to shut down the Municipal Corporation of Delhi (MCD): 'Stop farmhouse weddings or we will shut MCD: HC'[11] or 'Catch monkeys or shut down, HC tells MCD'.[12] Slums labelled 'encroachments' were being demolished all over the city under court orders, the incidents reported with relish by new periodicals like *Neighbourhood Flash* and local sub-city supplements such as *South Delhi Live* that had begun to come bundled with major newspapers like the *Hindustan Times*. The city news became the site of both the demand and supply of the courts' attention. Any political intervention against any of this – or even the intention of an intervention – would be declared 'populist'. In those days, if one followed the city news at all, PIL was inescapable. The legal correspondent for a daily newspaper who reported from the Delhi High Court later described the period to me thus: 'I would have seven bylines in the first six pages. The government used to function with contempt of court hanging over it.'[13] There were PILs pending related to so many aspects of the city's governance that newspapers would periodically carry random lists of such cases – the case topics in one such list included simian trouble, stray menace, urinals, no-parking zone, tinted glasses, save Yamuna, nursery admissions, Blueline buses, traffic fines, MCD demolitions, plastic ban, India Gate subways, free beds in hospitals, free seats in schools and illicit liquor – all of these were just in the Delhi High Court and this was by no means an exhaustive list.[14]

The city was being remade through the means of PIL. Indeed, Delhi had already been transformed significantly because of PIL cases over the past decade, as we shall see in Chapter 2. Every aspect of Delhi's transport – for example, auto rickshaws, cars, buses, cycle rickshaws – had been reconfigured because of PIL. Urban heritage was another arena of PIL's regular intervention: in November 2006, I was a witness to a well-connected lawyer specializing in heritage conservation cases threatening a local government official with the words 'Main toh bas PIL thok doongi (I will just slap a PIL [on you]).' Later, in December 2007, I heard an environmental scientist heading a new biodiversity park express the worry that the foreign species he had planted would be challenged by a PIL (This actually did happen, a year later.)

PIL procedure had enabled the court to monitor and micromanage every aspect of the city's governance, making the whole city the direct object of its reformative attention. The all-encompassing nature of the court's control over the city through PIL was slowly brought home to me as I began to follow the leads thrown up by newspaper headlines. In 2006, for instance, I was struck by the headline 'Supreme Court chides Delhi Government for Power Muddle'.[15] The story turned out to involve a PIL about the lack of access to adequate electricity in the capital city that had been admitted in 1999 by the Supreme Court at the instance of a senior advocate. The case came to be legally titled 'Power Crisis in National Capital Territory of Delhi vs Union of India'. The senior advocate in question was made the amicus curiae, meaning 'friend of the court'. The court went on to supervise the privatization of electricity in Delhi from 1999 onwards. By 2003, when privatization was complete, the PIL came to focus on transmission and distribution losses attributed to power theft. By 2006, this particular PIL's remit had turned to inadequate power supply in Delhi, and the court heard big power-generating companies talk of setting up 1,000 megawatt gas-based power plants. In May 2006, the judges in this case reportedly expressed the worry that if the power situation in the capital did not improve, 'how will we organize the Commonwealth Games in the year 2010 here?'[16] More than four years before the scheduled games, the PIL court's worry about the availability of electricity in Delhi was expressed through anxiety about the high-profile event. The court's ire in this case throughout this period was particularly excited by power theft in 'illegal' settlements – unauthorized colonies and especially slum clusters. While ostensibly the court's concern was the city as a whole, it were these communities that had emerged as the most visible symbols of illegality in its eyes. It was this conspicuousness that it wished to erase.

***

I will illustrate the qualitatively transformed nature of the relationship between the court and the city's heterogenous publics in this period by discussing three revealing vignettes from three PIL proceedings I encountered during my fieldwork. The first was in March 2007 during the hearing of a case in which a two-judge bench of the Supreme Court was supervising the formulation of the Municipal Corporation of Delhi's draft scheme for grant of *teh bazaari* (vending rights) to street vendors in Delhi. The case was *Sudhir Madan vs MCD*.[17] The MCD scheme had envisaged a process that would require first identifying sites in the city where hawking could be carried out, then inviting applications from interested eligible people and then granting such rights. During the day-long hearing, an alternative was suggested to the MCD scheme by one of the vendors' organizations. They suggested instead that first a census be conducted for the existing street vendors in the city and based on that ground-level mapping, vending rights be formalized at the already existing sites. The judges were livid at such a suggestion. If such a suggestion was accepted, Justice B. P. Singh interjected, Delhi would have to be renamed 'Hawker Nagar (lit. 'hawker city')'. There would soon be hawkers selling food in the Supreme Court building, he exclaimed[18].

The second vignette is from a hearing before a two-judge bench of the Delhi High Court in 2009, where a PIL against begging on the streets of Delhi was being heard.[19] The presiding judge, Sanjay Kishan Kaul, was particularly agitated about the proliferation of beggars in Delhi. He was specifically concerned about having come across beggars even while being chauffeured around the India Gate roundabout, the heart of the imperial capital. If the situation remained unchanged, he said, the day was not far when there would be beggars in the High Court building itself. The bench went on to order the active implementation of 18 'zero tolerance zones' for beggars in Delhi, including road intersections near New Delhi's court complexes as well as all railway stations and bus terminals in the city.

My final vignette is from a hearing in a PIL about traffic congestion in Delhi in 2006,[20] which was narrated to me in an interview by one of the lawyers in this case. As part of this PIL, the High Court had ordered the removal of a slum called Nangla Machi, which abutted an arterial road in Central Delhi and was allegedly causing traffic jams. When arguments were raised by a lawyer for the slum-dwellers in a court hearing, Justice Vijender Jain pointed out that currently the slum concerned was less than two kilometres from the High Court. If action was not taken immediately, he said, the slum dwellers would soon invade the court premises itself and squat there.

A spectre was haunting the court. The spectre of the unruly masses of the city – street hawkers, beggars and slum dwellers – invading its pristine environs. These were precisely the unwashed masses that PIL had originally invited into the courtroom. But now, PIL seemed to have adopted a path where it wanted to devour its own.

Political commentators Nivedita Menon and Aditya Nigam called the fantasy of 'Delhi-en-route-to-Paris' being played out in the city around 2006, the result of a 'judicial coup d'etat':

> Propelled by a judiciary with no accountability and a media that is deeply implicated in this new game, there has emerged a technocratic elite which desires hypermodern cities cleansed of all the 'mess' and 'irrationality' that comes with democracy and the people.[21]

Clearly, the higher judiciary with PIL as its principal weapon had taken over Delhi by 2006, affecting changes significantly different from the pious original aims of the PIL jurisdiction.

How did this jurisdiction of PIL, which arose with the court speaking in the name of the people, become parasitical on the very same people? Delhi in the 2000s was going through a process of dramatic transformations that seemed recognizably along the lines that were being affected in cities all over the world, usually termed as 'neoliberalism'. What marks Delhi's dislocations as distinct is their source and their basis – they were not based, as in the past, on administrative or municipal policy or executive directions, but on judicial directions in a series of PILs concerning the city. Delhi had emerged as the most relentless laboratory of the PIL jurisdiction. The question worth asking is how and why PIL emerged as the primary agent of 'neo-liberalism' in Delhi. Or rather, why did 'neoliberalism' in Delhi take the PIL route? This is what I will explore in this book.

A clue to understanding the new role played by the PIL court can be found in the other commonalities shared by all three of the cases mentioned above. These were all PILs which dealt squarely with three major problems that Delhi was perceived as having an excess of – street vending, begging and traffic congestion. In each case, the city as a whole was the site for reform. Even more crucially, in all of these PILs, the petitioner was either irrelevant, had been excised or had never even existed. All three were PIL cases owned and led by the court itself. A different form of adjudication – if one can call such PILs adjudication at all – was at work in all three of them.

I will briefly examine each of these three cases to highlight the strange new powers with which PIL had empowered the court. The street vendors' case, *Sudhir Madan vs MCD*[22] had been deployed to supervise policy formulation on this issue since 1987, when it was first filed. The petitioner had been made irrelevant and an array of parties concerned with street vending involved. The begging case was slightly different. *Court on Its Own Motion vs In Re: begging in Public* did not have a petitioner in the first place. The court initiated it as a *suo motu* case and appointed an *amicus curiae* to assist it. The third case, *Hemraj vs Commissioner of Police,* began with a plea to curtail goods traffic in a specific locality of Delhi called Chhattarpur. But, after this specific issue had been resolved, *Hemraj*'s remit was expanded to deal with the problem of traffic congestion in the entire city. The petitioner was made redundant and an 'amicus curiae committee' appointed.

A new kind of judicial process had emerged, entirely court led and managed, sometimes even initiated and implemented by its own machinery. The court appointed its own lawyers and instrumentalities. Such radical departures from basic norms of adjudication could be honed to perfection in PIL cases as they were never envisaged to have any procedural limitations in the first place. There was almost no institutional control of these cases at all, except such self-control that the court wished to exercise.

A new kind of PIL had emerged – what I call an 'Omnibus PIL'. A PIL that had originally been filed to address a specific problem in a specific part of the city could now be turned into a matter that dealt with that particular problem *all over the city*. In such an Omnibus PIL, the petitioner with his specific concerns about a particular place would be removed, and an amicus curiae appointed to guide the court. The whole city would be subject to intervention and correction through this process.

Through this new maneuver, PIL became a means to target those populations living on the margins of legality, who had hitherto been protected by their elected representatives. These illegalized citizens were ordinarily not even made parties to these omnibus PIL proceedings. These conspicuously illegal communities of the urban poor were seen as obstructing the neat solutions to the problems of the city. They would have to go as collateral damage. That they were there in the first place was because of the everyday political networks that Partha Chatterjee has called 'political society'.[23] These were the networks most drastically unravelled by this new kind of PIL.

The Omnibus PIL-led judicial interventions in almost every area of urban governance were cumulative and interlinked and are perhaps better understood as an aggregation rather than as isolated instances. The multiplicity of court-appointed bodies, the lack of clarity about their terms of reference and procedures, the extent of their investigative or executive powers and the non-availability of their records or minutes together made the entire adjudicatory process of PIL impenetrable and almost impossible to challenge. I came across an example of such opacity on a blazing hot morning in May 2007 when I received a frantic call from a friend in Nizamuddin Basti, informing me about shops being demolished near the famous Sufi shrine of Hazrat Nizamuddin Aulia. On reaching there, I came across a municipal 'demolition squad' going about their 'job' with large hammers and pickaxes (the lanes in this area are far too narrow for bulldozers.).

My persistent questions to the Assistant Engineer in charge of this demolition, about the orders under which it was being carried out, fetched only a vague response from him about it being a Supreme Court order in the 'M. C. Mehta case'.[24] I knew, however, that there were half a dozen 'M. C. Mehta' cases pending in the Supreme Court, so this wasn't particularly useful. I made at least 20 phone calls from my mobile phone, standing next to the demolition squad, just calling all the phone numbers of the various court-appointed committees I knew of, to try and figure out which of them had ordered this particular action. But, to no avail. After further requests, the best the leader of the demolition squad would do was to give me the phone number of the Deputy Commissioner of that particular municipal zone, for further following up. I mention this instance as an illustration of the incredible legal illegibility that characterizes the materiality of PIL procedure. At that point of time, there were so many PIL cases pending under which both the Supreme Court and the Delhi High Court were ordering demolitions that it was virtually impossible to keep track of them, and people living and working in the fringes of legality had come to expect the worst.

The orders in these cases were often specific directions, which were unreported and difficult to access, as they were given in a bewildering array of 'interim' applications in open-ended Omnibus PILs. Indeed, PIL cases did not often end up in any 'judgments' at all but in an endless spiral of 'orders', which are not reported in law journals. However, much of the scholarship on PIL has continued to concentrate on the 'completed' judicial process, i.e. judgments and other reported decisions of the courts, and the discursive charge they have. Yet because of the way in which the PIL jurisdiction has developed, most of its concrete actions are based on interim orders. These are in the nature of what legal scholar Upendra Baxi has called 'creeping jurisdiction', where the court regularly hears reports about the status of compliance with its orders, and gives further interim orders, usually without passing a final judgment.[25] Researching PIL in all its materiality required me to focus attention on such minutiae rather than rely solely on judgments as traditional legal scholarship tends to do.

This book tries to engage in a method that Kim Lane Scheppele has described as 'constitutional ethnography', defined as 'the study of the central legal elements of polities using methods that are capable of recovering the lived detail of the politico-legal landscape.'[26] The focus throughout is on 'a set of repertoires that can be found in real cases and that provide insight into how constitutional regimes operate.'[27] PIL emerges as a robust instance of constitutionalism seen:

> As a set of practices in which the transnational ambitions of legal globalization flow over and modify the lived experience of specific local sites, and as a set of practices in which local sites inescapably alter what can be seen as general meanings.[28]

The higher judiciary has hardly ever been the locus of such an anthropological study, and this book hopes to address this lack. While legal academia in India is obsessed almost exclusively with the higher judiciary, legal anthropology has solely focused on trial courts and panchayats. This perhaps is related to the fetishization of the unmediated face-to-face interaction with the litigants in a dispute or trial that the ethnographer can represent, and a discomfort with the heavily mediated drama of an appellate court – where the litigant is marginal or even absent and the lawyers represent their cases through heavily textualized presentations. Of course, part of the reason PIL is anthropologically interesting is because it is very deliberately presented as providing substantive, popular justice, unmediated by legalese and with an emphasis on questions of fact rather than law (even if it is actually ill-equipped to adjudicate on disputed questions of fact, as we will see).

***

The research for this book was done over a 30-month period in Delhi between March 2007 and August 2009. The research began with the following up on one particular demolition notice of one particular slum. The notice listed a writ petition under which its demolition had been ordered, which none of the inhabitants of the settlement had ever heard of. I started helping with the legal response to this action. But understanding and legally responding to this order required the unravelling of one of the great omnibus PILs then pending in Delhi High Court – the *Kalyan Sanstha* case. Understanding the enormity and the bizarreness of this case led me to start following a series of cases relating to slum demolitions in Delhi. For the first one year, my research focus was purely on PIL cases related to demolitions. But gradually I realized that court-led slum demolitions had to be studied in the context of other PILs, particularly those related to urban governance. Thereafter, my fieldwork was aimed at understanding PIL per se by studying the practices around it. My research involved participant observation in various PIL courts over a long period. Being a qualified lawyer, I had no problem accessing the appellate courts, which would otherwise be difficult, especially the Supreme Court. Having earlier practiced in Delhi as a lawyer for a year, I was somewhat familiar with the daily life of these court complexes and could be a fly in the wall when needed.

I would regularly attend hearings of PIL cases and followed some of the key cases over a long period. In those days, the Chief Justice's court in the Delhi High Court would exclusively hear PIL cases on Wednesdays. This weekly day-long event was a perfect place to witness the theatre of PIL. The other regular weekly event was the Forest Bench in the Supreme Court every Friday afternoon. This one case had set the pace for so many of the innovations of PIL that witnessing its proceedings helped me get a sense of just how far gone PIL really was. There was also the biweekly *tamasha* of the 'miscellaneous days' of the Supreme Court on Mondays and Fridays, when matters for admission would be heard. After the hearings of the specific PIL, the action moved outside where the journalists would congregate to get bytes and documents from the litigant lawyers.

During this period, I conducted interviews with several lawyers, judges, journalists, litigants, court commissioners and court-appointed monitoring committee members, many of whom were old PIL hands. A remarkable aspect about interviewing lawyers was the effortless ease with which they would move from cynicism to sincerity – from being supremely gossipy and irreverent on court corridors to being dead earnest during interviews, mouthing well-practiced platitudes.[29] Because the conversation involved PIL, the transition was even more extreme, moving from the sheer randomness of its everyday reality to its so-called ideal. During this fieldwork period however, PIL was not just in the courtroom. It was literally everywhere in the city. Everybody had something to say about PIL, especially in the media. The extent to which the English newspapers drove the PIL discourse in the city during this period was astonishing. They performed as chorus, prompters, critics as well as of course the devoted audience of PIL. Interacting with regular court reporters both inside and outside the courtroom was always insightful, especially because unlike the lawyers, they would not so easily put on masks of sincerity.

This book is aimed at addressing the politics of PIL per se. Because PIL is primarily a revolution in judicial procedure, the focus is on the transformation in the nature of adjudication itself that PIL enables. Instead of focusing on specific areas of substantive legal doctrine enunciated in PIL cases, the attempt here has been to think through the quotidian realities of the PIL process. I argue that the fundamental nature of PIL is to be understood in terms of its protean nature that its departures from basic legal procedure make possible, rather than in terms of the themes it addresses, whether it be gender, environment or urban affairs. The instances of PIL that have been taken for critical study here are, therefore, meant to illustrate the kinds of powers that PIL confers to appellate judges. The fact that there are many PIL judges, who do not necessarily take the liberties that the judges in the cases I discuss do, does not take away the fact that the PIL jurisdiction empowers them to do so. These cases illustrate the extreme extent to which PIL enables judges to go. The emphasis here is not so much on the unjust outcomes of these cases, rather it is on the profound injustice of the judicial process adopted in them.

To adapt David Scott's memorable turn of phrase in *Conscripts of Modernity*[30] to my purposes: PIL has often been talked of as a romance – if anything, as a romance gone wrong. In this book I will argue that PIL was a tragedy to begin with and has over time become a dangerous farce.

Chapter 1 provides a revisionist account of the origin of PIL in India. For a long time, there has been a general consensus that PIL arose as the court's attempt at exorcism its guilt for its emergency era performance. The question that is generally elided is why the response of the court had to be in the form of PIL. The chapter examines how and why the court chose to perform the rhetorical performative labour of populism through PIL. This is followed by an analysis of some of the early controversies around PIL focusing on the radical innovations in judicial procedure being introduced through this jurisdiction, culminating with a discussion of the decline of the role of the public interest petitioner.

Chapter 2 is a study of a PIL case filed in the Supreme Court of India in 1985, which is still pending. This case has single-handedly been responsible for the de-industrialization of Delhi and has had many significant avatars, with its cause of action changing multiple times: from pollution caused by stone-crushing units to pollution in the river Yamuna to removing 'encroachers' from the ridge forest to mining in areas of neighbouring Haryana's tourist resorts and Aravalli hills to its closing down of all 'hazardous' and large industries in Delhi to its closing of all 'non-conforming' industries, finally moving to its most famous avatar – as 'the sealing case'. A key attribute common to all of these 'environmental' causes taken up in this case was that most of the poor adversely affected parties were not even heard by the court while passing far-reaching orders. Class-based exclusions were materially inscribed within the adjudicatory processes of PIL.

Chapter 3 examines how the radical nature of PIL procedure enabled it to function as a highly effective slum demolition machine. Almost a million people were made homeless by the wonders of PIL in the first decade of the twenty-first century in Delhi. This ferocious campaign utilized the undemocratic potential of PIL to the fullest. The chapter will focus on the mechanisms of court-appointed fact-finding entities, from court commissioners to monitoring committees to amicus curiae. These were combined with the steamrolling quality of omnibus PIL cases to devastating effect.

Chapter 4 examines in some detail the two principal strands of critique that PIL has attracted – one which I call narrowly consequentialist led by the left-liberal and activist constituency, and the other a more institutional response led by critical self-reflection from the Bench itself. In the conclusion, I examine as to how the pathology of PIL has infected Indian legal culture more generally and the challenge it poses to democracy in India.

Endnotes

1 See Razzaque, *Public Interest Environmental Litigation in India, Pakistan and Bangladesh*. For Pakistan, see Khan, 'Genesis and Evolution of Public Interest Litigation in the Supreme Court of Pakistan.' For Nepal, see Paudel, 'Public Interest Litigation in Mountainous Ecosystem.' The Indian Supreme Court noted the rise of PIL in some of these countries in the *State of Uttaranchal vs. Balwant Singh Chaufal & Ors.* (18 January 2010). Since 2009, Pakistan's appellate courts have invoked their PIL powers so often that novelist Mohammed Hanif joked, 'Even the half of Pakistan that can't read or write will tell you what a *suo motu* is,' http://www.theguardian.com/commentisfree/2012/jun/22/yousuf-raza-gilani-chief-justice-pakistan

2 Ramanathan, Review of SP Sathe's *Judicial Activism in India.*

3 Vandenhole, 'Human Rights Law', pp. 147–48.

4 Rajamani, 'Public Interest Environmental Litigation in India', p. 294.

5 Moog, 'Judicial Activism', p. 271.

6 Moog, 'The Significance of Lower Courts in the Judicial Process', p. 1392. At the same time, legislative attempts to address the notorious delay in India's mainstream legal system have been undone by interpretations from the appellate courts which make these reforms meaningless. When strict timeframes for completion of various processual steps in civil proceedings were introduced in the Civil Procedure Code, the Supreme Court repeatedly relaxed the timeframes inserted by the amendments and restored to the courts discretion to dilute them in accordance with the courts' perceived sense of justice. Ranjan, 'Supreme Court of India and the Jurisprudence of Delay.'

7 Moog, 'The Significance of Lower Courts in the Judicial Process', p. 1393.

8 Moog, 'The Significance of Lower Courts in the Judicial Process', p. 1392.

9 Moog, 'The Significance of Lower Courts in the Judicial Process', p. 1400.

10 I am borrowing this term popularized by Jerome Frank (1970) in his famous attack on Benjamin Cardozo's writings on judicial process. My interest is not in the celebration of serenity in appellate court process which Frank was attacking, or the lack of it in India, but the normativization of appellate court behaviour as ideal typical judicial behaviour per se.

11 *Indian Express*, 14th January, 2006.

12 *Times of India*, 18th January, 2006.

13 Interview conducted in March 2009.

14 http://archive.indianexpress.com/news/paperjam-in-lawcourts/446253/0

15 http://www.thehindu.com/todays-paper/supreme-court-chides-delhi-govt-for-power-muddle/article3094106.ece

16 http://timesofindia.indiatimes.com/india/Power-crisis-SC-steps-in-seeks-explanation-from-Centre/articleshow/1518285.cms

17 Writ Petition (Civil) 1699 of 1987.

18 The reality of course is that almost all Indian cities are already 'hawker nagars'. The planned heart of Lutyens' Delhi is perhaps the only exception – but that is where Delhi's appellate judges live and work. The organization's lawyer in this case countered the judge, saying that the 'most modern of cities' have hawkers on the streets, including London and New York. There followed a factual disagreement with Justice B.P. Singh insisting that in his biannual trips to London, he had never seen street vendors on Oxford Street while the lawyer said there indeed were.

19 *Court on Its Own Motion vs. In Re:begging in Public*, Writ Petition (Criminal) No. 1840/2006. For an insightful description of the history of this case, see Ramanathan, Ostensible Poverty, Beggary and the Law, pp. 33–44.

20 *Hemraj vs. Commissioner of Police*, W.P.(C) No. 3419 of 1999. This case is discussed in some detail in Chapter 3.

21 Menon and Nigam, Lambs at the Law's Guillotine.

22 Earlier in this same case, while instructing the MCD to formulate such a scheme, the court had already shown its hand, 'The scheme need not be populist in its appeal, but must be practical and consistent with the rights of citizens, who have a fundamental right to use the roads, parks and other public conveniences provided by the State.' *Sudhir Madan vs. MCD*, 3 March 2006.

23 Chatterjee, *Politics of the Governed.*

24 M. C. Mehta is a Delhi-based lawyer who is probably the most well-known PIL petitioner in India, having filed dozens of such cases, most related broadly to the environment and many which have been now going on for more than 20 years.

25 Baxi, *Taking Suffering Seriously.*

26 Scheppele, 'Constitutional Ethnography', pp. 89–148.

27 Scheppele, 'Constitutional Ethnography', pp. 89–148.

28 Scheppele, 'Constitutional Ethnography', pp. 89–148.

29 See Goffman, *The Presentation of Self in Everyday Life*, pp. 17–24.

30 Scott, *Conscripts of Modernity: The Tragedy of Colonial Enlightenment.*

1

Competing Populisms

Revisiting the Origins of Public Interest Litigation in India

> It is by no means merely a matter of misguided theory that the French concept of *le peuple* has carried, from its beginning, the connotation of a multi-headed monster, a mass that moves as one body and acts as though possessed by one will; and if this notion has spread to the four corners of the earth, it is not because of any influence of abstract ideas but because of its obvious plausibility under conditions of abject poverty.
>
> —Hannah Arendt, *On Revolution*

The Indian Supreme Court is widely considered the most powerful judicial institution in the world.[1] The rise in its power follows the reconfiguration of Indian political life in the aftermath of the Emergency of 1975–77. In the last 35 years, it has acquired a central role in Indian public discourse.[2] The principal means by which the court has acquired its new importance is the phenomenon of 'Public Interest Litigation', or more commonly PIL – a term that is too easily translated into its American (and hence 'global') counterpart but in fact has little in common with it. PIL is a unique feature of the Indian appellate judiciary. It is not simply *pro bono* lawyering, something that a certain tribe of lawyers do, like in the United States. In India, PIL is a jurisdiction – that is, what some judges are empowered to do in a specific capacity provided or interpreted in the law. As Canadian scholar Jamie Cassels wrote in 1989, 'Unlike the case of public interest litigation in Canada or the United States, the legal aid/public interest movement in India has been almost entirely initiated and led by the judiciary.'[3]

The Indian form of PIL jurisdiction was born in the immediate aftermath of the Emergency, through the ingenuity of the Supreme Court commonly seen as trying to undo the legacy of its capitulation to the political rulers of that period. PIL, right from the start, was marked by impatience with technical formalities and a key rhetorical mode increasingly deployed by judges: arguments made in the name of 'the people'. In other words, the court redefined itself as the fount of substantive justice: portraying itself as the 'last resort for the oppressed and bewildered'.[4]

In this article, I will map the discursive context that PIL responded to and reconfigured with enormous popular appeal – locating its roots in the political language of India of the 1970s. In fact, the emergence of PIL was famously hailed in the early 1980s by the leading Indian legal scholar Upendra Baxi, indicating that the court had 'at long last' become the 'Supreme Court for Indians'. I will explore here this 'people's court'[5] aspect of the Indian Supreme Court. My effort, in particular, is to understand why the court needed to position itself as speaking for 'the people', and how it managed to do so. I will first address the 'why' and then, the 'how' of the journey that the Supreme Court of India undertook in the post-Emergency period in order to be able to ventriloquize 'the people'.

Constitutional roots of PIL

The first question here is this: Why did the Supreme Court emerge so powerfully only in the post-Emergency period? After all, the court's powers under the Indian Constitution have remained largely unchanged since the constitution first came into force in 1950. The answer to this conundrum lies partly in the text of the constitution and partly in the specific political conjuncture of 1970s India. Sudipta Kaviraj has argued that, 'the political history of independent India can be divided into two distinct historical periods to date.'[6] The first lasted until the late 1960s, and its political life could be 'fit unproblematically into the liberal-individualist format of constitutional arrangements'. By the late 1970s, Kaviraj argues, there emerged a new 'vernacular' to Indian politics based on the languages of caste, region and religion.[7] A similar periodization, I argue, can be made for the Indian Supreme Court, though in its case, as we shall see, gestures towards vernacularization were self-consciously adopted to mimic trends in the larger Indian political domain.

The Indian Constitution, in the words of its most famous historian, Granville Austin is a seamless web of three mutually dependent and intertwined strands : first, a federal governance structure that has its roots in the late colonial era Act of 1935; second, principles of democracy and universal adult suffrage providing popular sovereignty and drawing from the Congress party and the freedom movement; and finally, and most crucial for our purposes, ideas of social revolution that stemmed, in an immediate sense, from the Objectives Resolution adopted during the December 1946 Assembly session.[8] The most radical departures signifying a move towards a postcolonial constitutional framework were incorporated in parts III and IV of the Constitution, both parts being products of elaborate comparative constitutional scholarship by the framers. Part III lists 'Fundamental Rights: mostly negative rights borrowed from Euro–American history, with some interesting departures facilitating state intervention to ensure socio-religious equality. But, it is part IV that makes the Indian Constitution a teleological text, a transformative constitution that squarely tries to deal with 'the social question' of widespread poverty. Its key provisions prescribe the direction to which the state must aspire (The idea of having 'Directive Principles of State Policy', as these provisions are called, was borrowed from the Irish Constitution.). Uday Singh Mehta has argued that the incorporation of such constitutionally prescribed futures implied that 'the nation was now conceived as a project.'[9] Unlike the U. S. Constitution, the Indian Constitution was not primarily a procedural document, as American Constitutional scholar John Hart Ely has argued, but a substantive one.[10] To place it in a comparative frame made famous by Hannah Arendt, and applied to India by Mehta, the Indian Constitutional revolution follows the French example, not the American one. It sets out to deal with 'the social question', i.e., with how the issues of material destitution and inequality might be addressed. As Mehta writes, 'For Arendt, the American Constitution served as an ideal in which political power was limited, public freedom secured, and national unity anchored in the structures of political institutions – and all this was possible only because social questions were kept at bay.'[11] But, it is not the American model that the Indian and most other postcolonial constitutions adopt. American Constitutionalism 'stemmed from a deep distrust of power. . . . The first impulse of this constitutionalism was thus to limit political power, to be suspicious of it, and to constrain its reach.' Indian Constitutionalism, on the other hand, constitutes power and 'celebrates its ambit'.[12] Channeling Arendt's famous warning that 'every attempt to solve the social question by political means leads to terror'[13], Mehta suggests that in India too, with such a vision, 'freedom is recessed, and the tendency for political power to operate without limits deeply ingrained.'[14]

The socially revolutionary agenda of the Indian Constitution, as mentioned above, is incorporated into the Directive Principles of State Policy. These principles, though non-justiciable, unlike the Fundamental Rights, were declared to be 'fundamental in the governance of the country'. As Austin summarized it, the Directive Principles contain 'a mixture of social revolutionary – including classically socialist – and Hindu and Gandhian provisions.'[15] Mehta explains the teleological nature of part IV thus:

> This constitutionally enshrined vision of the future is what has often been seen as implying an activist and capacious state, responsible for the eradication of poverty, undoing the stigmas of casteism, improving public health and education, building large industry, facilitating communication, fostering national unity, and, most broadly, creating conditions for the exercising of freedom.[16]

But this freedom itself needed to be postponed and seen 'as a future prospect' that would come about as a result of the project of social revolution. The Indian Constitution would make the assertion of freedom conditional on achievements that could be at best prospective. As Mehta argues, 'The successful culmination to free oneself from imperial subjection led almost immediately to freedom itself becoming a subsidiary concern; that is, subsidiary to national unity, social uplift, and a concern with recognition.'[17]

The tension between this implicit ideological devaluation of freedom, which had been enshrined in the Fundamental Rights chapter and thereby made justiciable, with the project of the new state, as incorporated in the Directive Principles, would soon become the principal juristic battleground of the post-independence period. The political discourse that emerged around it saw Fundamental Rights as an obstacle to the realization of the social revolution as enunciated in the Directive Principles. This conflict framed the fraught relationship between the judiciary and the Congress regimes in the immediate aftermath of the adoption of the constitution. The most obvious reason for the conflict was that the Supreme Court had specifically been made the custodian of Fundamental Rights by the constitution, while the Directive Principles were after all, legally speaking, merely the aims of the state without any force of law.

The powers of the Supreme Court under the new constitution are important to note here. The Indian Supreme Court is not a constitutional court alone. It is a successor not only of the Federal Court set up under the 1935 late colonial constitutional statute, but also of the Privy Council located in London, which had, throughout the colonial period, the discretion to entertain and decide all Indian cases as the final court of appeal. Most important, the Supreme Court brought into being by the Indian Constitution in 1950 acquired a new original jurisdiction – to hear writ petitions to enforce fundamental rights against the state. Insofar as it decides disputes between the central government and the states and between states, it also functions as a federal court. And insofar as it has the power to grant 'special leave to appeal' under Article 136, it can hear any appeal from any court in India.

The granting of this last power led to an interesting debate in the Constituent Assembly. One of the members of the assembly, Pandit Thakur Das Bhargava, discussed the court's powers with regard to Article 136 in terms that would come to haunt later.[18] I quote below Bhargava's remarks on Article 136, which was then numbered 112, and Article 142, then numbered 118.

> Our Supreme Court shall be fully omnipotent as far as a human court could be and it shall have all kinds of cases.... *My humble submission is that Article 112 is the remnant of the most accursed political right of the divine right*

> *of kings. At the same time the jurisdiction of the article is almost divine in its nature*, because I understand that the Supreme Court will be able to deliver any judgment which does complete justice between states and between the persons before it. If you refer to Article 118, you will find that it says
> 'The Supreme Court in the exercise of its jurisdiction may pass such decree or make such order as is necessary for doing *complete justice* in any cause or matter pending before it, and any decree passed or order so made shall be enforceable throughout the territory of India in such manner as may be prescribed by or under any law made by Parliament.'
> So far so good, but my humble submission is that the Privy Council also, which as a matter of fact belonged to Great Britain and which was a sign of our judicial domination by the British, had very wide powers and proceeded to dispense justice according to the principles of natural justice. What is this natural justice? This natural justice in the words of the Privy Council is above law, and I should like to think that our Supreme Court will also be above law in this matter, in this sense that it shall have full right to pass any order which it considers just; and in this light, I beg to submit before the House that this is a very important section and gives almost unlimited powers and as we have got political swaraj, we have judicial swaraj certainly. Thus, the Supreme Court will be in this sense above law. I want that this jurisdiction which has been enjoyed by the Privy Council may be enjoyed and enlarged by our court and not restricted by any canon or any provision of law.[19] (My emphasis).

We see here a recognition of the 'accursed' genealogy of the vast powers given to the Indian Supreme Court, making it in a sense 'above the law'. But the knee-jerk desire to nationalize this potentially despotic power ensured its survival. Indeed, another prominent Constituent Assembly member even called the Supreme Court a potential 'Frankenstein monster'.[20] The 'divine' powers of the Supreme Court would, however, remain dormant for the first three decades of its existence but would be essential to the court's new political role in post-Emergency India.

It's interesting to note here, in light of the future growth of PIL ostensibly as a form of accessing the Supreme Court, that a member of the Constituent Assembly had suggested that:

> Those citizens who are so poor as not to be able to move the Supreme Court, should be enabled under proper safeguards, of course at the cost of the State, to move the Supreme Court in regard to the exercise of any of these fundamental rights.[21]

Such a simple means to provide access to the Supreme Court to the indigent was on nobody's agenda at the time. But over time, the court's relative inaccessibility emerged as the stick to beat it, as we shall see, with long-term consequences.

The great constitutional conflict: 1950–77

The constitutional provisions underlying the powers of the higher Indian judiciary would come into play immediately after the constitution came into force on 26 January 1950, with the legal battles on land reform – the signature post-independence programme meant to bring about the promised social revolution. The first move came on 5 June 1950, when the Bihar High Court struck down as unconstitutional – as a violation of the right to property – a law enabling the government to take over zamindars' estates without compensation. Nehru's response to this judgment was immediate and extreme. The first constitutional amendment was pushed through Parliament, which would, among other things, declare land-reform statutes beyond the scope of judicial review.[22] The mood of the moment can be gauged from Nehru's famous comment in Parliament while debating the amendment: 'Somehow we have found that this magnificent constitution that we have framed was later kidnapped and purloined by the Lawyers.'[23] The First Amendment implied, according to an apocryphal statement by a later chief justice, that 'the Indian Constitution became the only one that contained a provision providing for protection against itself.'[24] The more the Supreme Court fought for a higher market-value compensation for the landlords, the stronger Nehru's response was: he kept amending the constitution to reverse court decisions.[25] According to the eminent legal scholar Rajeev Dhavan, by the mid-1950s, the courts had 'backed off – but gracefully, without wholly surrendering their power of judicial review.'[26] What emerged from the episode was a détente with the court and an embrace of what Dhavan calls 'Nehru's Planning Commission model of law and social change.'[27] This was very much of a piece with the then dominant modernization theory and its approach to 'law and development', which privileged the state's desire to carry out social engineering through law. The lead figure in this *modus vivendi*, the first of many, was Justice Gajendragadkar. Dhavan describes his approach as being 'to assure the government that judges would strive for social justice by playing a supportive role in empowering the government to achieve its goals.'[28] The court, in this period, repeatedly upheld the Parliament's absolute right to amend the constitution.

This compact imploded in 1967, when the Supreme Court gave a decision in *I. C. Golaknath vs. State of Punjab* that would bar any amendment of the Fundamental Rights chapter in the constitution. The rationale for this decision had been explained by Justice Hidayatullah in an earlier minority decision from the Gajendragadkar era, where he wrote,

> The constitution gives so many assurances in part III [the Fundamental Rights chapter] that it would be difficult to think that they were the plaything of a special majority. To hold that would mean prima facie that the most solemn part of our constitution stands on the same footing as any other part.[29]

This time around, in 1967, the court was taking on an apparently much weaker Congress party, with Indira Gandhi as the new Prime Minister. But, this turned out to be a miscalculation of Himalayan proportions. In response, Mrs Gandhi not only passed constitutional amendments to reverse the recent dictum of *Golak Nath* that had made fundamental rights unamendable; she also launched a ferocious political attack on the court itself.

Thus began what Austin would call 'the great war, as distinct from earlier skirmishes, over parliamentary versus judicial supremacy.'[30] For the next six years, there would be many moves and countermoves by the two sides. The court would declare unconstitutional some of Mrs Gandhi's key 'socialist' political measures of the time – bank nationalization, withdrawal of privy purses and indirect control of private newspapers. Her response was to launch a massive political campaign against the Supreme Court, casting it as antisocialist and pro-property. She was re-elected with a huge majority in 1971, with enough political capital to radically amend the Constitution, pack the court and declare the need for 'a committed judiciary'. A series of amendments – the 24th, 25th and 26th – followed. The first undid *Golak Nath* and restored Parliament's absolute power to amend the Constitution. The second replaced the term 'compensation' in the right to property with 'amount', thus restricting the possibility of judicial review of land reform. The third amendment was really radical. It inserted a new Article 31C that restricted judicial review of all laws that 'claimed' to implement two key classically socialist directive principles: Articles 39(b) and 39(c). Violation of the fundamental rights of equality, freedom and property could no longer be the basis for challenge, as per this amendment. The architect of Mrs Gandhi's onslaught on the judiciary was an ex-communist lawyer named Mohan Kumaramangalam. He relentlessly attacked the court's defense of the right to property as elitist and instead demanded a 'committed judiciary'. While debating Article 31C in Parliament, Kumaramangalam directly attacked Supreme Court judges as coming from 'the class of men of money and property that undemocratic collection of very respectable gentlemen.'[31] Mrs Gandhi was now at the height of her political powers, and it would require something special from the Supreme Court to take her on.

A truly special judicial response did emerge in the next crucial battle of this great war: the case of *His Holiness Swami Kesavananda Bharati vs. State of Kerala*.[32] This was to become the most influential constitutional case in Indian history.

The legal challenge was to the constitutionality of the far-reaching post-1971 amendments: did Parliament have absolute power to amend the constitution, or could its amending power be subject to judicial review? This was the 'inner conflict of constitutionalism'[33] – political theatre at the highest level. It was heard by a bench of 13 judges, the largest in the history of the Indian Supreme Court, who met daily for four and a half hours, over 70 working days, between October 1972 and March 1973.[34] The judgment that emerged on 24 April 1973 was a puzzle, with 11 opinions running over more than 600 pages. Nine of the judges made a special statement clarifying the view of the majority, with its famous dictum that Parliament could not alter the basic structure or framework of the constitution. And while Parliament could henceforth amend any part of the constitution, the judiciary could declare the amendment unconstitutional if it violated the 'basic structure'. This was the enduring *modus vivendi* achieved by the court: conceding a lot, but retaining its final say. It stands as binding precedent to this day, with the prospect of its being reviewed receding every year.

To return to 1973: Mrs Gandhi's response to the *Kesavananda* judgment was swift and devastating. The next day, when the new chief justice was to be appointed, she chose to violate, for the first time in India, the principle of seniority conventionally followed in the appointment to this constitutional office, superseding three of the senior-most judges who had been part of the majority in *Kesavananda*, and thus compelling all three to resign immediately. This was a frontal attack on the Supreme Court as an institution, and it was the lowest point in executive–judicial relations in post-independence Indian history. It is important to note here the defense that her then chief ideologue, Kumaramangalam, gave for this decision. He told the Parliament that they wanted a 'forward - looking judge' and not a 'backward - looking judge'.[35] This language of 'progressive' and 'regressive' judges was to be the enduring legacy of this period to Indian juridical discourse.

By June 1975, when the Internal Emergency was declared by Mrs Gandhi, the negative political discourse about the court as an impediment to socialism was only strengthened further. The Emergency regime constituted a committee to review the constitution, resulting in the 42nd Amendment. With 59 different clauses, this was to be the most thoroughgoing and radical constitutional amendment in Indian history. Its official aim, according to the 'Statement of Objects and Reasons', was 'to spell out expressly the high ideals of socialism, secularism and integrity of the nation and give [the Directive Principles] precedence over those Fundamental Rights that had frustrated the Principles' implementation'.[36] It declared India a 'socialist' and 'secular' republic. Not only was Article 31C (that had been struck down by *Kesavananda*) reintroduced, it was expanded to provide that all laws 'declared' to be implementing any of the directive principles, and not just Articles 39 (b) and (c) as earlier, could no longer be declared invalid even if they violated the fundamental right to equality, freedom and property. The shocked opposing voices included H. M. Seervai, who had only recently been the central government's lead counsel in *Kesavananda*. Arguing against the then widespread belief, he wrote, 'It was an unfounded assumption, based on the battles over the right to property, that the Directive Principles were to secure social justice and the Fundamental Rights were 'mere selfish individual rights'.[37]

Directive Principles had by now explicitly come to be deployed not just as general constitutional goals, but effectively as resources to empower the legislature and immunize it from judicial review.[38] This approach put the judges under considerable pressure. As Dhavan calls it, 'the 1971–76 empowerment/immunization' approach to Directive Principles placed the judges in an uncomfortable bind. Confronted by an appeal to lofty ideals, they found themselves 'carried away to concede absolute powers to the government in the name of socialism and to abnegate their own judicial role'.[39] The Supreme Court had to respond and out-radicalize the political masters, but the ground for this battle had been already laid by the apotheosis of the Directive Principles. As Dhavan argues, the post-Emergency Supreme Court ended up performing this manoeuver by declaring that the constitution did not just have a basic structure, 'but a distinct socioeconomic goal of ameliorating poverty and achieving an egalitarian distributive justice.'[40] The court declared its constitutional duty to fulfil the Directive Principles.

Such was the context in which PIL was born. With the birth of PIL, says Dhavan, the court claimed a partnership with government.

> It seemed to be arguing that these duties could not be deferred or left to the legislature. [The Directive Principles] had to be dealt with immediately. Of course, they had to be grounded in some guaranteed constitutional or statutory right. But an underlying sense of purpose was derived not from these *entitlements*, but from the *goals* of the Constitution.[41]

It is important to note here that even the new rights discourse of the Supreme Court in the post-Emergency period was more embedded and interested in Directive Principles than Fundamental Rights. Dhavan continues:

> [The judges] declared a strong constitutional commitment to what they claim to be the primary purpose of the Constitution, enlarged the role of activist citizens, and became the mediator of both the values and processes by which this purpose can be achieved.[42]

An analogy can be drawn here from Kaviraj's essay about Indira Gandhi's politics, where he argues that even the fierce opposition to Mrs Gandhi, the response of Jai Prakash Narayan and the Sampoorna Kranti[43] movement were actually carried out in the language of populism adopted by her. The Supreme Court, too, in search of a new legitimacy, responded by mimicking Mrs Gandhi's populism. The battle henceforth was between the competing populisms of the court and the political class. I would argue that the Supreme Court eventually did become a 'committed judiciary' with the path it adopted in the early 1980s. There was, however, one vital difference from this early 1970s ideal – the court itself became the self-proclaimed vanguard of the social revolution.

Understanding the rise of PIL

The axiomatic explanation for the rise of PIL in India has been that it was an attempt by the post-Emergency Supreme Court to restore its image in the public eye after the crisis of legitimacy created by its ignominious role during the Emergency. Yet why did the court have to respond to that crisis of legitimacy in the *form* of PIL? To understand why this might not be so obvious, let us first rehearse the court's infamous Emergency performance. The most widely known instance of its capitulation during this period was in the *Habeas Corpus* case[44], where the court upheld the validity of the draconian Maintenance of Internal Security Act (MISA). A five-judge bench of the court decided by a four to one majority that habeas corpus rights had been entirely suspended by the Emergency and that even a mala fide detention order could not be challenged before the courts.[45] In the hall of infamy of the Indian Supreme Court, these observations by Justice Beg in this case will always hold pride of place: 'The care and concern bestowed upon the welfare of detenus who are well housed, well-fed and well-treated is almost maternal.' The good judge even felt gratuitously obliged to defend the internal Emergency, holding that it was justified 'not only by the rapid improvements' in the seriously dislocated national economy and discipline, but also because 'the grave dangers of tomorrow, apparent to those who have the eyes to see them, have been thus averted'.[46] Justice Beg was soon duly rewarded and made Chief Justice by Mrs Gandhi's regime, superseding Justice Khanna, the only judge with the courage of conviction to give a dissenting opinion in this case.

The *Habeas Corpus* case is generally considered the lowest point in the history of the Indian Supreme Court, and it is the damage done to its reputation by this judgment that the post-Emergency court is often said to be trying to undo through PIL. But this still begs the question: Why did the post-Emergency court choose to craft their political response through the innovation of PIL when, strictly speaking, there were other means available? Soon after Mrs Gandhi was re-elected in 1980, she reintroduced a preventive detention statute called the National Security Act (NSA), which took the place of the now-repealed MISA. It was challenged before the Supreme Court immediately. Some of the judges who were part of the majority in 'Habeas Corpus' (Justices Bhagwati and Chandrachud) also heard this case[47], giving them a neat opportunity to exorcise the demons of the Emergency and depart from their ignominious judicial approval of the clampdown on personal liberty. The Supreme Court, however, did no such thing. It upheld NSA unanimously. The path not taken here is as interesting as the path taken – that of PIL. Even where the court did take on Mrs Gandhi, like in the 'Minerva Mills' decision, which struck down Article 31C as unconstitutional, the language of the court – particularly Justice Bhagwati's partially concurring judgment – mirrored Mrs Gandhi's language in astonishing fashion: both declared Directive Principles part of the 'basic structure' of the Constitution.[48] One of the interesting corollaries is that, as Pratap Bhanu Mehta argues, 'all the Supreme Court's celebrated 'activist' decisions stemmed from a concern for equality rather than civil liberties. Indeed, civil liberties concerns have been palpably weak in Indian courts.'[49] Throughout the post-Emergency era, the concern has rarely been negative liberty from the state; much more often, it is positive liberty through the state. The court was henceforth more interested in expanding its role through judicial populism than in performing its classical function of judicial review. The legacy of MISA was not really undone; instead a new front was opened, that of PIL. Indeed, the court's cavalier approach to basic civil liberties has continued in the post-Emergency period, and it has consistently upheld the so-called anti-terror statutes and other draconian laws throughout this period. In fact, I would argue that the delegitimization of legal procedure that accompanied the rise of PIL in India, as we shall see, has actually made it easier for courts to justify and overlook departures from the basic principles of criminal procedure that mark such statutes.

Dhavan, writing in 1987, called the emergent PIL turn optimistic in the face of a widespread state of lawlessness.[50] But in a sense, the legal constituencies for PIL and for 'state lawlessness' largely diverged. The latter was the concern of civil liberties lawyers who typically worked in lower courts, dealing with trial litigation in criminal cases or appeals therefrom, as opposed to the high-profile Supreme Court and High Court lawyers who wanted to influence policy at the highest level through PIL. It is quite rare that these two subspecies of lawyers overlap and the divergence has only increased over the years. Very rarely will one find that a civil liberties lawyer has filed a PIL. In fact, in the sociology of the Indian legal profession, there is a clear distinction between trial lawyers and appellate lawyers. Trial lawyers do, of course, get involved in appeals in the higher courts, but they are rarely optimistic enough to engage in policy making through litigation. On the other hand, PILs are increasingly filed as an incitement for judges to enter the legislative domain. Pious homilies (generally in the form of 'guidelines'[51]) get delivered in such PILs, allowing the appellate court to sound morally superior, although these guidelines hardly ever travel to the adjudicative domain, where the violations of these judicial legislations could actually have any real repercussions. Increasingly, the court prefers to formulate such legislative guidelines rather than evolve legal principles on the issue in a considered way. To illustrate this trend, a useful example would be to compare two recent judgments on extra-judicial killings by the police, known as 'encounters'. The legal question was on the need to initiate a criminal investigation against the police by the mandatory filing of a First Information Report (FIR) in such cases. In 2009, a five-judge bench of the Andhra Pradesh High Court gave a detailed ruling on this issue with a careful examination of the provisions relating to investigation in the Indian code of criminal procedure.[52] This case was argued by some of the leading criminal lawyers of the country. The decision given was that an FIR had to be filed against the police to start an investigation in all encounter cases. Soon after, an appeal was filed against this judgment in the Supreme Court, which promptly stayed the High Court Judgment. After more than six years, this appeal is still pending, but the Supreme Court has not found the time to adjudicate on it. Meanwhile, the Supreme Court heard another appeal on the same broad issue, but this time it was asked to decide on guidelines relating to this question. The judgment laid down guidelines in a cavalier manner without a careful understanding of the existing practices on the issue and without considering the statutory framework in any depth. The result of this judgment has arguably been counterproductive, as it decreed that a FIR has to be lodged, but did not specify that it has to be against the police, and not the dead victims as is currently the practice.[53] This trend of 'continual and clamorous legislative activity'[54] through PIL is very much part of the story of law as panacea that emerged in the early 1980s, with the growing trend of social reform through law reform that has been the subject of much recent critical reflection.[55]

It is useful here to return to Dhavan's account of the rise of PIL. '[A] new public interest or social action law movement has developed', he writes, 'led, essentially, by middle-class judges, academics, newspapermen and social activists who feel that law can be 'turned around' to provide solutions for the poor.'[56] Notice here that the talk is of a solution to the problems of the poor, not of taking the law off their backs so it gives them less trouble. This is what makes it optimistic, and part of the law reform trend of the post-Emergency period. This new optimism was fundamentally different from E. P. Thompson's famous argument that even with the existence of 'the black act' in eighteenth-century England, the 'rule of law' understood as 'the imposing of effective inhibitions upon power and the defense of the citizen from power's all-intrusive claims' was 'an unqualified human good'.[57] Thompson retained a defensive idea of law. With PIL, on the other hand, recourse to law is not a defensive strategy but a possible solution to social problems. Here, the law is not the oppressive tool that can be turned against itself but is the very source of social revolution. The romance of the Indian state as being able to reform the unruly social gets significantly strengthened through PIL. The eminent lawyer Shyam Divan argues that 'until the 1970s, the role of the court was largely "negative" – to confine governmental action within constitutional bounds.'[58] With PIL, as Dhavan suggests, the concern becomes distributive justice.

> It [the court] can no longer fall back on a conservative concern for protecting life, liberty, property and religious freedom. Rather, it needs to think about those social welfare, social justice and civil and political rights which might give its vast millions a real chance both to withstand the pressures of India's unruly acquisitive capitalism and to fight for their individual and collective entitlements as full citizens and not just beneficiaries of welfare.[59]

'The People' in judicial discourse

In 1979, when PIL, as we know it now, had barely been born, Baxi reflected on the Indian Supreme Court's new avatar in a lecture. He said,

> There are more references to the people in the constitutional decisions of the Court since the Sixth General Elections [of 1977] than ever before in the Court's history.[60] He is here referring to the period between 1977 and 1979 – already 'the people' appear more often in the court's language in these two years than they had in its prior 27 years of existence. The post-Emergency court, Baxi observed, was 'seeking legitimacy from the people', and 'in that sense (loosely) there are elements of populism in what it is doing'.[61]

Lloyd and Susanne Rudolph, writing in 1981, discussed the 1970s battle of 'Judicial Review versus Parliamentary Sovereignty' as revolving around the question of who spoke for the people:

> Judges of state high courts and of the Supreme Court claimed to speak from the authority of the written constitution, which expressed the people's will as well as the fundamental law of the land. Ruling Congress governments claimed to speak with the authority of constitutional majorities in parliament, based on electoral mandates that expressed the people's will.[62]

We have seen so far why the Indian Supreme Court chose to imitate Indira Gandhi's populism to survive her political onslaught. We shall now see how the court actually went about developing its legal arsenal to accommodate 'the people'.

The ground for this transition to a 'people's court' was prepared in 1973, in the landmark 'Kesavananda' judgment itself. Justices Hegde and Grover, speaking for the majority of the Supreme Court bench in this case, questioned the assumption that the Parliament speaks for the people as a whole, but they still did not claim any access to the people. According to the two judges:

When a power to amend is given to the people, its contents can be construed to be larger than when that power is given to a body constituted under that constitution. Two-thirds of the members of the two Houses of Parliament need not represent even the majority of the people in this country. Our electoral system is such that even a minority of voters can elect more than two-thirds of the members of either House of Parliament. Therefore, the contention on behalf of the Union and the States that two-thirds of members in the two Houses of Parliament are always authorized to speak on behalf of the entire people of this country is unacceptable.[63]

A spoke had been put in the wheel of parliamentary legitimacy and, in particular, its monopoly on speaking for the people. Soon after the Emergency, this issue re-emerged in *State of Rajasthan vs. Union of India*. In 1977, the newly elected Janata Party government dissolved all the Congress-ruled states' assemblies, invoking Emergency powers under Article 356. Called on to decide the constitutionality of such a dissolution, the Supreme Court enthusiastically supported it and, interestingly, based its decision on the sentiments of the people – as expressed in the recent parliamentary election results of 1977. J. Bhagwati was the most eloquent. Interpreting the electoral mandate, he surmised: 'There is a wall of estrangement which divides the Government from the people and there is resentment and antipathy in the hearts of the people against the Government.' He argued that the consent of the people was the basis of democracy, and 'when that is withdrawn so entirely and unequivocally', there is 'no room for doubt about the intensity of public feeling against the ruling party'. J. Bhagwati continued,

> On account of total and massive defeat of the ruling party in the Lok Sabha elections, the Legislative Assembly of the State has ceased to reflect the will of the people and there is complete alienation between the Legislative Assembly and the people.

While the court had begun to claim rhetorical access to the people, it was still a claim mediated by its interpretation of the election results. But, a pattern had been set; a decision disastrous for the institutional viability of Indian federalism was legitimized by the court with hyperbole for reasons of political pragmatism.

Soon after this, we see the birth of Public Interest Litigation (PIL). The Supreme Court's first programmatic statement about this new phenomenon came in 1981. In the *Judges' Transfer* case that year, the rule of locus standi ('standing' is the American legal equivalent) was relaxed, opening up the doors of the Supreme Court to 'public-spirited citizens' – both those wishing to espouse the cause of the poor and oppressed (who were referred to as having 'representative standing') and those wishing to enforce performance of public duties (who were said to have 'citizen standing').[64] Representative standing in Indian PIL was characterized by American legal scholar Clark Cunningham as enabling litigation similar to class-action suits, except with a non-class member representing the larger group.[65] A petitioner under citizen standing, on the other hand, sues not as a representative of others but in his own right – as a member of the citizenry at large to whom a public duty is owed.

J. Bhagwati's judgment in the *Judges' Transfer* case was a kind of manifesto for PIL. Bhagwati took this opportunity to reflect on the question of standing as

> of immense importance in a country like India where [with] access to justice being restricted by social and economic constraints, it is necessary to democratize judicial remedies, remove technical barriers against easy accessibility to justice and promote public interest litigation so that the large masses of people belonging to the deprived and exploited sections of humanity may be able to realize and enjoy the socio-economic rights granted to them and [so] these rights may become meaningful for them instead of remaining mere empty hopes.[66]

J. Bhagwati makes a statement here that would be repeated ad nauseam in later years:

> But it must not be forgotten that procedure is just a handmaiden of justice and the cause of justice can never be allowed to be thwarted by any procedural technicalities. *The Court would therefore unhesitatingly and without the slightest qualms of conscience cast aside the technical rules of procedure in the exercise of its dispensing power* and treat the letter of the public-minded individual as a writ petition and act upon it. Today, a vast revolution is taking place in the judicial process; the theatre of the law is fast changing and the problems of the poor are coming to the forefront. *The Court has to innovate new methods and devise new strategies for the purpose of providing access to justice to large masses of people* who are denied their basic human rights and to whom freedom and liberty have no meaning.[67]

We see here a tirade against technicalities and a plea for adapting the inherited British legal system to Indian realities. The rhetoric of indigenization is mobilized to make a case for legal informalism in the form of PIL.

Kaviraj has argued that 'the evasion of institutional controls' during Mrs Gandhi's rule was 'accompanied by a rhetoric of radicalism – a particularly dangerous combination of a bourgeois leader invoking socialist principles to evade encumbrances of bourgeois constitutionalism.'[68] Bhagwati would adapt Mrs Gandhi's strategy to the judiciary – here was a judge invoking 'the poor' to evade constitutionalism, the judge himself facilitating a discourse by which legality was constructed as the enemy of justice. Kaviraj has discussed analogous political dilemmas more generally:

> The politics of community assertion in India has created a potential conflict between these two principles of participation and proceduralism. Political parties representing large communities with a strong sense of grievance have often regarded procedures of liberal government as unjustified obstacles in their pursuit of justice. Procedures are sometimes threatened by the politics of intense participation.[69]

While the nationalist movement initially spoke in the participatory language, the first two decades of post-independence politics saw a clear attempt to suppress it and adopt the procedural path.[70] We can see strong parallels to this trajectory in the judiciary. The court had made a clear choice with PIL – choosing participation over procedure. And the language it deployed to justify that choice was that of indigenization.

The indigeneity of PIL

Later writers on PIL have emphasized this discourse of indigeneity and decolonization to establish PIL's status as a 'distinctly Indian' legal phenomenon[71], arguing, for instance, that PIL 'has cut the umbilical cord between the Indian legal system and its mentor systems in the "white" common law world'[72] and that it 'entails reconceptualization of the role of judicial process in at least the Third World societies'.[73] This culturalist manoeuver to justify the need for PIL as a peculiarly Indian achievement would be part of its enduring appeal.

The need for a truly 'Indian' jurisprudence achieved through a gesture as grand as PIL had not always existed. In 1968, the most well-known American commentator on Indian law, Marc Galanter, was struck by the fact that for Indian legal professionals, modern Indian law is 'notwithstanding its foreign roots and origin... unmistakably Indian in its outlook and operation'.[74] Mrs Gandhi's assault on the Indian judiciary in the early 1970s tried to undo such a consensus. She would use the indisputable fact of the relative lack of access to Indian legal institutions to delegitimize the higher judiciary. Soon after the Emergency was declared, Mrs Gandhi derided the Indian legal system, saying, 'We have adopted the Anglo-Saxon juridical system, which often equates liberty with property [inadequately providing] for the needs of the poor and the weak.'[75]

In 1973, the Expert Committee on Legal Aid, chaired by a recent appointee to the Supreme Court, Justice Krishna Iyer, submitted a report commissioned by the government that 'viewed itself as a radical critique of Indian legal arrangements' and spoke glowingly of *nyaya panchayats* as part of a larger scheme of legal aid and access to the courts.[76] The follow-up Emergency era 'Report on National Juridicare: Equal Justice – Social Justice' was headed by Justice P. N. Bhagwati. This report argued that '*panchayats* would remove many of the defects of the British system of administration of justice, since they would be manned by people with knowledge of local customs and habits.'[77] Galanter would later reflect on how these visions of paternalistic indigenous justice, published during the 1975–77 Emergency, provided the basis for future developments like PIL. As he recounted in 2004, 'In the Krishna Iyer and Bhagwati reports, the imagery of indigenous justice was combined with celebration of conciliation and local responsiveness under the leadership of an educated outsider.'[78]

In an essay written a few years after the Emergency, Baxi described the role these two judges, later the chief architects of PIL, had played as 'legitimators of the [Emergency] regime':

> During the 1975–76 [E]mergency, legal aid to the people was one of the key points of the 20-point programme launched by Indira Gandhi, to which Justices Krishna Iyer and Bhagwati, themselves deeply committed to the spread of the legal aid movement, readily responded. They led a nationwide movement for the promotion of legal services. They organized legal aid camps in distant villages; they mobilized many a High Court justice to do *padayatras* (long marches) through villages to solve people's grievances. They, through 'camps' and *lokadalats* (people's courts), sought to provide deprofessionalized justice. They also in their extracurial utterances called for a total restructuring of the legal system, and in particular of the administration of justice. In a sense, their movement constituted a juridical counterpart of the 1971 *Garibi Hatao* (eliminate poverty) campaign, as well as of the 20-Point Programme.[79]

The 42nd Amendment to the constitution, which was introduced during the Emergency, contained a new Directive Principle titled 'equal justice and free legal aid'. It read:

> The State shall secure that the operation of the legal system promotes justice, on a basis of equal opportunity, and shall, in particular, provide free legal

> aid, by suitable legislation or schemes or in any other way, to ensure that opportunities for securing justice are not denied to any citizen by reason of economic or other disabilities.

Legal aid was to be the means to mitigate the expense and the general lack of access to courts – by making legal aid itself into a directive principle. However, while legal aid ordinarily ought to have provided access to legal services in courts at a cost borne by the state, what instead transpired in post-Emergency India was that the legal process itself was selectively transformed ostensibly to make it easier for people to access the court. Tribunals were created in various arenas as replacements to regular courts. While legal aid was meant to make access to lawyers less expensive or free, it was decided instead that the judicial apparatus would be transformed to make it so accessible that people could approach them directly. Dhavan saw in this trend a desire 'to design alternative structures, processes and normative understanding to show a far greater proximity to notions of law and justice in civil society.' The principal means of solving this problem of judicial access was through institutional changes: at the lowest level, by creating *lok adalats*, or 'people's courts'; at the intermediate level, by creating tribunals with non-lawyers at the helm; and at the highest level, by innovating the concept of PIL. Legal technicalities, the colonial nature of the Indian legal system and complicated procedures were seen as the principal problems plaguing the system. Law itself, or rather legal procedure – especially the standard adversarial nature of legal proceedings – was perceived as the enemy of access to justice.

Thus began, as Galanter and Krishnan have argued, the phenomenon of 'debased informalism' in Indian law.[80] While legal aid was neglected and poorly funded, these other institutional innovations were widely adopted. It was not as if informal non-state institutions were given power. What happened instead was that state institutions themselves were transformed and made to behave according to inchoate ideas of what informal 'traditional' institutions were like. The state's legal institutions were now set to mimic their fantasy of what they imagined an informal institution would look like.

Anticipating and leading this trend, during the Emergency both Justices Krishna Iyer and Bhagwati 'called for thoroughgoing judicial reforms, minimizing reliance on foreign models of adjudication, including the system of s*tare decisis*. They advocated a return to "swadeshi" jurisprudence including justice by popular tribunals.'[81] Bhagwati spoke of the Indian judicial system as being ill-suited to 'a country where the majority lived in villages and was ignorant of its legal right'.[82] Here, we see another symptom of what Kaviraj has diagnosed as the crisis of institutions in India during that period:

> Legitimacy of institutional power was increasingly giving place to a legitimacy of individuals; and perhaps still more significant, the new rhetoric of socialism, indiscriminately used by nearly all political forces, signified something often fatally misunderstood. Socialist rhetoric often gave a respectable cover for the re-emergence of an essentially pre-capitalist alphabet of social action. It looked upon impersonal rules and application of rationalistic norms with derision, as forms of 'bourgeois' fastidiousness.[83]

Justice Bhagwati summed up his PIL agenda in clear populist terms in the 'Judges' Transfer' case:

> It is necessary for every judge to remember constantly and continually that our Constitution is not a non-aligned national charter. It is a document of social revolution which casts an obligation on every instrumentality including the judiciary, which is a separate but equal branch of the state, to transform the status quo ante into a new human order in which justice, social, economic and political will inform all institutions of national life and there will be equality of status and opportunity for all. The judiciary has therefore a socio-economic destination and a creative function. It has to use the words of Granville Austin to become an arm of the socio-economic revolution and perform an active role calculated to bring social justice within the reach of the common man. It cannot remain content to act merely as an umpire but it must be functionally involved in the goal of socio-economic justice.[84]
>
> He followed it up with a dig at:
>
> The British concept of justicing, which to quote Justice Krishna Iyer (*Mainstream*, 22 November 1980), is still 'hugged by the heirs of our colonial legal culture and shared by many on the Bench' is that 'the business of a Judge is to hold his tongue until the last possible moment and to try to be as wise as he is paid to look'.[85]

To undo such perceived anachronisms, the Committee on Implementation of Legal Aid Schemes (CILAS) was established in 1980 by Indira Gandhi, just back in power, with Justice Bhagwati as chair to effectuate his earlier Emergency-era report. On 8–9 May 1981, a seminar was organized by CILAS under his leadership, with many of India's legally active social groups participating. From the bench and otherwise, the PIL court under Justice Bhagwati 'extended to journalists, activists, academics, and anyone else who may have been witness to constitutional neglect and lawlessness' an invitation to participate in this new kind of judicial process.[86] Right from these early years, therefore, these occupational groups emerged as PIL's principal constituency. The fact that the birth of PIL in this post-Emergency period coincided with the rise of new social movements and investigative journalism in India is not coincidental. Interestingly, PIL was identified so closely with Justice Bhagwati that most of the early PILs in 1980–82 arose out of letters written by individuals to him in his twin capacities as a judge of the Supreme Court and the chairperson of CILAS.[87]

Early controversies around PIL

In this early phase of PIL, a controversy broke out over Justice Bhagwati's actively soliciting petitions, a fact that drew attention to the judge-led nature of PIL. Arun Shourie, then editor of the *Indian Express*, gave an interview in 1983 where he observed:

> A judge of the Supreme Court asked a lawyer to ask me to ask the reporter to go to these areas, get affidavits from some of the victims who are still alive and some of them who were dead, from their families. The affidavits were [*sic*] compiled, sent and he entertained a writ. Eight months later, someone came to me saying that the same judge had sent him to ask me to ask the respondent to file such and such information in a letter through so and so. A third time a civil rights activist asked that the same thing be done. He said the judge had asked him. The point that the opponents of the case were making was that the litigants were choosing a judge. As it turns out, some judges were choosing their litigants.[88]

From the beginning, the PIL petitioner was a crutch that judges could rely on to further their own agenda, but as we shall see, even this crutch soon became unnecessary.

A famous PIL that showcased many of the innovations of the PIL jurisdiction was the 1984 case of *Bandhua Mukti Morcha vs. Union of India*, filed by an organization dedicated to ending 'bonded labour'. As analyzed in a much-cited article on PIL from the late 1980s:

> When the petition was first received, the court appointed two lawyers to visit the quarries where the bonded labourers were said to be held. This was followed by a 'socio-legal' investigation of the area undertaken by an academic, funded principally by the state government in whose area the offending quarry was sited. The defendants objected to the admission of this evidence, arguing that it was based only on *ex parte* statements which had not been tested by cross-examination, nor were any such investigations within any of the relevant Supreme Court rules.[89]

Justice Bhagwati rejected this objection by reverting to his standard trope of Indian difference. He argued that insisting on a rigid legal procedure 'in a country like India beset by problems of "poverty, illiteracy, deprivation and exploitation" would be to place fundamental rights beyond the reach of the common man.' In a far-reaching precedent, he declared that in such PILs, it was not necessary to be bound by the normal conception of an adversarial trial in which each party produced witnesses who were then cross-examined by the other side. The introduction of such evidence could not be resisted by assertions that it was of no evidentiary value since it could not be subjected to direct cross-examination. To accept such a conclusion would be to introduce the adversarial procedure in a situation to which it was totally inapposite.[90]

Justice Bhagwati's usual flourish can be usefully contrasted with another concurring judgment by Justice Pathak in the same case, which clarified that any such procedural flexibility would be limited by any contrary statutory provision as well as by 'principles of natural justice'. But, it was Justice Bhagwati's judgment that carried the day. One could either be charitable here and recall the old adage 'hard cases make bad law', or bemoan this fateful departure from constitutionalism, 'as a version of precommitment related to an ability not to take courses of action which might offer immediate relief but are fraught with dangers of long-term calamity', as Kaviraj calls it.[91]

In 1979, Baxi was the first to use the framework of 'judicial populism' to explain the then imminent rise of PIL, deploying Edward Shils' definition:

> Populism proclaims that the will of the people as such is supreme over every standard, over the standards of traditional institutions, over the autonomy of institutions and over the will of other strata. Populism identifies the will of the people with justice and morality.

Interestingly, clear-eyed as Baxi was, he did not view this new trend as a problem but saw it instead as strategically opportune. He wrote in the same book that 'the politics of the Court represents the best hope for the millions of Indians for a new constitutional dawn'.[92] He even went so far as to argue that 'the interests of the people require the Court to "lead" and the legislature to "follow"[93], citing as explanation "the nagging political realities of India".'[94] Many years later, in 1993, Baxi would write about PIL as the court's response to the executive's demand for a 'committed judiciary':

> Throughout the seventies, the executive made its wish public that the judges and courts should be committed to the Constitution and the promise of progress and justice within it. Now, led by the Supreme Court of India,

> judges and courts have shown their 'commitment'; the executive did not have this kind of 'commitment' in view at the same time, it cannot repudiate it publicly.[95]

In an interview in 2011[96], Justice Bhagwati proudly discusses his sole authorship of PIL and the circumstances that led him to invent it. He talks of visiting the poor states of Bihar, Orissa and UP as a judge, of seeing the 'stark naked poverty' there, and of being moved because 'his' justice had not been reaching them. In what is still the most widely cited article on PIL, written soon after its birth, Baxi famously celebrated PIL by arguing that it took 'suffering seriously', as a result of which 'the Court is being identified by justices as well as people as the "last resort for the oppressed and the bewildered".'[97] This mobilization of suffering by the Supreme Court through PIL is evocative of what Hannah Arendt called, in the context of revolutionary France, 'eloquent pity' as counterposed to 'mute compassion'.[98] While the latter 'has no notion of the general and no capacity for generalization,' the former ends up 'depersonalizing the sufferers, lumping them together into an aggregate the suffering masses, et cetera.' Talking of Robespierre, Arendt says that even if he

> had been motivated by the passion of compassion, his compassion would have become pity when he brought it out into the open where he could no longer direct it towards specific suffering and focus it on particular persons. What had perhaps been genuine passions turned into the boundlessness of an emotion that seemed to respond only too well to the boundless suffering of the multitude in their sheer overwhelming numbers. Measured against the immense sufferings of the immense majority of the people, the impartiality of justice and law, the application of the same rules to those who sleep in palaces and those who sleep under the bridges of Paris was like a mockery.[99]

In Uday Mehta's gloss on the uses of such pity in Indian constitutionalism, following Arendt, he argues:

> Since pity maintains a distance from its object, it can conceive of the object as embodying an abstraction, or representing a type, such as the poverty-stricken or the disadvantaged castes or the people of India. And because it is not limited by the injunction to share in the plight of those it perceives, it can imagine a redress to their condition that corresponds to the generality of its perspective.[100]

The Indian Supreme Court soon put the political legitimacy it had accumulated through PIL to dramatic use. After the gas leak disaster in Bhopal in 1984, a complex tort litigation ensued.[101] By 1987, while the civil suit was still extant in a district court in Bhopal, an appeal was pending in the Indian Supreme Court to decide whether the interim compensation of 2.5 billion rupees was legally appropriate. This interim relief was meant to address the urgent needs of the victims before the final compensation amount could be decided by the district court. But instead of adjudicating this limited issue, the Indian Supreme Court in January 1988 presided over a secret final settlement between the Indian government, as the sole representative of all the gas victims, and the defendant multinational company Union Carbide, allowing the company to get away with the relatively minuscule amount of 470 million dollars.[102] Castigated widely for this apparently unethical act, the court went on to give a series of post-facto rationalizations over the next four years. Veena Das's analysis of this judicial discourse reveals how the Supreme Court would persistently mobilize 'suffering' to perform an 'ornamental function' and justify itself (150). Thanks to years of PIL, the court was very much at home in the language of suffering and could deploy it masterfully, if cynically. The court legally justified the expropriation of the grievance of the victims – declaring them 'judicially incompetent' – by the government that had emerged as the surrogate victim (157). The mobilization of 'suffering' and 'agony' of the victims 'allowed the judiciary to create a verbal discourse which legitimized the position of the government as guardian of the people and the judiciary as protector of the rule of law (159).' Das lays out the justifications given by the court for its strangely hasty settlement:

> The first imperative to arrive at the meagre settlement was the 'suffering' of the victims. The second imperative to do this with complete secrecy, and to present the victims with a fait accompli, was the irresponsibility and inability of the victims to understand the issues that affected their lives (160).

Das concludes, 'In the judicial discourse every reference to victims and their suffering only served to reify "suffering" while dissolving the real victims in order that they could be reconstituted into nothing more than verbal objects (164).' In classic post-PIL language, the court went on to justify itself, 'Legal and procedural technicalities should yield to the paramount considerations of justice and humanity' (171). The constitutional provision that the court invoked to give itself a legal fig leaf in this case was Article 142, the same Draft Article 118 that would literally allow the court to do 'complete justice', which Thakur Das Bhargava had said in the Constituent Assembly enabled the court to be 'above law'. This provision had never been used to violate statutory provisions, but Bhopal opened the floodgates, and since then the court has routinely deployed its 'divine' power.[103]

The Curious Case of the Disappearing Public Interest Petitioner

After having been around for more than a decade, PIL had apparently begun to change.[104] This change is usually explained in ideological terms as coterminous with the larger changes in India's political economy since the 1990s, when economic liberalization was initiated. While that may well be the case, the attempt here is to understand why PIL could serve as such a powerful weapon in the changed political economic context. I argue that this is precisely because of its (in)formal characteristics. Our focus here is therefore on a key formal manoeuver signifying a new phase of judicial populism: the PIL petitioner became an increasingly redundant figure. At the time of the birth of PIL, the court had needed a public-spirited petitioner to stand in for the public at large. But over a period of time, even this became unnecessary and the court could fold the public into itself.

Cunningham, one of the earliest American commentators on PIL, noted the trajectory of this change from the cases of representative standing to those of citizen standing. In early PIL cases:

> In each case, behind the public spirited petitioner the court could see the faces of particular people in urgent need of justice. However, in more recent years Indian public interest litigation has come to include cases involving matters of general public policy in which the petitioner stands for the entire citizenry of India rather than individual victims of injustice.[105]

And in this latter role of a petitioner citizen, she was merely an informant bringing an issue concerning the people at large to the court and was no longer the representative of the victims. She could be superfluous once her minimal role was performed. This was in accordance with the general trend in the populist trajectory of the court, which Baxi usefully summarized thus: 'If in the seventies lawyers and justices achieved a proper conception of judicial power as people's power, in the eighties the SAL movement innovated a more direct, unmediated form of people-judiciary partnership.'[106]

The first sign of things to come, indicating the changing fortunes of the public-spirited petitioner, was in 1988. Sheela Barse, a journalist, had filed a case regarding the rights of children in prison. Later, Barse wanted to withdraw the PIL, saying that the court had become dysfunctional and that she was frustrated with the slow progress of the case as a result of repeated adjournments.

J. Venkatachaliah called this withdrawal application 'a walk-out of the court'. He dismissed Barse's application for withdrawal after dwelling on her arguments at length:

[Her] ground is that the proceedings are brought as a 'voluntary action' and that applicant is entitled to sustain her right to be the 'petitioner-in-person' in a public interest litigation and that the proceedings cannot be proceeded with after de-linking her from the proceedings. This again proceeds on certain fallacies as to the rights of a person who brings a public interest litigation. Any reconnection of any such vested right in the persons who initiate such proceedings is to introduce a new and potentially harmful element in the judicial administration of this form of public law remedy. That apart, what is implicit in the assertion of the applicant is the appropriation to herself of the right and wisdom to determine the course the proceedings are to or should take and its pattern. This cannot be recognized. The petition cannot be permitted to be abandoned at this stage. Only a private litigant can abandon his claims.

The court removed her as petitioner and appointed the Supreme Court Legal Aid Committee as petitioner. The *Sheela Barse* case marked the beginning of the process that has since become a characteristic feature of PIL: the court claiming ownership of a PIL case and deciding what direction it was to take.

From the mid-1990s, this process went one step further. The court now began to wilfully displace the petitioner and appoint a senior advocate as amicus curiae to assist it. This happened most famously in the *Vineet Narain* case (relating to political corruption as indicated in the Jain Hawala Diaries). As Chief Justice Verma observed in this case:

> Even though the matter was brought to the court by certain individuals claiming to represent public interest, yet as the case progressed, in keeping with the requirement of public interest, the procedure devised was to appoint the petitioners' counsel as the amicus curiae and to make such orders from time to time as were consistent with public interest. Intervention in the proceedings by everyone else was shut out but permission was granted to all, who so desired, to render such assistance as they could, and to provide the relevant material available with them to the amicus curiae for being placed before the court for its consideration.

The appointment of the amicus curiae is recorded in one of the interim orders passed in this case:

> Anil Diwan has been requested by us to appear as Amicus Curiae in this matter.... It is open to anyone who so desires, to assist Shri Anil Diwan and to make available to him whatever material he chooses to rely on in public interest to enable Shri Diwan to effectively and properly discharge functions as Amicus Curiae. Except for this mode of assistance to the learned Amicus

> Curiae, we do not permit any person either to be impleaded as party or to appear as an intervenor. In our opinion, this is necessary for expeditious disposal of the matter and to avoid the focus on the crux of the matter getting diffused in the present case by the appearance of many persons acting independently in the garb of public interest.[107]

This dispensation of the petitioner in PIL cases has since become a routine. Public-spirited petitioners now often appear as impediments to justice rather than its allies. The court seems to manage just fine without them. A leading commentator on PIL, S. Muralidhar, now a judge of the Delhi High Court, has been one of the few voices critical of this trend. He argues that it defeats the very purpose of the PIL jurisdiction and renders petitioners redundant as mere informants. He writes, 'The petitioners are then entirely at the mercy of the amicus curiae who as the delegate of the court's screening power can decide who can or cannot petition the court and what can and cannot be said by them.'[108] In effect, these public-spirited petitioners are deprived of their right to espouse the public cause because of this procedural innovation. The PIL petitioner, who might often have greater knowledge and understanding of the issue than the amicus curiae, is thus silenced without his or her consent.

Once petitioners were made dispensable, the remit of PILs could be enlarged and extended in unanticipated directions according to the whims of the court. While a new form of PIL had been made possible by *Vineet Narain*, its full implications took some time to manifest themselves. Let me provide here three revealing examples of the unique imbroglios that this new avatar of PIL gave rise to.

The first of these is the so-called Forest case[109], one of the most influential and egregious instances of this new version of PIL, in which forest governance for all of India has been taken over by the Supreme Court and the amicus curiae Harish Salve has been requested by the court to screen all applications for intervention.[110] Any person with any grievance has to first approach the amicus curiae and the special body appointed by the court called the Central Empowered Committee (CEC), which can then place it before the court, at its discretion. The far-reaching effects of such a judicial policy can be gauged from a controversy that arose in 2009. This was regarding the non-recusal of Justice Kapadia in the case before the Forest Bench relating to permission given to Vedanta Alumina Ltd. to mine bauxite in the Niyamgiri Hills of Odisha, the traditional home of the Dongria Kondh tribe. Justice Kapadia apparently held shares in Vedanta's sister company, Sterlite and announced it in court as per the 1999 resolution passed in the Chief Justices Conference, which required a judge to disclose any involvement with a company under litigation before him. But the resolution also said, assuming a normal adversarial proceeding, that if no objections were raised by the lawyers for either party, it would be presumed that the parties have no objection to the judge.

But in this new kind of PIL, as we know, the only parties heard are the state and the amicus curiae. So, as advocate Prashant Bhushan explains:

> ...the only lawyers represented in the case were those of Vedanta Alumina Ltd (the project proponent), Odisha Mining Corporation (the mining lease holder), the Odisha government (the promoter of the project), the Centre's Environment Ministry (which granted the approval to the refinery), and the junior Amicus Curiae, Uday Lalit (since the senior amicus, Mr Harish Salve, had a retainership from Vedanta). The only lawyer who could have objected to Justice Kapadia's hearing the matter was Sanjay Parikh who was representing the tribals in a connected writ petition. He was, however, prevented from speaking by Justice Pasayat on the bench, on three occasions when he tried to get up to speak. He was told in no uncertain terms that the amicus could take care of the interests of the tribals and that he would not be separately heard.[111]

We see thus the removal of representative voices from PIL proceedings, the assumption being that these voices could be subsumed and represented by the court and the state, thanks to this new kind of PIL.[112]

Another example of the difficulties that arise because of this trend of the Supreme Court appointing an amicus curiae and making the petitioner irrelevant is provided by the case relating to the miscarriage of justice in five criminal trials relating to some of the most heinous incidents during the Gujarat pogrom of 2002. The statutory National Human Rights Commission (NHRC) and the Citizens for Justice and Peace (CJP) led by Teesta Setalvad were the petitioners in this case. Here, too, the court chose to appoint Harish Salve as amicus curiae and has paid little attention since to the petitioners. In the court hearings of this case that I attended in 2009, the bench would hear only the amicus and the counsel for the Gujarat government. To provide a sense of the power that the amicus had vis-à-vis the petitioner, let me quote from Setalvad's interview with the news magazine *Tehelka* in 2011:

> Nearly six years after our criminal writ petition praying for the transfer of investigation in nine major riot cases to the CBI was filed, . . . on 26 March 2008 . . . the Supreme Court appointed a SIT. Though it was headed by a retired CBI director, it comprised . . . Gujarat police officials. When the matter of who would constitute the team came up, the CJP on behalf of the victim survivors pleaded that only those officers from Gujarat who enjoyed reputations of neutrality and impeccable integrity should be included. But

> to our shock the amicus accepted the names of officers given by the state of Gujarat without even consulting us. We placed our objections to this unfair procedure and suggested alternate names but nothing happened.[113]

The petitioners were keen here that an independent investigation be conducted only by the Central Bureau of Investigation (CBI), but Salve did not think it would be a good idea. The court finally appointed a Special Investigation Team (SIT) to independently conduct the investigation in the five riot violence cases. However, when the SIT's report was given to the court, it chose to keep it confidential and give copies to the amicus and Gujarat government alone. No copies were given to any of the petitioners. The day after the report was submitted in the Supreme Court, the *Times of India* reported that 'the SIT led by the former CBI Director R. K. Raghavan told the Supreme Court that the celebrated rights activist cooked up macabre tales of wanton killings'.[114] It was later revealed that the *Times of India* article was based on its interpretation of the SIT report that had been leaked to the *Times* correspondent, while the actual petitioners in the case were not privy to the information. The resultant widespread media reportage made it appear as if the report had indicted these NGOs rather than the Gujarat government. But because of the systemically skewed nature of this PIL case, where the amicus and the state were the only parties with access to the actual report, the state government's misinformation campaign could not be adequately contested.

The final logical culmination of this new kind of PIL is that the court entirely does away with the requirement of a petition with the widespread use of *suo moto* powers, or as it is called in India, 'court on its own motion'. Thus, a 1994 *Hindustan Times* article on pollution in Yamuna, titled 'And Quiet Flows the Maily Yamuna', led the court to convert it, on its own motion, into a writ petition to clean up the river Yamuna. The case is usually called 'And Quiet Flows the Maily Yamuna', or sometimes 'AQFMY'. This particular case is still pending after two decades, and the court has been supervising a 30 billion rupee project involving the institution of interceptor drain sewers with the assistance of the amicus curiae Ranjit Kumar.

But even more amazing things have happened in this case. While this writ petition was pending, the amicus curiae filed I.A. No. 27[115] in 2002, referring to the national address of Dr A. P. J. Abdul Kalam, then President of India, on the eve of Independence Day. It related to the need to interlink various rivers in the country, to deal with the apparently paradoxical situation of floods in one part of the country and droughts in other parts. On 16 September 2002, the court, while considering the said I.A., directed that the application be treated as an independent writ petition and issued notice to the various state governments as well as the attorney general for India and passed the following order:

> Based on the speech of the President on the Independence Day Eve relating to the need of networking of the rivers because of the paradoxical phenomenon of flood in one part of the country while some other parts face drought at the same time, the present application is filed. It will be more appropriate to treat it as independent Public Interest Litigation with the cause title 'IN Re: Networking of Rivers __v.__' Amended cause title be filed within a week.[116]

Thus, I.A. No. 27 in AQFMY [Writ Petition (Civil) No. 725 of 1994] was converted into In Re: Networking of Rivers [Writ Petition (Civil) No. 512 of 2002]. In the course of one *suo moto* case, the court had taken up another. The first involved the cleaning up of one of India's bigger rivers; the second, piggybacking on the first, would be India's largest engineering project if it came through. The latter culminated in the court's final judgment in 2012, which appointed a committee to execute this project, estimated to cost 5,60,000 crore rupees in 2002, i.e. a little under a hundred billion dollars.

The *reductio ad absurdum* of the legal process had been reached, as presaged by Justice Hidayatullah in 1984, when he predicted that PIL would result in the 'annihilation of all procedure'.[117] Whether this new post-petitioner PIL could even be called an adjudicative proceeding at all is a moot question. With no procedural norms to control it and with even the minimal crutch of a petitioner deemed unnecessary, what was unveiled was a new beast, of a kind perhaps unknown in modern legal history. The PIL judges could now give free rein to their ideological predilections; their awesome power had no limits except their own sense of judgment.

Endnotes

1 See, for example, Cunningham, 'The World's Most Powerful Court'.

2 There are other related changes that accompanied the PIL phenomenon, which gave the Supreme Court a much higher profile – the expansive interpretation given to Article 21, pronouncing all kinds of unlisted rights within the rubric of right to life.

3 Cassels, 'Judicial Activism and Public Interest Litigation in India: Attempting the Impossible?', p. 497.

4 Baxi, 'Taking Suffering Seriously', p. 107.

5 For an early use of this term for PIL, see Singh, 'Access to Justice', p. 173. For a more recent use, see Robinson, 'Hard to Reach'.

6 Kaviraj, 'Ideas of Freedom in Modern India', p. 77.

7 Ibid. p.78.

8 See Austin, *Working a Democratic Constitution*, pp. 6–7.

9 Mehta, 'Constitutionalism', p. 17.

10 Ely, *Democracy and Distrust: A Theory of Judicial Review*, 92. 'The original Constitution was principally, indeed I would say overwhelmingly, dedicated to concerns of process and structure and not to the identification and preservation of specific substantive values' (92). And again, 'As a charter of government a constitution must prescribe legitimate processes, not legitimate outcomes' (101).

11 Mehta, 'Constitutionalism', p. 25.

12 Mehta, 'Constitutionalism', p. 26.

13 Arendt, *On Revolution*, p. 108.

14 Mehta, 'Constitutionalism', p. 27.

15 Austin, *Working a Democratic Constitution*, p. 8.

16 Mehta, 'Constitutionalism', p. 20.

17 Mehta, 'Constitutionalism', p. 17.

18 The full text of this debate can be found at parliamentofindia.nic.in/ls/debates/vol8p16a.htm. See also, Prakash, 'Complete Justice under Article 142'

19 H. V. Pataskar from Bombay responded to Bhargava and supported Draft Article 112, asserting its need in the language of an archaic sovereignty. 'The Supreme Court may, in its discretion grant special leave to appeal from any judgment decree or final order in any cause or matter' because 'the Supreme Court is intended in this country to serve the functions of the King in some other countries where he is the fountainhead of all justice. Here, there is no King, and naturally therefore we must have some independent body which must be the guardian of administration of justice and which must see that justice is done between man and man in all matters whether civil, criminal or revenue.' See parliamentofindia.nic.in/ls/debates/vol8p16a.htm. Emphasis is by the author.

20 T. Krishnamachari, quoted in Dhavan, Judges and Indian Democracy, p. 314. Around sixty years later, Justice Markandey Katju used strikingly similar language in a Supreme Court judgment: 'Public Interest Litigation which was initially created as a useful judicial tool to help the poor and weaker section of society who could not afford to come to courts, has, in course of time, largely developed into an uncontrollable Frankenstein…' Common Cause (A Regd. Society) vs Union of India, (2008) 5 SCC 511

21 Comments by N. G. Ranga, *Constituent Assembly of India*, vol. 3, book 1, 29 April 1947. In Banerjee, *Constituent Assembly of India*.

22 See Menon, 'Citizenship and the Passive Revolution'.

23 Parliamentary Debates 12–13 (Part II) Col. 8832 (16 May 1951).

24 Austin, *Working a Democratic Constitution*, p. 85.

25 See Dhavan, 'Governance by Judiciary', pp. 78–79.

26 Dhavan, 'Governance by Judiciary', p. 79.

27 Dhavan, If I Contradict Myself, pp. 56–57.

28 Dhavan, *Governance by Judiciary*, p. 85.

29 *Sajjan Singh vs. State of Rajasthan*, 1965 1 SCR 762.

30 Austin, *Working a Democratic Constitution*, p. 198.

31 Ibid. pp. 245–46.

32 While the literature on this case is vast, for a book-length study, see Krishnaswamy, *Democracy and Constitutionalism*.

33 See Mehta, 'The Inner Conflict of Constitutionalism.'

34 See Austin, *Working a Democratic Constitution*, p. 264.

35 Ibid. p. 283.

36 Ibid. p. 370.

37 Ibid. p. 367.

38 Dhavan, 'The Constitution as the Situs of Struggle', p. 414.

39 Ibid. p. 415.

40 Ibid.

41 Ibid. p., 416.

42 Ibid.

43 'Sampoorna Kranti' literally means 'Total Revolution.'

44 *A. D. M. Jabalpur v. Shivkant Shukla*, 1976 2 SCC 521. For a brilliant in-depth analysis of this judgment, see Baxi, *Indian Supreme Court and Politics*, 79–115.

45 Baxi, *Indian Supreme Court and Politics*, p. 112.

46 Ibid. p. 113.

47 *A. K. Roy vs. Union of India*, 1982 1 SCC 271.

48 See the discussion in Mehta, 'The Inner Conflict of Constitutionalism', pp. 198–200.

49 Ibid. p. 205.

50 His full statement was 'A more optimistic approach, undeterred by the dismal reality of State oppression, argues that as long as the legal machinery retains some autonomy of standards and decision-making, State law is up for grabs in the hands of those, including the disadvantaged, who acquire the skills to use it.' In *Dhavan, Means, Motives, and Opportunities*, p. 745.

51 For an early critique of the judicial tendency to issue guidelines in PIL cases, see Hidayatullah. For a very different view on the importance of such discursive production in PIL cases, see Lokaneeta, 'Debating the Indian Supreme Court', pp. 1–16.

52 The judgment was called *A.P. Civil Liberties Committee (APCLC) vs. Government of Andhra Pradesh*, 2009(1)ALT 754.

53 People's Union for Civil Liberties vs. State of Maharashtra, Criminal Appeal No. 1255 of 1999. For a critique of this judgment by eminent lawyer Colin Gonsalves, see http://indianexpress.com/article/opinion/columns/showing-weak-judgment/

54 Foucault, *The History of Sexuality*, p. 144.

55 See Agnes, Protecting Women against Violence? and Menon, *Recovering Subversion*.

56 Dhavan, 'Means, Motives, and Opportunities'.

57 Thompson, *Whigs and Hunters*, p. 266. For a very different take on Thompson's argument about 'rule of law' in the context of PIL, see Thiruvengadam, 'Swallowing a Bitter PIL? Brief reflections on Public Interest Litigation in India,' p. 134.

58 Divan, 'A Mistake of Judgment'.

59 Dhavan, 'Means, Motives, and Opportunities', p.746.

60 Baxi, *Indian Supreme Court and Politics*, p. 246.

61 Ibid. p. 126.

62 Rudolph and Rudolph, The Struggle over Stateness, p. 107.

63 *Kesavananda Bharati Sripadagalvaru and Ors. v. State of Kerala and Anr.* AIR 1973 SC 1461. Justice Chandrachud, who would later preside over the Supreme Court for most of the 1980s and the concomitant rise of PIL, gave a minority opinion in *Kesavananda* that upheld the absolute power of Parliament to amend the Constitution, but he shared the new judicial concern for popular legitimacy: 'The Court is not chosen by the people and is not responsible to them in the sense in which the House of the People is. However, it will win for itself a permanent place in the hearts of the people and augment its moral authority if it can shift the focus of judicial review from the numerical concept of minority protection to the humanitarian concept of the protection of the weaker section of the people.'

64 *S. P. Gupta vs. Union of India* AIR 1982 SC 149. The court defined 'representative standing' thus, 'If a legal injury is caused to a person, and such person or determinate class of persons is by reason of poverty, helplessness or disability or socially or economically disadvantaged position, unable to approach the court for relief, any member of the public can maintain an application for an appropriate direction, order or writ in the High Court under Article 226 and in case of breach of any fundamental right of such person or determinate class of persons, in this court under Article 32 seeking judicial redress for the legal wrong or injury caused to such person or determinate class of persons.' Further, in some cases, the court claimed that it 'will not insist on a regular writ petition to be filed by the public spirited individual espousing their cause and seeking relief for them, This Court will readily respond even to a letter addressed by such individual acting pro bono publico.'

65 Cunningham, Public Interest Litigation in the Supreme Court of India. In some early cases, PILs were filed in the name of a class member even though the public-spirited individual was the real petitioner (as in Hussainara Khatoon's case). In some cases, both actual class members (pavement and slum dwellers) and public-spirited individuals (two journalists and a civil liberties organization) were among the petitioners, as in *Olga Tellis vs. Union of India.*

66 *S. P. Gupta vs. President of India.*

67 Justice Bhagwati emphasized this stand in even more vehement terms in *People's Union of Democratic Rights vs. Union of India*: 'We wish to point out with all the emphasis at our command that public interest litigation which is a strategic arm of the legal aid movement and which is intended to bring justice within the reach of the poor masses, who constitute the low visibility area of humanity, is a totally different kind of litigation from the ordinary traditional litigation which is essentially of an adversary character where there is a dispute between two litigating parties, one making claim or seeking relief against the other and that other opposing such claim or resisting such relief.' *People's Union of Democratic Rights vs. Union of India*, 1982 3 SCC 235. Emphasis by the author.

68 Kaviraj, 'Indira Gandhi', p. 1700.

69 Kaviraj, The Post-colonial State.

70 For a trenchant critique of this post-independence Nehruvian language, see Chakrabarty, 'In the Name of Politics: .

71 Vandenhole, 'Human Rights Law', p. 155.

72 Dhavan, 'Ambedkar's Prophecy', p. 27.

73 Baxi, 'On How Not to Judge the Judges', p.233.

74 Galanter, *Introduction*, p. 215. Galanter here relies on a famous public lecture by M.C. Setalvad, India's first attorney general.

75 Austin, *Working a Democratic Constitution*, p. 348.

76 Galanter and Krishnan, Bread for the Poor, p. 793. *Nyaya panchayats* were a post-independence attempt at recreating an idealized version of traditional village-based dispute settlement bodies with elected members and democratic fellowship. According to studies, it was almost moribund by 1970. See Meschievitz and Galanter, *In Search of Nyaya Panchayats: The Politics of a Moribund Institution.*

77 Galanter and Krishnan, 'Bread for the Poor', p. 794.

78 Ibid. p. 795.

79 Baxi, 'Taking Suffering Seriously', p. 113.

80 See Galanter and Krishnan, 'Debased Informalism'.

81 Baxi, 'Taking Suffering Seriously', p. 113. 'Stare decisis' is a Latin maxim that literally means 'let the decision stand.' This maxim refers to the principle of precedent in common law. *Swadeshi* loosely translated as 'autochtonous'.

82 Quoted from Austin, *Working a Democratic Constitution*, p. 349.

83 Kaviraj, 'On the Crisis of Political Institutions', p. 234.

84 *S.P. Gupta vs. Union of India* AIR 1982 SC 149 (para 27).

85 Kaviraj, 'On the Crisis of Political Institutions'.

86 Ramanathan, Review of *Judicial Activism*,

87 Baxi, 'Taking Suffering Seriously', p. 118.

88 Agrawala, *Public Interest Litigation in India*, pp. 16–17.

89 Craig and Deshpande, 'Rights, Autonomy, and Process', p. 363.

90 Ibid. p. 364.

91 Kaviraj, 'On the Crisis of Political Institutions', p. 235.

92 Baxi, *Indian Supreme Court and Politics*, p. 248A.

93 Ibid. p. 248.

94 Ibid. p.184.

95 Baxi, 'Judicial Discourse: Dialectics of the Face and the Mask', p. 7.

96 View the full interview at www.youtube .com/watch?v=OrXO8CAi98E

97 Baxi, 'Taking Suffering Seriously', p. 107.

98 Arendt, *On Revolution*, p. 85.

99 Ibid.

100 Mehta, 'Constitutionalism', p. 26.

101 The literature on the litigation around the Bhopal disaster is vast. Particularly notable are Baxi, *Inconvenient Forum and Convenient Catastrophe*; and more recently Fortun, *Advocacy after Bhopal.*

102 To put this figure in context, the Indian government had originally sued Union Carbide for 3.2 billion dollars in a New York court in 1986. One can only agree with Veena Das's remark that what the Bhopal victims had to settle for was multinational charity, not multi-national liability. See Das, 'Suffering, Legitimacy, and Healing', p. 163.

103 For an extended analysis of the transformation in the interpretation of Article 142 brought out by the Bhopal case, see Ramanathan, In the name of the People, pp. 44–53.

104 For an excellent account of PIL till the early 1990s, see Dhavan, 'Law as Struggle'. For a turn of the century exhaustive survey of PIL, see Desai and Muralidhar, 'Public Interest Litigation'. For such a detailed treatment more recently, see Robinson, 'Expanding Judiciaries'.

105 Cunningham, 'Public Interest Litigation'.

106 Baxi, 'On Judicial Activism'.

107 *Vineet Narain and Others vs. Union of India.*

108 Muralidhar, India: Public Interest Litigation.

109 *T. N. Godavarman Thirumalpad vs. Union of India*, Writ Petition No. 202 of 1995.

110 Rosencranz et al., 'The *Godavarman* Case: The Indian Supreme Court's Breach of Constitutional Boundaries in Managing India's Forests'. Since then, multiple amici have been appointed in the case, though Salve is still the 'senior amicus'.

111 Bhushan, 'Prashant Bhushan's Reply'.

112 Meanwhile, the court gave its permission for mining in this case by its old rhetorical strategy of speaking for the poor: 'According to CEC, use of forestland in an ecologically sensitive area like Niyamgiri Hills should not be permitted. On the other side, we have a picture of abject poverty in which the local people are living in Lanjigarh Tehsil, including the tribal people. There is no proper housing. There are no hospitals. There are no schools and people are living in extremely poor conditions which are not in dispute. . . . Keeping in mind the two extremes, this court thought of balancing development vis-à-vis protection of wildlife ecology and environment in view of the principle of Sustainable Development.'

113 Khetan, 'Whose Amicus Is Harish Salve?'

114 Mahapatra, NGOs.

115 I. A. is an acronym for Interlocutory Application.

116 See courtnic.nic.in/supremecourt/temp/512200232722012p.txt

117 Hidayatullah, 'Highways and Bylanes of Justice'.

2

The Case that Felled a City

A PIL with Nine Lives

> The new role of the Supreme Court is that of a policymaker, lawmaker, public educator and super administrator all rolled in one. In the US, they have the Congress, the Federal Environment Protection Agency and bags of money to protect the natural environment. Here, we have our Supreme Court.
>
> –Shyam Divan[1]

> In Delhi, in 2000, so much of the government's activity in so many matters boiled down to securing compliance of court orders in PIL that one might have been excused for thinking of it as the court's bailiff.
>
> –Gita Dewan Verma[2]

In 1984–85 a lawyer named M. C. Mehta filed a bunch of Public Interest Litigation (PIL) cases in the Supreme Court of India. These cases were fated to be landmarks in the history of PIL in India. They are generally discussed as the archetypical environmental PILs, which set the pace of judicial intervention in urban governance and environmental regulation in India.[3] In narrating the story of PIL, these cases are usually read as signalling a new era, shifting the focus of PIL away from the dominant concerns of poverty and judicial reform to the subject of environment. My focus in this chapter, however, will be on the pioneering innovations introduced in these PIL cases. These cases have been trailblazers in exploring the boundless potentialities of PIL in India, particularly in Delhi. I will foreground these trendsetting procedural novelties and the politics immanent in them. The shifts that these cases brought about in PIL were not only in terms of its ideological concerns, but also in terms of the very nature of its process. This is the story I shall try to narrate here.

Four of these M. C. Mehta PILs from 1984–85 are still going on after three decades, with no end in sight. The unending nature of these cases provides us a hint as to their unique nature. These four vintage PILs still thriving are the cases popularly known as the Taj Mahal Pollution case[4], the Ganga Pollution case[5], the Delhi Vehicular Pollution case[6] and the particular case that I will be focusing on here, Writ Petition (Civil) 4677/1985. No such simple moniker would work for the latter case as its very cause of action, i.e. its central dispute shifted, not once, but multiple times in the last three decades. It started with a plea against stone-crushing units, then concerned itself with pollution in the river Yamuna, then with the condition of Delhi's Ridge Forest and with mining in the Aravalli mountain ranges, but its most famous targets were Delhi's hazardous large industries, then 'non-confirming' industries and finally and most spectacularly, it became known as the 'sealing' case against commercial establishments in residential areas in Delhi. The story of this PIL case can be narrated as the story of Delhi's urban transformation in the last three decades as it singlehandedly led to large-scale deindustrialization of the city, and it performed this task assiduously and relentlessly. But the question that is worth posing here is: why and how did PIL emerge as the primary agent of this transformation. While Delhi, just like many other cities, saw massive changes in its political economy in this period with a move from industry to services, what marks Delhi's dislocations as distinct is their source and their basis – they are based not, as in the past, on administrative or municipal policy or executive directions, but on judicial directions in a single PIL case concerning pollution in the city. The spectacular efficacy of a PIL case in carrying out such a role, I would argue, can be explained not just by the external ideological trends prevailing at the time, but also by the peculiar nature of PIL itself. While WP 4677/1985 became a means of spectacular urban transformation, it also broke fresh ground for PIL itself as a perennially unstable and fundamentally malleable jurisdiction.

WP 4677/1985 has been dealt with by most of the leading charismatic PIL judges of the last three decades from Justice Bhagwati to Justice Kuldip Singh and Justice Sabharwal, making it particularly fertile as a case study for the history of PIL. While the focus of this chapter will be on this one case, I will begin with a brief discussion of another of the still surviving M. C. Mehta cases of 1985, the vehicular pollution case, in so far as it resonates with the particular case at hand. While the M. C. Mehta cases were first admitted by Justice Bhagwati in 1985, these cases scaled new heights in the early 1990s with Justice Kuldip Singh at the helm, enabling him to establish a reputation as a 'green judge'. The style of functioning of his court at this time can be discerned from the following description provided in 1995 by Shyam Divan, then a young environmental lawyer:

> A public interest litigation to clean up the Ganga has caught the judge's fancy. Each Friday a huge shoal of advocates, administrators, company executives, and public officials attentively follow the court proceedings as a

> range of snappy judicial directions are issued… The Ganga court functions a bit like a village panchayat dispensing justice in the shade of a banyan tree. The rigour of formal court procedures and statutory requirements are diluted in favour of a summary, result-oriented process.[7]

To characterize such a peculiar attempt to mimic 'traditional justice' in the hallowed portals of India's Supreme Court with its liveried attendants in turbans and full Raj-style regalia, perhaps a more appropriate analogy would be the medieval court or *durbar* rather than a village panchayat. Justice Hidayatullah had anticipated this and as early as 1984, he thought it fit to compare PIL with Moghul Emperor Jehangir's:

> Zanjir-e-Adl – a gold chain which he had hung from his apartment to the ground. Supplicants used to give a tug to ring a bell in his private apartment and the emperor would before a jharoka (window) and hear and decide the complaint in person.[8]

While J. Kuldip Singh's judicial conduct set new standards for PIL judges, it was not fated to be exceptional for too long, as we shall see.

The Delhi Vehicular Pollution case

Writ Petition (Civil) 13029/1985, better known as the Delhi vehicular pollution case, was to lead to a complete overhaul of public and private transport in the city. Its impact started to be felt with a series of orders in the mid-1990s. Its initial orders included the phasing out of leaded gasoline, the introduction of pre-mixed fuels for two-stroke engine vehicles and the removal of 15-year-old commercial vehicles. But, soon to come in this case was the most famous of its decisions – to order all commercial public transport vehicles to change from diesel or petrol to Compressed Natural Gas (CNG), which was seen as a 'green' fuel. The decisions were actually taken at the behest of a fact-finding body called the Environment Pollution (Prevention and Control) Authority, abbreviated as EPCA and commonly referred to as the Bhure Lal Committee after its chairman, who was then a member of the Central Vigilance Commission. The EPCA had been appointed as a statutory body on 28 January 1998 under the orders of the court. This five-member committee was initially composed of a representative from the Central Pollution Control Board, the Automobile Manufacturers Association of India, the Centre for Science and Environment (an environmental NGO) and the Transport Department of Delhi, besides the Chairman.[9] Because the committee was designed to express the interests and expertise of the major affected parties, the Supreme Court has since 1998 consistently looked to the committee as its fact-finding commission and has relied almost exclusively on its findings when making its decisions in this case.[10] Of course, the court did not always follow EPCA recommendations – the most prominent example of such an instance being the fate of diesel-fuelled private vehicles. As a 2004 article on this case notes:

> The Environment Pollution (Prevention and Control) Authority (EPCA) recommended that private diesel cars should not be registered and that the Supreme Court should freeze sales of diesel cars. Lawyers for the automobile industry strenuously opposed this. Instead of following the EPCA recommendation, the Court ordered only that all private cars must conform to engine standards by new, tighter deadlines.[11]

Another glaring instance of the court's skewed sense of priorities in this case was when it did follow EPCA recommendations and made a direction (on the same day as the CNG order) to augment the number of public transport buses in Delhi to 10,000 by 1 April 2001.[12] But the court did not make any significant effort to implement this order (while its other orders were causing havoc) and even in 2016, Delhi has much less than 10,000 public buses in its fleet.

The petitioner M. C. Mehta was active in the Delhi vehicular pollution case till 1995. Thereafter, the court relied on Harish Salve, a senior lawyer who was appointed as the amicus curiae – literally 'friend of the court', a court-designated position that became increasingly common in PIL cases around this period, as we saw in Chapter 1. The crucial role that the amicus played here has been described thus: 'In this case, the amicus curiae was a combination of special master and advisor to the justices'.[13] He collected and sorted out factual material and distilled from the numerous affidavits and other representations submitted to the court a précis of their perspectives. At several critical junctures, Salve did factual research to debunk what he described as 'extravagant claims' and otherwise played a central role in moving the case forward.[14] For a case of citywide scope, only a relatively small number of stakeholders actually played much of a role in the deliberations.

On 28 July 1998, the Supreme Court issued its order that all public transport in Delhi would be converted to run on CNG by 1 April 2001.[15] The CNG order included buses, taxis and auto rickshaws, some 100,000 vehicles in all.[16] This was immensely controversial because the science behind it was severely contested, with two committees giving diametrically opposite reports regarding the advisability of adopting diesel or CNG.[17] Even if the problem of pollution in Delhi was widely acknowledged to be severe, many alternative solutions to this dismal situation had been suggested. The most controversial aspect of the court's solution was that private vehicles were relatively unaffected, while public transport was made to bear the brunt – directly affecting the livelihoods of people employed in public transport. There was a sudden drop in the number of public buses available. The effect of this forced change of fuel on bus personnel and commuters was drastic.

The drivers of auto rickshaws (officially known as TSRs: 'Three-wheeled scooter rickshaws') were particularly badly hit. The changeover from petrol to CNG engines required a relatively large monetary investment, which most auto rickshaw drivers were not in position to make and bank loans were hardly available to them. They ended up taking usurious loans from private financiers. Besides, CNG was not actually available in sufficient quantity for many years, even after it had been imposed as the only fuel for auto rickshaws. This led to extreme hardship, as auto rickshaw drivers would normally have to queue for 3–4 hours to refuel their vehicles, which affected their workdays very adversely. Serpentine queues of dozens of auto rickshaws outside gas stations were to become a normal sight in Delhi in the first few years of the twenty-first century.

The auto rickshaw drivers' situation was further exacerbated by an earlier order of the Supreme Court in this same case in 1997, which stated that:

> It would be in the interest of the environment, to freeze the number of TSRs for the present at the level at which they are actually in use in the city. We, therefore, direct that there would be no grant of fresh permits in respect of the TSR, save and except by way of replacement of an existing working TSR with a new one.[18]

The result of this court-ordered permit freeze was catastrophic for auto-rickshaw drivers. In 2010, the EPCA found that, according to the Transport Department of the Government of Delhi, the number of registered three-wheelers in the city was 55,236, while 72,429 of them had existed in 1997.[19] There was, thus, a substantial 'decline' in absolute numbers of auto rickshaws in Delhi between 1997 and 2010. Simultaneously, by 2010, as the EPCA observed, the city was registering over 1,000 new private vehicles every day. In the period from 1997 to 2011, thus while private vehicles increased manifold, the Supreme Court's freeze on TSRs resulted in an artificial scarcity of permits.

The decline in the number of auto rickshaws in Delhi's streets was thus due to the combined effect of the Supreme Court's TSR freeze order of 1997 and its enforcement of CNG conversion soon after. In 2002, the court did allow a minuscule 5,000 new permits to be issued, but otherwise the number of TSRs remained stagnant till 2011, when the court finally allowed 45,000 new permits after the TSR unions approached it in August 2009 and prayed for relief from the freeze 'in view of the increase in population and increase in the number of vehicles during the past several years'. The court asked the EPCA to examine the matter afresh and requested it 'to give a report as regards the needfulness for fresh permissions for three wheelers'.[20]

The situation that then prevailed was explained in a 2010 report on auto rickshaws in Delhi:

> The permit cap created a gap between the supply of autos and the growing demand from Delhi's increasing population. A black market for auto permits soon emerged and the price of an auto permit rose dramatically. Just a year later owner-drivers were ordered to replace their autos or convert them to CNG by fitting expensive conversion kits. Unable to afford the Rs.25-30,000 CNG kits, thousands of owner drivers had no option but to sell their autos and permits to financiers at bargain prices, further focusing power in the hands of the consolidating finance 'mafia'.[21]

The black market price of an auto rickshaw with the permit increased to 6.5 lakh rupees by 2011, while the cost of the auto rickshaw itself was only 1.4 lakhs – a difference of more than 5 lakhs.[22] In November 2011 when the Supreme Court finally allowed 45,000 new autorickshaw licences to be granted, the market price immediately crashed and went down to as low as 2.5 lakh rupees.[23] The creation of this black market in TSRs was purely a result of the Supreme Court's decision, as can be gauged from the results of revoking it. Already, the order about change in fuel had made many auto rickshaw owners take loans from private financiers, and when they were unable to pay these back, they had to transfer their permits to these financiers. Studies have shown that before the Supreme Court's double whammy, most auto rickshaws were owned by drivers themselves, but the effect of the fuel change and the permit freeze was that almost the entire fleet of auto rickshaws came under the control of financiers and drivers were converted into wage labourers.[24] Even the EPCA recognized in 2010 that 'the bulk of the vehicles on road are owned by a limited number of people who rent these to drivers on a charge of around '250–300 for an 8-hour shift.' By the time the EPCA recommended the removal of the cap on auto rickshaws, recognizing their importance as public transport and finally understanding the impact of the court-ordered freeze, great harm had been done to all concerned. As its 2010 report noted:

> EPCA has noted that the current crisis of pollution in the city and its adjoining areas is largely because of the exponential growth of private vehicles. The only option for the city in the future is to provide a viable and reliable public transport system, which will restrain the use of private vehicles on the roads. The three-wheeler plays an important role in providing an intermediate

> public transport facility. It remains cheaper to operate as compared to any four-wheeled vehicle and removal of the cap and the high transaction costs associated with it will bring down the cost of capital drastically and provide space for improvement of the service on road. Removal of cap will also help in eliminating the dominating hold of 'financier's mafia' who are exploiting not only the drivers but also general public by pushing up artificially the capital cost of 3-wheelers and hence the operational cost.

Both these decisions – the permit freeze and the CNG changeover – in the Delhi pollution case were taken without even giving the city's auto rickshaw drivers and their representatives a chance to argue their side of the story. I was witness in August 2009 to the proceedings of this case. An application had been filed in the Supreme Court for its permission to increase the number of permits for auto rickshaws that had been fixed in 2002. The lawyer for the autorickshaw union had just begun his oral submission pleading for notice to be issued in this case because seven years had passed since the freeze and the rationale for the original order of 1997 – that auto rickshaws were polluting vehicles – was now irrelevant since the CNG fuel now used was eco-friendly. If notice had been issued, the application would in any case have been examined by EPCA, and based on their recommendation, the court would have considered granting permission. But the amicus curiae Harish Salve weighed in, opposing the application itself. His contention was that the presence of auto rickshaws on Delhi roads led to traffic congestion, because of which motor vehicles generally had to spend more time in stationary mode with engines on, leading to further pollution, therefore even CNG-fuelled auto rickshaws would cause pollution. Presumably, in Salve's reasoning, the introduction of thousands of motor vehicles in the city on a daily basis would cause no such problem. No authorities were cited by Salve and this was an extempore objection by him. This is just to provide an inkling of the kind of judicial processes through which decisions are made in such PIL cases.

In this case, which transformed Delhi's roads, the Supreme Court displayed a stark preference for imposing disproportionate environmental costs on public transport while allowing private transport to thrive, even though the latter was the cause of most of the vehicular pollution in Delhi. The case induced a marked increase in private transport, which expanded so exponentially since the court's actions of the late 1990s that the reduction in carbon emissions of public transport vehicle was over a period more than compensated for by the rise of private vehicles, particularly diesel vehicles.

An ideological interpretation of this case can rightly be made, as it significantly worsened the livelihood of thousands of poor informal sector transport workers in the name of environmental problems and the need for clean fuel, while stimulating the demand and supply of private automobiles, just when this sector was opening up in a post-liberalization Indian economy. While such an interpretation would not be incorrect, I would instead ask a different question: why was the court the instrument of such a major policy change? And how was this forced transition carried out?

The Supreme Court acted supposedly on purely environmental grounds, marshalling the spectre of vehicular pollution without adequately considering the impact its interventions would have on vulnerable sections of the population who live a hand-to-mouth existence, and without making any effort to cushion them from the harsh economic effects of such a transition. There was a callousness at work in which a blinkered and absolutist idea of environmentalism – sociologist Amita Baviskar called it 'bourgeois environmentalism'[25] – was imposed, where the poor are bizarrely and conveniently seen as responsible for urban pollution and have to bear disproportionately the costs of moving to a more ecologically benign system. While Baviskar's diagnosis of such a trend is persuasive and spot on, it is worth reflecting on why PIL emerged as the most powerful weapon for this phenomenon of 'bourgeois environmentalism'. While a class-based ideologically inflected worldview among appellate judges is hardly new and indeed is part and parcel of any realist understanding of judicial behaviour, PIL empowers judges to take their predilections much further than ordinary adjudication. It is the ability to enact and materialize a particular worldview that makes PIL so especially effective. I would argue that PIL was uniquely suited to impose such a worldview, not just because many judges shared it, but also because the extreme malleability of PIL empowered them to carry it out. In fact, the repeated exclusion of adversely affected parties from even getting a hearing that we see throughout the history of these 'environmental' PIL cases is symptomatic of the fact that the class-based exclusions of 'bourgeois environmentalism' gets materially inscribed within the adjudicatory processes of PIL.

Soon after this forced change of fuel to CNG, there was an appreciable drop in vehicular pollution in Delhi. The effects seemed to last for about a decade, after which the problem resurfaced, as the number of private vehicles had increased so much in the meantime that their combined emissions neutralized the reduced pollution caused by public transport. But the interesting thing about this is not the ideological aspect as much as the ability of the Supreme Court to ride roughshod over the interests of tens of thousands of people employed in 'non-corporate capital'[26], with the unspoken assumption that they could be made redundant or ignored. This kind of blinkered obliviousness is simply not conceivable by any democratic regime in India. The only time the Indian state could carry out such a draconian measure was perhaps during the Emergency regime. And therein you have the unique power of the court, which as many critics have argued[27], play a very careful negotiating role when it comes to high politics, but as we have seen here, can take an intransigent stand when it comes to vulnerable groups. It is not irrelevant that many of these decisions were made during the period of 1998–2004, when Jagmohan, the principal architect of the Emergency era 'cleaning up' of Delhi as the then Vice Chairman of the Delhi Development Authority, held office in the NDA government at the Centre, as we will see in the next section.

WP(C) 13029/1985 continues to thrive in the Supreme Court with the same amicus curiae Mr Harish Salve, who has held this position in this PIL for two decades now. This means, he is much more conversant with this case than any judge who hears it, because typically a Supreme Court judge would officiate in such a case for 2–3 years at the most. In the other unending mammoth PIL, popularly known as 'the forest case', in which Salve has served as amicus for a similar period, I have had a chance to witness him address and brief a new incumbent judge joining 'the Forest Bench', so that the latter would also be acquainted with the background and glorious history of the case.[28] The story of many landmark PIL cases is often written, with good reason, in terms of the judges heading the bench and is identified with their charisma, Justice Kuldip Singh being a good example. But perhaps the time has come to narrate the history of some other more recent PILs in terms of the charismatic amicus curiae involved in them, as they play a no less crucial role in steering the case in new directions. During its hearings during 2014–15, the veteran amicus in WP(C) 13029/85 was assisting the court in supervising the construction of two big road projects – the Western and Peripheral Expressway, which would re-route vehicular traffic away from Delhi and thus reduce traffic and pollution in the city.

WP(C) 4677/1985: The many-headed Hydra

The focus of the rest of this chapter will be on one of the other still active PIL cases [Writ Petition (Civil) Number 4677] filed by M. C. Mehta in 1985, which changed the face of Delhi more than any other case. It is generally regarded as a case concerning industrial pollution in Delhi as it famously led to the removal of industries from the city, in the name of implementing city-zoning laws[29], but this was just one of the many achievements of this PIL. The Master Plan of Delhi would get so much attention as a result of this case that it became a paperback bestseller during the mid-2000s. But WP(C) 4677/1985 initially started with a plea against stone-crushing units, which were alleged to be causing dust pollution in the city. Three hundred such units were closed down under court orders in 1992.[30] Already, in a sign of things to come, after discussing the chaos in implementing these closure orders, leading legal commentators observed, 'one may wonder whether the Supreme Court of India can have the time and resources for the above sort of micro-management'.[31] No lessons were learnt from this experience, however.

Such chaos was repeated cyclically multiple times in the future avatars of this case and in ever-increasing scale, as we shall see. The PIL case did not come to a close with the achievement of the objective with which it was first filed. The continuation of the case after the decree of closing down the stone crushing units was passed was not merely to monitor the implementation of its judgment, but to take up fresh causes of action. The closure of the units, in retrospect, was merely an unmarked blip in the juggernaut that this case became.

The petitioner M. C. Mehta soon thereafter filed a number of interlocutory applications (IAs) in this same case relating to other aspects of pollution in Delhi. The initial ones related to pollution in the river Yamuna and led to the setting up of sewage treatment plants and common effluent treatment plants.[32] But a big area of intervention in this phase of this case was the ridge forest of Delhi, which the court wanted to protect in its 'pristine glory'. On 9 May 1996, the court directed that the ridge be made free of all 'encroachers', as per the terms of the Delhi Master Plan. This would impact over 30,000 residents living in three colonies adjacent to the Asola Wildlife Sanctuary. The affected residents were nomadic tribals, who used to work in the erstwhile Bhatti mines of this area. As Ravi Agarwal notes, 'under direction from the Supreme Court they were asked to relocate, even though many adjoining private farmhouses were left untouched.'[33] Some of the tribal residents managed to resist eviction through political negotiations, but their fate remains precarious.

Another application, IA no. 29, relating to mining operations near Badkal Lake and Surajkund tourist resorts in the state of Haryana near Delhi, was filed in this PIL by the petitioner. The court barred any mining activity within two kilometres of these resorts by an order dated 10 May 1996.[34] A spin off of these IAs was the court's intervention in curtailing mining in the Aravalli hills, a matter that this case continues to grapple with even after nearly two decades. The nature of the orders passed in this PIL under each of these heads was such that even after the court definitively pronounced on many of these issues, the implications of each of these were so wide and implementation so complicated with so many affected parties who were often not even represented, that each of them took years of the Supreme Court's time and some are still on. As the case became larger and larger, the numbering of the numerous IAs filed by various parties in the various branches of this case became more and more unwieldy. As early as 11 November 2002, the order sheet of a hearing in this case lists an item it was dealing with as I.A.No.1782/2001 in I.A.No.1172 in I.A.No.22 in Writ Petition (Civil) No.4677/1985.[35] This one writ petition had so many heads that it really was like a many-headed hydra. Conventional modes of legal analysis would struggle to make sense of a juridical beast such as this PIL.

With Justice Kuldip Singh at the helm in the 1990s, this case almost single-handedly led to the deindustrialization of Delhi (before Justice Y. K. Sabharwal led it in a slightly different tangent from 2005). The first significant step in this direction culminated on 8 July 1996 with the court ordering the relocation of 168 large industries from Delhi within five months. The court reasoned:

> Delhi is recording heavy population growth since 1951. As the city grows, its problems of land, housing, transportation and management of essential infrastructure like water supply and sewage have become more acute. Delhi is one of the most polluted cities in the world. The quality of ambient air is so hazardous that lung and respiratory diseases are on the increase. The city has become a vast and unmanageable conglomeration of commercial, industrial, unauthorised colonies, resettlement colonies and unplanned housing. There is total lack of open spaces and green areas. Once a beautiful city, Delhi now presents a chaotic picture. The only way to relieve the capital city from the huge additional burden and pressures is to deconcentrate the population, industries and economic activities in the city and relocate the same in various priority towns in the NCR.[36]

The court's order was as per the 'Second Master Plan for Delhi – Perspective 2001' (henceforth, the Master Plan) notified in 1990 which specifically provided that the hazardous/noxious/heavy/large industries were not permitted to operate in the city of Delhi and the existing industrial units falling in these categories were to be shifted/relocated outside city limits. These industries were either characterized in the Delhi Master Plan's Annexure III as 'H(a) category' meaning 'Hazardous and noxious industries' or 'H(b) category' meaning 'heavy and large industries'.

The court ordered that if the factory owners choose to relocate to a neighbouring district, they would have to pay each worker monthly wages during the period of the move, as well as one year's salary as a resettlement bonus. If owners opted to close their factories, workers would be entitled to six years' wages as a retrenchment allowance. Two years later, it was found that only one out of the 168 industries had paid any compensation to the workers.[37] In any case, the liability of the factory management was limited to the narrowest possible definition of 'workmen', those who were on the rolls as permanent employees.[38] An estimated of 35,000–50,000 workers were rendered jobless because of this court-enforced relocation, but were not even heard by the court until after the closure of the factories.[39] A new federation of trade unions and other human rights organizations was formed in December 1996 as a response to the Supreme Court's orders called Delhi Janwadi Adhikar Manch (DJAM—Delhi Socialist

Rights Forum).[40] The Manch tried to intervene in court, but as Amita Baviskar records:

> Three trade unions affiliated with the Manch approached the bench separately through their lawyers, asking to be heard in the air pollution case. The judges brushed them aside, merely remarking that the court would protect workers' interests and did not need the intercession of the unions. This verbal assurance was not recorded as a part of court proceedings.[41]

Later again:

> ...when the Manch approached the Supreme Court and pointed out that the judges' orders were being violated, the court suggested that they take their complaints to the labor commissioner, an official whose previous inaction had already demonstrated his total lack of interest in protecting workers' rights.[42]

The closure suited many of the industries. The bigger ones were anyway keen to shut down or relocate, but Indian labour laws made closure of an industrial establishment almost impossible. The court's intervention gave them a timely opportunity. Not only that, this order provided them a real bonanza as they were free to dispose at least 32 per cent of the industrial land as commercial real estate, land that had been earlier given to them by the government at heavily subsidized rates. The court was not unaware of this as it noted, 'In view of the huge increase of prices of land in Delhi the reuse of the vacant land is bound to bring a lot of money which can meet the cost of relocation.'[43] On the other hand, it was estimated that the total number of people directly affected by loss of employment (workers and their families) as a result of these orders exceeded 250,000.[44]

Within three months of the July 1996 order, the court also ordered in the same case the relocation or closure of another 513 factories, 46 hot mix plants, 21 arc/induction furnaces and 243 brick kilns, all of which were to be closed down or moved by 1997. This spate of 1996–97 orders was only the first of the many major developments in this case that completely reordered the city. Already, even at that early stage, it was perceived as signalling a new trend. As Baviskar noted:

> The partnership of environmentalists M. C. Mehta and Kuldip Singh, advocate and judge, which resulted in directives that affected the lives and livelihoods of hundreds of thousands of workers and their families, people who had no representation in court, exemplifies the new efficient dispensation of justice in the 'public interest' that middle-class people acclaim.[45]

The case continued though the dramatis personae changed. By the late 1990s, an amicus curiae was appointed in this case – senior advocate Ranjit Kumar – as was the general trend in PIL cases. The public interest petitioner M. C. Mehta now participated only intermittently, if at all, and henceforth Kumar was to play a key role in the future directions that the case took.

In 2000 came the next major development in the deindustrializing trajectory of this case. This time, the scale was even bigger as the order was to close/relocate all 'non-conforming' industrial units, i.e. factories located in areas designated as 'residential' in the Delhi Master Plan, the attempt being to strictly enforce Delhi's zoning laws.[46] The stage was set in 1996 itself when the court asked Delhi Pollution Control Committee (DPCC) for information on the number of polluting and non-polluting units running in non-conforming areas. The resulting survey put the figure of industries in Delhi at 126,218 units, with 97,411 of them being non-conforming.[47] It was decided that only 'household industries' – those that did not pollute, employed fewer than five workers, used no more than one kilowatt of power and occupied an area smaller than 30 square metres – would be licensed and allowed to continue where they were. But only 5 per cent of 51,000 units that applied for these licences could meet these stringent criteria.[48] On 1 April 1996, the court ordered the rest to be relocated by 1 January 1997. But a fundamental problem arose. There was no place to relocate them as there were not enough industrial plots as envisaged in the Master Plan. Only after the order was passed in 1996, a government developer called the Delhi State Industrial Development Corporation (DSIDC) began to acquire land in Bawana, on the Northern outskirts of the city, where small factories from residential areas could relocate. The court meanwhile allowed those factory owners who had applied to the DSIDC for alternate plots temporary licenses to continue operating in their old locations. The court asked the government to submit quarterly reports about the progress in complying with its orders. In September 1999, the court heard the case again and fixed the deadline for relocation for 31 December 1999. Eventually by July 2000, 52,000 factories had applied for alternate plot allotments, but not a single factory had been relocated. Because it had still not finished developing the industrial land, DSIDC in 2000 asked the Supreme Court for an extension until March 2004 to develop the Bawana industrial properties.[49]

The court at this point lost all patience with the relocation process and on 12 September 2000, it ordered that 'all polluting industries of whatever category operating in residential areas must be asked to shut down'. This judicial exasperation with the mendacity and inefficiency of the government would lead to massive devastation in the lives of Delhi's labouring class. As factory owners later complained, 'They were bearing the brunt of the punishment that ought to have been meted out to the state for its inaction'.[50]

It was as if the court had no duty to take care of workers' interests in this massive relocation exercise – that duty was the concern of the government alone. When, after the 31 December 1999 deadline lapsed and the process was nowhere near completion, the Supreme Court issued a notice in November 2000 to the government representatives that they would be hauled up for contempt for not implementing the court's orders, the government panicked and 'ordered the immediate closure of 'all' nonconforming industrial units (and not just the polluting ones)'.[51] Almost a hundred thousand factories were thus closed down within a week. Government officials, escorted by heavily armed policemen, went around sealing factory premises, locking their doors, disconnecting electricity and water supply. Riots ensued, with a general strike on 20 November 2000. The accompanying violence led to three workers being shot dead by the police and hundreds injured.[52] The court, soon after these incidents, scolded the government for closing not just polluting but also non-polluting units. However, its new deadline for closing all polluting units now was not much later, fixed for 7 January 2001, which was eventually extended till 31 December 2002.[53] In the intervening chaos of the 2000–03 period, thousands of factories closed down, though the Delhi government tried and eventually succeeded in liberalizing the Master Plan norms for factories. The definition of 'household' factories was liberalized as well as 24 areas with about 20,000 factories and a land use concentration of 70+ per cent industrial usage re-designated as 'industrial' and thus regularized. This issue led to a major political battle between the central and the state governments, as Delhi's land use planning is in the hands of the central government.

Kaveri Gill has analyzed the impact of this Supreme Court action on a specific 'polluting and non-conforming' urban informal industry, that of plastic recycling, which could ironically otherwise be seen as environment-friendly. This community of workers, belonging to a Dalit caste called 'Khatik' and working in the plastic scrap trade, had prior to this case been quite successful in exercising their political voice around a caste identity. But the interventions of the PIL court in this case negated their ability to mobilize politically. The usual democratic channels were bypassed by the Supreme Court. In Gill's analysis:

> The elected representatives of the people, in this case Outer Delhi MLAs and others, such as former and present chief ministers from both political parties, were given no avenue to contest the order and influence the course of policy on the basis of larger trade-offs with poverty and livelihoods in their constituencies.[54]

The court was thus able to ride roughshod over the negotiations of political society and able to impose its vision of the city via its apotheosis of zoning laws as incorporated in the Master Plan.

In September 2000, the court had taken the implementation of the order out of the hands of the Delhi government, instead appointing 'an independent nodal agency under the auspices of the Central Government to ensure that the relocation took place within the desired timeframe'.[55] The Central Minister for Urban Development was to head this nodal agency. It was not a coincidental choice of appointee, as the then incumbent was none other than Jagmohan, the man responsible for the massive Emergency era social engineering in Delhi. The court showed its hand here, knowing full well that 'Delhi governments lacked the political will to carry out relocation orders, as it would adversely affect the livelihood and business of hundreds of thousands of voters,'[56] and that if there was one person in government who could implement these far-reaching orders, it was Jagmohan. And soon enough, the relocation orders 'came to be associated with Jagmohan's office and person' and in the discourse of the displaced, with the Emergency-era dislocations.[57] The court's actions reminded the factory owners of the Emergency years, specifically, as Gill notes, because:

> The Supreme Court refused to hear the lawyer representing the collective body of small-scale traders and manufacturers affected by the relocation order. Various locality- and community-based trade associations had spent a considerable amount of time and effort raising substantial sums of money in order to hire a lawyer willing to defend them, only to have the Supreme Court have him sit down without an adequate hearing.[58]

As with the auto rickshaws, affected parties were not heard by the PIL court, before sealing their fate. Jagmohan was eventually removed from the Urban Development Ministry in 2001 at the behest of his own party leaders from Delhi, when he refused to ratify the change in land use norms to regularize de facto 'industrial areas'. He was now made the Tourism Minister, a position in which he wreaked further havoc, as we shall see in the next chapter.

WP 4677/1985 becomes 'the Sealing case'

After having successfully deindustrialized the city through this single PIL, Writ Petition (Civil) 4677/1985, the Supreme Court went further down the path of making Delhi a 'world-class city' with a judgment on 16 February 2006 in this same case, proclaiming that all commercial units in residential areas would be closed down. This directive took the zoning logic of the Delhi Master Plan further, with its clear separation of residential and commercial establishments. This PIL 4677/1985, which till 2005 was officially called 'RE: Shifting of Industries from Residential Area of Delhi, New Delhi' in its recorded orders, took a new direction after 17 March 2005, when a bench headed by Justice Y. K. Sabharwal, acting at the behest of Amicus Curiae Ranjit Kumar, decided 'to hear and decide the issue of commercialization of residential areas'.

This fateful move would make the case even more infamous than it already was – and both the judge and the amicus lawyer would be identified with this new chapter of the PIL. The court's intervention would affect hundreds of thousands of commercial establishments in Delhi as the desired zoning separation existed only on the map. The contradictions between the Master Plan's desired city and the city that in fact existed was so widespread that many even surmized that the majority of shops in Delhi would turn out to be in areas demarcated as non-commercial and would, therefore, be guilty of 'misuse of property'. In fact, the judgment of 16 February 2006 records that the lawyer for MCD had argued that 'since there is a large scale misuse of residential premises for commercial purposes, it is a physical impossibility to remove the misuser'. The court reacted with anger: 'Such a contention is not open to MCD. It is not merely a case of only lack of will to take action, it appears to be a case of predominance of extraneous considerations.' The state's role in this process, in the eyes of the court, was seen as tolerating these illegalities and indeed being complicit in them, partly explained as 'corruption' and partly as 'vote banks', but often narrated as a jumble of the two. Or, as Justice Y. K. Sabharwal wrote in a newspaper article about this case after his retirement, 'Judges decide on law and not on populism'.[59]

The municipal authorities were, therefore, ordered to seal these commercial properties so that they could no longer be (mis)used. The extreme mismatch between the de jure and de facto situation here has often been explained away in terms of the modernist state's attempt to impose Western zoning ideas alien to Indian sensibilities and, therefore, an impractical hope. But it could, at least partially, also be attributed to the abject failure of the state authorities, in being able to implement their own Master Plan. There were projections with a time frame in the Master Plan for a certain amount of commercial space to be developed for the expected populations by specific dates. The state, repeating its record with the industrial estates, did not end up developing even half the commercial space it was supposed to. The resulting mismatch of supply and demand of commercial land, not surprisingly, led to shops opening in areas demarcated as 'non-commercial'. The Delhi Development Authority (DDA) was the sole developer, having acquired agricultural land all over the city in the 1950s and 1960s and being given the responsibility to develop it. But the DDA completely failed to provide industrial or commercial or indeed residential properties in the measure estimated by its own plan document. Without holding the DDA and its failed monopoly accountable, the court repeatedly penalized the unplanned construction of industrial, commercial or residential establishments. It went about treating the symptom rather than the cause. Now, once again, the people who ran commercial establishments and worked in them were going to be penalized in the name of clamping down on illegality, without hearing them in this process. The state's fundamental failure in creating the demand for these illegalities by not delivering the commercial space it targeted in the Master Plan, was impatiently glossed over. While the court ignored this omission, it relied on the same document as gospel to insist on strict enforcement of zoning. It, thus, acted wilfully blind to the impossibility of what it was demanding, by harping on about illegalities while ignoring the underlying reason behind it. Because the court had ordered sealing of commercial establishments in areas not designated as commercial, the case came to be known as 'the sealing case'. It was under that name that the Supreme Court dominated the newspaper headlines in Delhi in 2006–07.

Once the court had decided to start the crackdown on 'misusers', it asked the MCD about the process it wanted to adopt to go about this mammoth operation. The MCD suggested a four-part plan – start first with a survey of misuse which would take six months, followed by notices issued to the misusers identified, then grant an opportunity to them of being heard and finally seal properties, focusing on the blatant and obvious cases of large-scale misuse. The court had no patience for following such a process. Instead, it wanted a public notice to be issued immediately (within 10 days) in major newspapers stating that violators would have 30 days to stop misuse on their own, and file an affidavit saying they would themselves close the shop and resume residential use. After 30 days, if misuse did not stop, MCD would start the process of sealing, starting with major roads. This was the court's plan of action. What followed, however, was much more complicated, as for once the court had taken on a really powerful lobby – the traders and shopkeepers of Delhi.[60]

Initially, things seemed to be following the court's script. The first public notice was issued on 26 February 2006, stating that the first phase of sealing would target those roads with more than 50 per cent commercial misuse as well as other major roads above a specified width. On 24 March, a little over a month after the court's initial sealing order of 16 February, some traders' associations approached the court for more time to stop misuse, and the court directed that the affidavits for voluntarily ceasing misuse would have to be filed within the next four days by 28 March, following which they would be given time till 30 June. But, for those who did not file any affidavits, the sealing action would commence on 29 March 2006. The 28 March deadline for affidavits was extended to 7 April, but sealing operations had started by then. Forty thousand eight hundred affidavits were filed in this allotted time, swearing to stop the misuse by 30 June[61] and 'giving an undertaking to the effect that violation of this would...subject him/her to offence of perjury and contempt of court for violation of the order of the Court.' But this large number who filed affidavits was still only a fraction of the total shops affected by the court orders. For the others, the sealing action had begun, a court-led campaign cheered on by the drumbeat of the daily newspapers.

Not trusting the municipal bodies' ability and willingness to carry out its orders without constant prodding, the Supreme Court on 24 March 2006 appointed a monitoring committee, 'in order to oversee the implementation of the law, namely sealing of offending premises in terms of the letter and spirit of this Court's directions.' The Committee was headed by Bhure Lal, the retired bureaucrat who also headed the EPCA, which continued to give reports on vehicular pollution related issues. The other two members of this Committee were K. J. Rao, another retired bureaucrat and Major General (Retired) Som Jhingan. They were allotted office space in Delhi's swanky NGO-cum-cultural hub, the India Habitat Centre. By this time, the petitioner advocate M. C. Mehta in whose name the original case was still continuing, 21 years after he filed it, hardly ever appeared in court. Instead, the amicus curiae Ranjit Kumar had taken charge. The court had 'directed that all the petitions relating to sealing in Delhi are to be routed through the learned Amicus-Curiae'.[62] This meant that any petition relating to sealing of any commercial establishment in Delhi had to be dealt with as part of this case and not independently. And the amicus decided when and how it was heard by the court. This was really important, as soon there were thousands of interlocutory applications (IAs) and Writ Petitions filed by owners of commercial establishments aggrieved by the sealing actions taken pursuant to court orders. As the court orders were broad and the sealing was to be done by the Municipal Corporation of Delhi (MCD), supervised by the Monitoring Committee, the question often arose of ascertaining whether in a specific case of an establishment being sealed, it was violating the Master Plan or not. Also, getting temporary relief for the removal of supplies already stocked up in the shops, became a repeated cause of affected parties approaching the court. In such a situation, with the number of applications proliferating in the same case, it became extremely cluttered and difficult to manage. The amicus, who had a monopoly on deciding which applications would be heard by the court and when, occupied an increasingly powerful position.

This 1985 PIL writ petition number 4677/1985 was what I call an 'omnibus PIL'. This meant that the case had become a juggernaut which dealt with, for example, all aspects relating to 'misuse of properties' at a citywide level, with the Master Plan being the reference point in deciding the scale of the problem and its geography, and all other individual cases filed pertaining to this issue would be deemed to be a part of the omnibus case. Since there were obviously a very large number of properties affected, only a relatively small number of them could be sealed every day. The newspapers approvingly reported this sealing process on a daily basis, with comments by the members of the monitoring committee as they accompanied the MCD sealing squad. The monitoring committee acquired a reputation for their zeal in removing the 'illegalities' from the city, and their activities were vociferously backed by the media and the Resident Welfare Associations (RWAs), organizations of middle-class residents of gated colonies that proliferated in Delhi in the 2000s.

The massive outcry from the traders and shopkeepers that followed the sealing actions under the orders of the court also got public attention, but it was seen by the newspapers and the courts as coloured by 'political society' and its illegalities. And 'political society' did indeed intervene, this time speedily unlike at the time of the relocation of industries. While the state had till now mostly allowed the court to shape the city as per its wishes, with the sealing matter the political stakes became too high. The shopkeepers and traders of Delhi had always been a powerful constituency and both the leading political parties were quite agitated about sealing, unlike the slum demolitions going on at the same time, as we shall see in the next chapter.

On 28 March 2006, the day before the sealing was to start, a notification was issued by the Delhi Development Authority (DDA) modifying the Master Plan insofar as the chapter on mixed use was concerned. The aim was to take a liberal view regarding mixed land use, i.e. the provision of non-residential activity in residential premises[63]. The attempt was to give relief to small shopkeepers affected by the Supreme Court directive, allowing some commercial activities to run in residential areas. The new policy to legalize commercial activities on the ground floor of residential premises would be applicable on 118 roads in the capital. This was, however, still too minuscule a relief and two days after the sealing started, the traders went on a 48-hour strike amid a flurry of political activity. On 10 April, Delhi traders met the President of India, APJ Abdul Kalam and sought his intervention, arguing that the business community was neither a petitioner nor respondent in the PIL under which action was being taken against them. Initially, the government tried to get a six-month reprieve from the court to 'complete the exercise of identifying mixed use roads and streets in residential areas within six months in a systematic and organized manner as per provisions of the Delhi Master Plan.' But this cut no ice with the court and it criticized the government for its 'policy of appeasement'. The Bench of Chief Justice Y. K. Sabharwal and Justice C. K. Thakker observed on 28 April:

> Appeasement causes confusion. We extended the time [for sealing] but meanwhile it [Centre] came out with a notification. By doing so what message you [Centre] want to convey to the law abiding citizen... It is a deliberate failure because of extraneous considerations at the cost of the citizen and the message is the law abiding citizen suffers.

The apex court also observed that it was because of the nexus between government officials, law-enforcing agencies and businessmen that there was unauthorized commercial use of the residential areas.[64]

Amidst the court's intransigence and bipartisan political support, the government finally introduced a new law in Parliament called the Delhi Laws (Special Provisions) Act, 2006. This proposed a one-year moratorium from punitive action against unauthorized development in the capital and provided for status quo as on 1 January 2006 of unauthorized development in respect of mixed land use, construction beyond sanctioned plans and encroachment by slum dwellers, hawkers and street vendors in the city. On 12 May 2006, the Delhi Laws (Special Provisions) Bill, 2006 was passed by the Lower House; the Upper House passed it three days later, and on receipt of assent of the President on 19 May 2006, it was notified the same day – an unusually fast pace for a Central legislation. The very next day, the Government of India issued a notification placing a moratorium for a period of one year in respect of all notices issued by local authorities regarding categories of unauthorized development. By the Act and this notice, the government tried to relieve those who had given an undertaking to the Court, and also issued directions for removal of seals that had been placed on the premises till then. As a result, the municipal authorities suspended their sealing drive. By the time the notification was issued, around 15,000 commercial establishments functioning in residential areas had already been sealed, out of which 6,000 were desealed after the court received affidavits from the owners.

The constitutionality of this new statute was challenged immediately and came up before the same 'sealing' bench of the Supreme Court. Initially, the court just expressed outrage in oral remarks calling this new law 'wholly invalid and void', and declared that 'this is pure and simple legislature over-ruling this court'. The court speculated that the statute might be unconstitutional, but refused to stay its operation until the constitutionality question had been adjudicated. On 10 August 2006, however, while the court still made oral statements from the bench that 'though prima facie the Act is an 'invalid' statute, we are not inclined to completely stay the legislation'[65], it insisted on suspending the notification that had been passed a day after the Act was passed, as it was seen as expressly trying to undo and overrule the actions that the court had already taken.

The premise was that even if the sealing of new areas covered under the moratorium was now barred, the government could not undo actions with respect to the specific establishments against which the court had already taken action, either in terms of affidavits filed, undertaking to stop misuse by 30 June or in cases of establishments already sealed. The court, therefore, ordered the Municipal authorities to reseal some 5,000 shops, which had been earlier sealed by the court and then unsealed by the government. The court also ordered the sealing of 40,800 shops that had given affidavits to stop commercial activities on their premises after 15 September (extended from the earlier date of 30 June). Two categories of shops had emerged – those who had given affidavits and those who had not.

The government was wrong footed at first and had to undo its earlier notification by a fresh notice. But amidst the resumption of the sealing, after three months and a fresh crisis, the Delhi government finally amended the Master Plan in September, declaring large areas that already had massive commercial presence but were still designated 'residential' instead of 'commercial'. The amended plan also declared that some residential colonies could have commercial establishments in their midst. Colonies, as residential neighbourhoods in Delhi are called, were categorized from A to G by size of residential plots and density of population (both being indicators of 'posh'ness, an English word that has successfully been adopted into Delhi Hindi). Except for 'A' and 'B' areas, where zoning was to be strictly enforced, with minor exceptions allowed only if the local RWAs agreed, the other categories were granted a reprieve. The government also issued two notifications in September 2006, clearing 2,183 roads for mixed land use, commercial stretches and pedestrian shopping streets in the C, D, E, F, G and H categories of colonies across the capital. As the sealing continued, a 'Bandh' against the sealing campaign called by the Confederation of All India Traders on 20 September 2006 led to violence and five people died in police firing in Seelampur, one of the poorest parts of East Delhi.[66] These actions by the government as well as the protests were of course immediately condemned by the media, the RWAs and the court as unseemly vote bank politics.

With the conflict heating up, the Court on 29 September 2006 criticized the government for these notifications, calling them 'ad hoc measures' and orally observed that 'the last minute notifications are causing utter confusion and chaos to the citizens... An impression is given as if judiciary is on one side and government on the other side.' It continued to insist that at least the 40,000-odd people who had filed affidavits that they would stop misuse would still have to comply with it or have their shops sealed to protect 'the dignity and authority of the Court'. The court allowed them time till 31 October 2006 on account of the festival of Diwali. With regard to the others saved by the new September notifications, the court required fresh undertakings to be filed by all before the Monitoring Committee by 10 November 2006 (later extended to 31 January 2007) that misuse would be stopped as per the court directions if the law was invalidated and/or the notifications quashed. It also declared that sealing would continue vis-à-vis others not covered by the notifications. The court restrained the government from issuing any other notification for conversion of residential use into commercial use except with the leave of the court.

With the deadline of 31 October approaching and another bandh call given by the traders at the perceived discrimination against the 40,000 traders who had given undertakings, the MCD and the government again approached the court. This time they were armed with a survey which said that 25,000 out of these 40,000 odd would be covered by the September mixed land use notifications. The court finally recognized the anomaly in insisting on action against the people who had filed affidavits in time, while others who had not filed would get away, and temporarily barred action against them. But after the experience of these shops whose shopkeepers had filed affidavits, the others covered by the new notifications were also now required to file fresh undertakings. They would be subject to the court's final decision on the legality of the notifications by 31 January 2007. They, now, hesitated to file any affidavits because they did not want to be in a similar boat in the future. As sealing could theoretically resume against all of them, the government deployed its final weapon on 7 February 2007. It notified a New Master Plan for Delhi, which incorporated the recent mixed-use notifications and relaxed many of the zoning norms.

***

The new plan – MPD 2021 – was declared an 'Anti-Plan plan' by the newspapers and was immediately challenged as invalid in the Supreme Court by the RWAs. The court reacted in a manner similar to its response to the prior amendments, and soon declared that it would examine the constitutionality of the Plan. It also made actions taken as per the new Plan norms subject to the court's final decision on its constitutionality. For instance, the Plan, for the first time, allowed a third floor to be constructed in a residential building. Initially the court barred the MCD from giving any permission for construction of a third floor in residential areas under this provision, but a year later (by an order in March 2008), the court allowed it, subject to an undertaking given by the home owners that they would abide by its final decision on the validity of MPD-2021. An MCD official explained the standard practice that had evolved on this issue after this order: 'The court had said neither the owner nor the person to whom the property would be sold or transferred could claim equity, if the verdict goes against them. We just take an affidavit from the owner stating this.' The MCD had already sanctioned almost 25,000 building plans for the third floor by 2011.[67] By 2013, this number was estimated to be many times larger.

The writ petition challenging the 2007 Master Plan that arose in this case and was heard along with it is still pending in court, and hundreds of thousands of people own and/or live in third floor residential units throughout the city. But permission to construct it is given subject to the court decision and if the court decides against the New Master Plan norms, these would be declared illegal and subject to demolition – a kind of Damocles' sword hanging over people in Delhi due to this case. Meanwhile, the drama of sealing and de-sealing continued off and on even after the MPD-2021 came into force, though with relatively fewer protagonists and lower stakes. After 2009, in particular since the retirement of Justice Arijit Pasayat, who headed this bench after Justice Sabharwal's retirement, hardly any effective hearing took place in this case.[68] The case had become impossibly unwieldy with hundreds of IAs pending, mostly for de-sealing of specific premises already sealed. For a bench hearing this case for the first time, it was a herculean task to get a handle on the sheer bulk of the files in this case. The cause list of this case alone, listing all the pending matters, would itself run into dozens of pages. By 2013, as many as 900 IAs connected to this case were still pending. Also pending were the writ petitions challenging the constitutionality of provisions of the Master Plan 2021, the Delhi Laws (Special Provisions) Act, which had been renewed every year and the DDA notifications allowing mixed land use. The court had had enough of it by then, and on 30 April 2013, the sealing case was divided into two parts and remanded to the lower judiciary. The IAs dealing with factual questions requesting for de-sealing were sent to the appellate tribunals of the respective Municipal Authorities in Delhi, and the writ petitions dealing with the more legal questions were referred to the Delhi High Court. The court had belatedly realized its own limitations in dealing with issues of such complexity and amplitude. Meanwhile, the Delhi Laws (Special Provisions) continue to be extended periodically and are still in force in 2016.

Conclusion

One of the reasons for the court easing off on sealing was the retirement in January 2007 of Chief Justice Y. K. Sabharwal, who had presided over the sealing matter from the beginning. In fact, he had initiated this matter by his order in 2005 and moved the focus decisively from relocation of 'non-conforming industries' to commercial 'misuse' of residential properties. On his retirement, he confessed that the 'sealing case' in the capital was the most difficult one of his career. He said that he had to earn the wrath of his friends and relatives on the issue:

> My friends and relatives even stopped talking to me. Yesterday one of my relatives [affected by the sealing order] told me sarcastically that I am a big man. I told him I cannot solve individual problems. The problem is because of corruption in the system and flaws in the Master Plan.[69]

Perhaps the uniqueness of the sealing case in Delhi's long history of PIL is not only the amazing alacrity and avidity with which the government and MCD fought the long-drawn out chess battle with the court, with one move following another, but also that the potential losers in this case could include the 'friends and relatives' of a Supreme Court judge, not something that could be said by the thousands made jobless by the relocation of industries in the same case or indeed, about the slum-dwellers who were made homeless by the PIL courts' intervention in the 2000s.

As Justice Sabharwal phrased his dilemma: 'The issue of sealing was difficult, as on the one hand it was a question of law and on the other it was the sufferings of people.' For once, at least, the judge was in a position to encounter (and potentially understand) the 'sufferings of people' caused by his PIL orders, unlike in the many other instances of people who lost their livelihoods because of the orders in this very case. The auto rickshaw drivers were easy sacrificial lambs for the cause of environment – unlike, say, diesel car manufacturers. Owners of large factories wanting to close sunset industries and convert them into profitable real estate were given a break by the court, while the labour working in the same factories paid a heavy price. Smaller factory owners had less space to manoeuvre in court, but a section of them managed to pull their political weight eventually. But the hundreds of thousands of traders and 'mom and pop shop' owners of Delhi were an immeasurably more powerful constituency, for political society and eventually, even for the court.

Perhaps this is why the sealing matter had a much stormier career in court – lasting for a whole year, and allowing the court at best a pyrrhic victory. It is not a story we encounter very often with PIL, but the exception is of interest precisely for that reason. When can people manoeuvre around an all-powerful PIL court and when can they not?

***

The most unsavoury aspect of the sealing case came to light four months after Justice Sabharwal's retirement – causing what writer Arundhati Roy then called a 'scandal in the palace'.[70] In May 2007, the tabloid *Mid-day* published a news item pointing out that just when Justice Sabharwal was kick-starting the 'sealing case' by turning the long-running PIL about relocation of industries into a case about misuse of commercial properties, his sons were entering into partnership with two major mall and commercial complex developers, resulting at the very least in a 'conflict of interest' as their father led a judicial campaign that indirectly benefited them. Suddenly, the repressed aspect of the sealing case was out in the open: that it was about mall owners versus shopkeepers. Closing down shops would create a demand for mall space. The sealing campaign had further limited the availability of commercial space for shops, and as Roy put it, 'The better-off amongst those whose shops and offices had been sealed queued up for space in these malls. Prices shot up. The mall business boomed, it was the newest game in town.' And ironically, the judge who initiated and presided over the sealing campaign against commercial use of residential property, himself simultaneously allowed his sons to use his private as well as official residence for commercial purposes, that too as their firm's registered office! Meanwhile, instead of starting any inquiry against Justice Sabharwal, the whistle-blower journalists of *Mid-day* were sentenced to four months' imprisonment for contempt of court, in a hurriedly decided *suo motu* case[71] initiated by the Delhi High Court.

Even if the charges of corruption against Justice Sabharwal are unproven and it was perhaps 'a borderline case',[72] the remarkable fact is that a jurisdiction like PIL enabled a judge to wilfully initiate a roving inquiry into a complex issue like zoning that affected millions. He could then decide on the path to be taken and force its implementation at a citywide level with supervision by his own chosen officials, with his own handpicked lawyer deciding the direction of the case and without necessarily hearing the parties affected by his decisions. In such a system, petty corruption is at the very least an occupational hazard. Ideological predilection leading a judge in such a direction is scarcely less dangerous.

Such an ideological slant in favour of corporate capital was clearly enunciated in a judgment made by the Supreme Court around the same time when it was leading the campaign against the toleration of illegalities in 'the sealing case'. On 17 October 2006, the court delivered its verdict on one of the most conspicuous cases of elite illegality in Delhi. The cause of the controversy was the construction of a huge complex of three 'world-class' shopping malls, intended to be the most exclusive in India. The location of these malls was to be the South Delhi ridge, hitherto designated a forest area, and with a history of acute water scarcity in the residential neighbourhoods in the vicinity. A PIL had been filed against the malls by concerned citizens of the area. No environmental clearance had been obtained. An 'expert committee' appointed by the court found blatant illegalities and noted that 'the location of large commercial complexes in this area was environmentally unsound'. But with substantial construction already completed, the committee recommended 'a compromise with de facto situation'. The environmentalist petitioners protested against such post-facto regularization and cited various decisions of the court where it had 'taken serious view of unauthorized construction'.

The court brushed aside all objections, having decided already that it was 'satisfied about the bona fides' of the mall developers. What the bench did here was to clearly specify its double standards:

> The stand that wherever constructions have been made unauthorisedly demolition is the only option cannot apply to the present cases, more particularly, when they unlike (sic), where some private individuals or private limited companies or firms being allotted to have made contraventions, are corporate bodies and institutions and *the question of their having indulged in any malpractices in getting the approval or sanction does not arise.*[3] (Emphasis mine)

Just 18 days before the above verdict, the Supreme Court had passed the following judgment in 4677/1985 at the height of its exasperation in the sealing case:

> The city of Delhi is an example of a classical case, which, for the last number of years, has been a witness of flagrant violations of municipal laws, town planning laws and norms, Master Plan and environmental laws. It is borne out from various orders and judgments passed by this Court and the Delhi High Court, whether in a case of shifting of hazardous and polluting industries or providing cleaner fuel (CNG) or encroachment of public land and streets or massive unauthorized construction and misuse of properties. It is a common knowledge that these illegal activities are also one of the main sources of corruption.

Through PIL, the appellate judges of Delhi launched a fierce drive to undo illegality and corruption in the municipal regulation of land use of Delhi, of which WP 4677/1985 is the definitive example. However, some of the most flagrant of such violations were the massive building complexes built clearly in violation of municipal norms – Akshardham Temple and Commonwealth Games Village on the Yamuna River Bed, Sainik Farms – the largest unauthorized colony in Delhi and of course, the Vasant Kunj malls. High profile PILs had been filed against all of these conspicuously illegal developments and these were all heard in the same decade that saw so much judicial action against illegally built structures all over the city. However, in each of these cases of egregious violations of municipal laws, the court rationalized their existence and refrained from intervening. All of these buildings survive unscathed. The wrath of PIL was clearly a selective one.

Endnotes

1 Divan, 'A Mistake of Judgment'.

2 Gita Dewan Verma, *Slumming India*, p. 88.

3 See Sivaramakrishnan, 'Environment, law, and democracy in India', pp. 905–28. For a more critical view, see Menon, 'Environment and the Will to Rule', Mayur Suresh and Siddharth Narrain, *The Shifting Scales of Justice*, pp. 59–78. For a detailed analysis of two large urban environmental PIL cases in Kolkata around the turn of the century, see Dembowski, *Taking the State to Court.*

4 Writ Petition (Civil) No.13381/1984

5 Writ Petition (Civil) No. 3727/1985

6 Writ Petition (Civil) No. 13029/1985

7 Divan, 'Cleaning the Ganga'.

8 Hidayatullah, 'Highways and Bylanes of Justice'.

9 The members of this committee were D. K. Biswas, Chairman of the Central Pollution Control Board, Anil Aggarwal of the Centre for Science and Environment, Shri Jagdish Khattar of Maruti Udyog Limited and Ms. Kiran Dhingra, Transport Commissioner of Delhi.

10 Rosencranz and Jackson, 'The Delhi Pollution Case', p. 15.

11 Bell et al., 'Clearing the Air'. See also Mathur, 'Battling for Clean Environment'.

12 See the Supreme Court judgment at *http://www.indiaenvironmentportal.org.in/files/file/28%20July%201998.pdf*

13 Bell et al, 'Clearing the Air', p. 39.

14 Ibid p. 39.

15 On 26 March 2001, the Supreme Court extended this deadline to 30 September 2001, provided auto rickshaw owners 'who have placed firm orders for new CNG vehicles or for conversion to CNG mode' 'give details on affidavits by 31st March, 2001 about their existing vehicles, as also details of the orders placed by them for new CNG vehicles or for conversion to CNG mode.' The difficulties in this process of getting an official document to prove that such an order has been placed is discussed in Faruqui and Sud, Auto-rickshaws in Delhi. This caused a situation where tens of thousands of auto rickshaw-owners had to file the requisite affidavits in the Supreme Court in five days' time, leading to an unprecedented situation in the Supreme Court registry. As a result of this melee and the confusion caused by the conversion process, the number of autorickshaw permits in Delhi declined from 83,000 to 50,000 in 2002.

16 Aman Trust, 'On the road to nowhere?'

17 Sharan, '"New" Delhi: 'Fashioning an Urban Environment through Science and Law', and Rosencranz and Jackson, 'The Delhi Pollution Case', p. 223.

18 Paragraph 9 of the Order of 16 December 1997.

19 EPCA Report Number 34, 'Review of existing cap on the number of three wheelers in Delhi and its implications for pollution and congestion', January 2010.

20 Order dated 3 September 2009. The EPCA accordingly submitted its Report Number 34 on 'Review of existing cap on the number of three-wheelers in Delhi and its implications for pollution and congestion' in January 2010. The court finally granted permission for an increase on 18 November 2011.

21 Aman Trust, 'On the road to nowhere?', p. 2.

22 Harding, 'A Few Questions about a Few Thousand New Auto-rickshaws in Delhi'.

23 The application on behalf of the auto rickshaw unions was first moved in this case in the Supreme Court in 2009.

24 In 2011, an estimated 90% of TSRs were owned by financiers as opposed to drivers, according to the Special Leave Petition (Civil) 22870–22871 of 2011 in Nyaya Bhoomi vs Transport Department, Delhi, available at *http://nyayabhoomi.org/autorickshaw-service/auto-finance-mafia* . On the other hand, in 2001, an estimated 65 per cent driven by their owners. See Mohan and Roy, Operating on Three Wheels.

25 Baviskar, 'The Politics of the City'.

26 Chatterjee, *Lineages of Political Society,*, p. 208–35.

27 See Mehta, 'The Rise of Judicial Sovereignty'. For older versions of this theory of *Modus Vivendi*, see Lloyd and Susanne Rudolph, 1981. The classic account remains Baxi, *The Indian Supreme Court and Politics.*

28 WP(C)202/1995. For a discussion of the role of the amicus curiae in 'the forest case', see Chowdhury, 'From Judicial Activism to Adventurism', p. 177. Chowdhury provides instances to 'illustrate how the amicus curiae in this case was able to repeatedly influence the Court's thinking.' (p. 185)

29 For a discussion of the writ petition filed in this case, see Sharan, In the City, Out of Place, p. 200.

30 Sudershan, In Defence of Judicial Activism.

31 Divan and Rosencranz, *Environmental Law and Policy in India*, p. 259.

32 Sudershan, In Defence of Judicial Activism.

33 Agarwal, 'Fight for a Forest'.

34 See Ahuja, *People, Law, and Justice,* p. 807

35 The most important of the many applications filed in this case turned out to be I.A. no. 22/1995, under which the orders in the next three phases of this case would nominally be passed.

36 AIR 1996 SC 2231

37 Dasgupta, 'Tall Blunder'.

38 Baviskar et al., 'Rethinking Indian Environmentalism Industrial Pollution in Delhi and Fisheries in Kerala', p. 199.

39 Delhi Janwadi Adhikar Manch (DJAM), 'The Order That Felled a City', p. 22. For the higher figure and contextualizing discussion, see Nigam, Dislocating Delhi.

40 Nigam, 'Whose Delhi Is It Anyway?

41 Baviskar et al., Rethinking Indian Environmentalism Industrial Pollution in Delhi and Fisheries in Kerala, p. 199. In Chapter 1, we saw a similar argument being deployed for an uncannily similar move to exclude affected groups from being heard in 'the forest case'.

42 Baviskar et al., 'Rethinking Indian Environmentalism Industrial Pollution in Delhi and Fisheries in Kerala', p. 200

43 (1996) 4 SCC 750

44 Baviskar et al., 'Rethinking Indian Environmentalism Industrial Pollution in Delhi and Fisheries in Kerala', p. 200.

45 Ibid. p. 211

46 While the July 1996 order about the 168 industries was about those falling under the highly polluting 'H' category (which needed to be relocated out of Delhi in a neighbouring district), industries belonging to Categories B,C, D, E, F and G, located in 'non-conforming' areas, as classified by the Master Plan were to be moved to designated industrial areas. See Gill, *Of Poverty and Plastic*, p. 225.

47 Ahmed, Khanduja, Sethi, 'Master plan for anarchy', *Down to Earth* 9(15), 31st Dec, 2000. Available at, http://www.downtoearth.org.in/coverage/master-plan-for-anarchy-19111 (Accessed on 28 February 2013).

48 Sudershan, In Defence of Judicial Activism.

49 Baviskar, 'The Politics of the City', p. 202

50 Gill, *Of Poverty and Plastic*, p. 214.

51 Ibid p. 203.

52 I remember being forced to walk to my then workplace, a distance of more than 10 kilometres, witnessing the scenes of complete breakdown, the like of which I have never seen before or after in my long stay in Delhi.

53 Gill, *Of Poverty and Plastic.*

54 Ibid. p. 217.

55 Ibid. p. 209.

56 Ibid.

57 Ibid. p. 209–15.

58 Ibid. p. 213.

59 'A former Chief Justice of India defends his honour', *Times of India*, 2 September 2007.

60 For an insightful account of the mobilisation of 'traders' against the sealing case, see Mehra, 'Protesting Publics in Indian Cities'.

61 'Delhi Corporation moves apex court', *The Hindu*, 1 November 2006. *http://www.hindu.com/thehindu/thscrip/print.pl?file=2006110115971400.htm&date=2006/11/01/&prd=th&*

62 This had become standard practice in PILs by then, as we saw in Chapter 1.

63 See *http://pib.nic.in/newsite/erelease.aspx?relid=16908*

64 Singh, 'Delhi: Demolitions and Sealings'.

65 Ibid.

66 Aman Sethi, 'Uneasy reprieve', *Frontline*, 23, No. 20. *http://www.flonnet.com/fl2320/stories/20061020002903400.htm*

67 Risha Chitlangia, 'Delhi: Future of Third Floors Hangs on SC Ruling', *Economic Times* 21 December 2011. *http://articles.economictimes.indiatimes.com/2011-12-21/news/30542927_1_third-floor-mpd-mcd-officials*

68 Bhadra Sinha, 'After 7 yrs, SC wants HC to Hear Sealing Cases'. http://www.hindustantimes.com/newdelhi/after-7-yrs-sc-wants-hc-to-hear-sealing-cases/article1-1042964.aspx

69 'Delhi Sealing Case most Difficult of My Career', *The Hindu*, 14 January 2007. *http://www.hindu.com/2007/01/14/stories/2007011416400100.htm*

70 Arundhati Roy, 'Scandal in the Palace.' (2007)

71 Or, as it is usually called in India, Court 'on its own motion'.

72 'Instead of helping shopkeepers, he made his sons rich', *Tehelka*, 18th August, 2007. *http://archive.tehelka.com/story_main33.asp?filename=Ne180807Instead.asp*

73 Judgment by Justice Arijit Pasayat, dated 17th October 2006, in I.A.NO. 1156 IN WP (C) NO. 202/1995.

3

Public Interest Litigation as a Slum Demolition Machine

Yeh High Court is *sheher par raaj karti thi*. (This High Court used to rule this city.)

–Delhi High Court correspondent for the *Hindustan Times*[1]

In the first decade of the twenty-first century, the Delhi High Court presided over the most comprehensive and ruthless campaign to remove informal 'slum' settlements that the city had seen in a generation.[2] According to the official statistics, in 1998, Delhi had about 3 million people living in 1,100 *Jhuggi-Jhompri* clusters. When the next such survey was conducted in March 2011, the official figure had fallen to 685 *jhuggi-jhompri* clusters housing around 2 million people.[3] The only other period when there was such a massive recorded fall in the slum population in Delhi was between 1973 and 1977, when it fell from about half a million to about a hundred thousand, with a decline of about 80,000 slum households. This decline in 1973–77 is infamous because this was the period in which the Internal Emergency was in force (between 1975 and 1977) and one of the most notorious 'achievements' of the Emergency was a massive programme of forced relocation of slums – a well-known aspect of Delhi's contemporary history.[4] But how did this other more recent decline in the slum population of Delhi take place? If the Emergency regime saw a breakdown of political negotiations as a technocratic elite ran amok, the period between 1998 and 2011 saw a very similar process unfold – only this time the vehicle was Delhi's appellate judiciary, particularly the Delhi High Court, acting principally in its Public Interest Litigation (PIL) jurisdiction. In this chapter, I will examine how the procedural departures made possible by India's peculiar PIL jurisdiction enabled it to function as a slum demolition machine.

This phenomenon of the court-led slum demolition drive in Delhi has recently been analyzed and explained by some scholars. However, the difficulty with the existing literature on this topic is that it treats PIL cases as if they are like any other. It tends to understate the specificities of the PIL jurisdiction which turned to be so uniquely well-suited to facilitate such an expansive and unconventional judicial role. The still common emphasis on the dilution of *locus standi* of the petitioner as the only significant attribute of a PIL case represses the other radical characteristics of such cases that in reality take it far beyond any understanding of an adjudicative proceeding. I argue, on the other hand, that to understand this phenomenon of the court-led remaking of the city in its materiality, the procedural departures of PIL, which the Delhi High Court took to its *reduction ad absurdum* in this period, have to be understood and foregrounded.

Much of the critique of the Indian appellate courts' interventions in urban governance has focused on its ideological predilections relying on a dissection of judgments. I argue that such discursive analysis, while useful, serves only a limited purpose in helping us understand this phenomenon. Perhaps the most persuasive of such analysis has come from Asher Ghertner. He discusses two key aspects of the early phase of the slum demolition cases.[5] First, he examines the language of a bunch of PIL petitions and judgments to demonstrate a perceptible shift in nuisance law, which recast slums as nuisance per se. Second, he demonstrates that these cases are clearly based on aesthetic judgments, i.e. the apparently unsightly nature of slums makes them appear illegal to the judges, the photographs of these settlements often serving as the only evidence against them. Both are important points, which help us decipher the shift in the substantive legal doctrine of nuisance, as well as account for the discursive context in which the courts were operating.[6]

However, on the first point, it is important to understand that a pure conceptual development in the law, like the change in legal interpretation of nuisance, can only go so far. It does not provide the apparatus to change the very nature of governance, to enforce their ideas via a takeover of the whole arena. PIL has made this possible in the arenas in which it has intervened. It provides the procedural framework to create a field for its operation and transform it. Secondly, I would argue that it is PIL with the kind of power it vests in judges which actually empowers them to act on their biases (aesthetic, anti-poor or otherwise) and that too with a free hand in a most expansive manner, unconstrained by technicalities and rules of adjudication, and on such flimsy evidence as random photographs. The particular unaesthetic slum might not even appear in any case before them, but they can *suo motu* (i.e. by their own initiative) invoke it in a PIL and make it the object of their judicial concern. And not just at the level of one slum, but at the level of the whole city, as we shall see. While I am sympathetic to the existing literature which maps the ideological shifts in judicial discourse and which usually explains such changing trends in PIL cases (relating to slum demolitions and otherwise) from 1980s to the twenty-first century in terms of shifts in political economy, I argue here that this still begs the question: why was the PIL court the principal agent of such radical urban transformation in Delhi?

Additionally, discursive analysis is inadequate to understand this process, as most of the city-related PIL cases of this era often did not end up in any 'judgments' at all, but in an unending series of interim 'orders', which are not reported in law reports. This is just another peculiarity of the twenty-first century PIL, among its numerous other anomalous features. The distinction is important because while orders carry the force of law, they are generally not reasoned and do not provide an explanation of why that order has been given. Only if such an explanation is present, it becomes a judgment. Much of the scholarship on PIL has ignored such specificities of this jurisdiction and has continued to concentrate on the *completed* judicial process, i.e. judgments and other reported decisions of the courts, and the discursive charge they have. This is also the case because traditionally in a common law jurisdiction like India, only judgments act as precedent for future decisions, orders do not. As the Indian legal academic world is, therefore, only focused on an analysis of such judgments, it is ill-equipped to deal with the peculiar manifestations of the twenty-first century PIL that we discuss here.

In this chapter, my focus is on the proliferation of a new legal juggernaut that emerged in this period, which I call 'omnibus PIL' that turns a PIL filed about a specific problem in a specific part of the city into a PIL that deals with that particular issue 'wherever it comes up in the city'. The biggest departure in omnibus PIL cases was that the city became the scale at which the court defined and addressed the problem. The optics through which the problem was framed and the city made legible was usually the Delhi Master Plan. The original petitioner in the PIL case with his or her specific concerns about a specific urban neighbourhood would be either removed or made irrelevant or never have existed in the first place, and instead an amicus curiae or a monitoring committee would be appointed to guide the court on the issue of a citywide basis. The whole city would then be made subject to judicial intervention and correction through this process steered by such a court-appointed figure. The informality of PIL procedure enabled the court to monitor and micro-manage key aspects of the city's governance and make the whole city the direct object of its reformative attention. The court no longer needed the crutch of middle-class Resident Welfare Associations as aggrieved PIL petitioners with concerns limited to a specific locality.

The 'omnibus PIL' enabled the court to legally extrapolate its own role in the widest possible manner, making it a powerful weapon that was repeatedly used to target the 'illegal' residents of the city, negotiating their precarious lives at the edges of legality. The Delhi High Court deployed such PILs to order a city-level 'cleanup' of Delhi's street vendors, beggars and cycle-rickshaw drivers, but the principal and persistent object of the Court's wrath were the city's slums. In this chapter, I will rely on my fieldwork in the Delhi High Court during this period when I followed a series of such cases to examine the changing material practices of adjudication introduced by PIL. I shall argue that it was the unbearable lightness of PIL procedure, which provided the juridical conditions of possibility for it to function as a slum demolition machine.

PIL cases against slums: The first phase

In the years after the Emergency, the slum population had returned to a steady rate of growth, as no regime in Delhi dared a repeat of that experience. By 1981, in fact, the slum population had already reached pre-Emergency levels.[7] In the 1980s and 1990s, there were a few evictions, but at least since 1990–91, a policy was in place that officially guaranteed relocation in case of any slum demolition, stating that any 'past encroachment which had been in existence prior to 31 January 1990 would not be removed without providing alternatives'.[8]

That political compact broke down from the late 1990s onwards, with the courts presiding over a spectacular and largely gratuitous campaign against slums that led to almost a million people being evicted. The most infamous pronouncement that announced this new phase came from the Supreme Court in 2000, in a PIL which had no obvious connection with slums at all. Almitra Patel, an engineer with long-standing experience in solid waste management, filed a PIL in 1996 in the Supreme Court against the municipal garbage disposal practices in 300 of India's largest cities. The court went on to appoint a committee in this case in 1998, to formulate the Municipal Solid Waste (Management and Handling) Rules for the country, which were then officially notified. But once this apparatus had been set in motion, the petitioner 'was unable to steer the course of the petition'[9] and the presiding judge Justice B. N. Kirpal turned the case towards the unrelated issue of slums in Delhi[10], through a bizarre logical jump: blaming the slums for the solid waste problem.[11] The petitioner Almitra Patel later observed in an interview that the court was trying to play 'Municipal Commissioner' and took the case on a tangent for over two years, for reasons unclear to her.[12] This is another instance of a definite trend in PIL cases since the late 1990s, where the petitioner is made redundant and the court steers the case in whatever direction it deems fit.[13] In such a situation, conventional modes of legal analysis distinguishing between the 'Ratio Decidendi' (literally 'the reason for a decision') and 'Obiter Dicta' ('by the way' remarks) of a judgment based on the issues around which the parties in the case actually fought have little relevance because the whole judgment has nothing to do with the *lis* (dispute) in the case at all.

I quote here two passages from the infamous outburst by Justice Kirpal in *Almitra H. Patel vs. Union of India*:

13. Domestic garbage and sewage is a large contributor of solid waste. The drainage system in a city is intended to cope and deal with household effluent. This is so in a planned city. But when a large number of inhabitants live in unauthorized colonies, with no proper means of dealing with the domestic effluents, or in slums with no care for hygiene the problem becomes more complex.
14. Establishment or creating of slums, it seems, appears to be good business and is well organized. The number of slums has multiplied in the last few years by geometrical proportion. *Large areas of public land, in this way, are usurped for private use free of cost. It is difficult to believe that this can happen in the capital of the country without passive or active connivance of the land owning agencies and/or the municipal authorities. The promise of free land, at the taxpayers cost, in place of a jhuggi, is a proposal which attracts more land grabbers. Rewarding an encroacher on public land with free alternate site is like giving a reward to a pickpocket. The department of slum clearance does not seem to have cleared any slum despite it's being in existence for decades. In fact more and more slums are coming into existence. Instead of 'Slum Clearance' there is 'Slum Creation' in Delhi.* This in turn gives rise to domestic waste being strewn on open land in and around the slums. This can best be controlled at least, in the first instance, by preventing the growth of slums. The authorities must realize that there is a limit to which the population of a city can be increased, without enlarging its size. In other words the density of population per square kilometer cannot be allowed to increase beyond the sustainable limit. Creation of slums resulting in increase in density has to be prevented. What the slum clearance department has to show, however, does not seem to be visible. *It is the garbage and solid waste generated by these slums which require to be dealt with most expeditiously and on the basis of priority.*[14]

These comments cited above, particularly the 'reward to a pickpocket' analogy, revealed the Supreme Court of India's contempt for any attempt at humane relocation, and soon became the basis of a ferocious slum removal campaign in the Delhi High Court. The Court's main grouse in these cases was that of 'public land' being encroached upon.

'Public land' was the land that had been acquired by the government, especially the Delhi Development Authority (DDA), which was designated the sole developer of all the urbanizable land in Delhi in 1957. Land was acquired and socialized in the 1950s and 1960s, and was to be developed according to the terms laid down in the 'Master Plan'. Almost all slums in Delhi are located on such public land, most of them on the land owned by DDA. Legal scholar Usha Ramanathan diagnoses this malaise: 'The cause of the 'illegal' occupation of public lands is… directly attributable to the non-performance of state agencies.'[15] The 10th Plan document of the Planning Commission of India itself noted that up to 90 per cent of the deficit in urban housing at the time pertained to the urban poor and was attributable to non-provision of housing to slum dwellers. The courts, throughout this period, ignored any attempt to bring its notice to any such systemic analysis.

Emboldened by the 'pickpocket' remark of the Supreme Court, the Delhi High Court saw a fresh impetus in PILs filed by middle-class Resident Welfare Associations to remove 'encroachments' on public land in their vicinity. The trajectory of a typical PIL for slum clearance would be as follows: a Resident Welfare Association (RWA) would file a writ petition in the High Court, praying for the removal of a neighbouring slum, alleging nuisance caused to them by its very existence. The court would grant the RWA's prayer, and the matter would only end when the landowning agency of the encroached public land abided by the court's direction of demolition and relocation of a slum.[16]

The procedural departures that the Delhi High Court was making in its PIL jurisdiction in these RWA cases can be best gleaned from a comparison with another case from another time and another city, but in the same jurisdiction. A remarkably similar petition to these Delhi RWA petitions had been filed in Ahmedabad in 1984, complaining of 'nuisance on account of emission of smoke, passing of urine on public street by the hutment dwellers who are residing in this area'. The case, however, was then dismissed by the Gujarat High Court – not because of the affluence of the PIL petitioners and the poverty of the slum dwellers, or any similarly ideologically inflected arguments, but for good old-fashioned procedural reasons:

> (1) As to whether there is encroachment or not is a question of fact and it is difficult to ascertain in a petition under Art. 226 of the Constitution as to who has caused encroachment. This cannot be determined without recording evidence and without allowing the parties to lead evidence. Normally this Court would not adopt this course in a petition under Art. 226.
>
> (2) The persons who are alleged to have made encroachment and who are alleged to be residing in hutments are not parties in this petition. Without hearing them no order which may adversely affect them can be passed.[17]

These kinds of legal arguments were given no play in the Delhi High Court of the twenty-first century. In hardly any of these RWA cases were the slum dwellers, who were to be evicted, made parties to the case at the court's instance and heard by it.[18] In fact, ordinarily, the name of the slum was not even mentioned by the court in its orders in these cases. They were simply designated 'encroachers' and ordered to be removed. In many instances, the first time they would only hear about the court order when the bulldozers would enter their colony. Omission of a 'necessary party' from civil proceedings, like the slum dwellers here obviously are, would ordinarily be considered 'non-joinder of parties'. This is a fundamental rule of civil procedure, also applicable to writ jurisdiction, under which all PIL cases are filed. A judgment of the Supreme Court in 1984 had clearly laid down the law on this issue:

> A High Court ought not to hear and dispose of a writ petition under Article 226 of the Constitution without the persons who would be vitally affected by its judgment being before it as respondents or at least some of them being before it as respondents in a representative capacity if their number is too large to join them as respondents individually, and, if the petitioners refuse to so join them, the High Court ought to dismiss the petition for non-joinder of necessary parties.[19]

But such 'technical' or 'legalistic' arguments, which still had appeal in the early 1980s even in PIL cases, stopped enjoying the same valence by the early twenty-first century as the radiating effects of the ideological onslaught against procedural formalism by the votaries of PIL had by then infected the entire appellate judiciary.

Similarly, the other procedural issue here, the question of fact regarding the alleged 'nuisance' caused by 'encroachers' was never really examined and adjudicated by the Delhi High Court in these slum demolition PILs. The only 'evidence' that the court would rely on to initiate such eviction was photographs showing the nuisance caused by the slum dwellers.[20] Such impressionistic 'evidence' was deemed to be adequate by the court in such cases. Conventionally, the High Court is not supposed to adjudicate upon questions of fact under the writ jurisdiction of Article 226, as there are practical difficulties because the court normally just relies on affidavits. However, such a rigid position has been difficult to sustain as the courts have inevitably needed to go into disputed questions of fact to adjudicate 'public law litigation', as Abram Chayes famously called complex civil litigation on issues of public law.[21] While this is inevitable perhaps, Chayes had warned that in such cases:

> The extended impact of the judgment demands a more visibly reliable and credible procedure for establishing and evaluating the fact elements in the litigation, and one that more explicitly recognizes the complex and continuous interplay between fact evaluation and legal consequence.

Any such clarity on evidentiary procedure and standard of proof has, however, not been forthcoming from the Indian PIL courts. As Sudhir Krishnaswamy has argued in the context of another PIL that relied on scanty evidence, 'the broader the factual claims sought to be relied on by a public law court, the greater the burden of proof that will need to be discharged.'[22] This situation is complicated further by the fact that the principle of not adjudicating on questions of fact in PIL cases continues to be paid lip service to, leading to its opportunistic deployment even in cases which are otherwise based on factual analysis.

By 2002, these RWA cases had reached such a scale that a High Court bench was constituted that heard 63 such combined petitions under the lead petition of *Pitampura Sudhar Samiti vs. Union of India*.[23] The judgment summed up the petitions as:

> Filed by various resident associations of colonies alleging that after encroaching the public land, these JJ Clusters have been constructed in an illegal manner and they are causing nuisance of varied kind for the residents of those areas.[24]

Interestingly, these 63 petitions were combined with another 'set of petitions filed by or on behalf of JJ Clusters who either want to continue in the same clusters and demand better facilities or are claiming their rehabilitation'. The court dealt with the problem of slums as 'encroachments' by dividing the issue into two aspects – one being the removal of slums and the other that of their rehabilitation as per government policies. What was deemed to be the second issue – the constitutionality of rehabilitation of these slum dwellers – was relegated to another bench, as we shall soon see. Meanwhile, the court accepted the RWAs' contentions, reasoning that 'humanitarianism must be distinguished from miscarriage of mercy...these residential colonies were developed first. The slums have been created afterwards which is the cause of nuisance and brooding ground of so many ills.'[25]

The governmental failure to provide minimum facilities like public toilets for slum dwellers and the resulting nuisance caused by public defaecation was to be solved by removing the slum itself, not by making the government provide those facilities.[26] The court also rejected the slum dwellers' petitions saying, 'Since they are encroachments of public land and are unauthorised occupants of public premises at public places, they have no legal right to maintain such a Petition.'[27]

The government's existing policy requiring the provision of alternative land before demolishing a slum was dealt with soon after this in a most astonishing judgment given by a two-judge bench of the Delhi High Court on 29 November 2002 in a PIL filed by the Okhla Factory Owners' Association.[28] The judgment continued in the vein of Justice Kirpal's 'pickpocket' remark, quoting it for support 'against the grant of indulgence to such encroachers' and went a long way further to delegimitize any need for relocation of 'encroachers' as a prerequisite for demolishing their houses. The judgment set the tone with its very first sentence: 'Benevolence in administration is a necessity but this benevolence has to be balanced against the rights of the residents of a town specially when dealing with one commodity which can never increase which is land.' After having cast the issue as the 'rights' of some versus 'benevolence' towards others, the court examined the legality of the government policy of allotting land to squatters as 'this problem of relocation of *jhuggi* dwellers was arising in a number of cases where public interest petitions were filed to clear public land'. The court went on to not only do away with the requirement of relocation, it actually declared it illegal even where it was possible. Providing alternative sites, according to the court, was self-defeating and 'it has only created a mafia of property developers and builders who have utilized this policy to encourage squatting on public land, get alternative sites and purchase them to make further illegal constructions', the court speculated. 'A populist measure need not necessarily be a legal one', said the court. This P-word would thus appear repeatedly in such cases.

The court raised a statistical spectre by spelling out the amount required for providing minimum housing to the estimated 3 million *jhuggi*-dwellers of Delhi – about 59.25 billion rupees (the largeness of the figure was subtly underlined by enunciating it in all its numerical splendour, with the requisite zeroes). Finally, after evaluating the speed at which rehabilitation had taken place in the past, the court stated that at this rate, it would take 272 years to resettle Delhi's existing slum dwellers. The court, thus, managed to ridicule the slum policy and made it seem impractical and impossible. The court finally managed to reach the conclusion that any rehabilitation by the government under its slum policy would itself be illegal. The logic of the judgment followed what Pratap Bhanu Mehta later called 'the jurisprudence of exasperation'. As Mehta explains:

> The function of law in this view is to express, both literally and figuratively, exasperation at the state of affairs...it expresses a certain impatience with reality...Much in our society would prompt us to tear our hair out in exasperation. Judges now see it as their job to give these sentiments expression in law.[29]

Where these millions of slum-dwelling people would go once evicted from their homes and why they were there in the first place was of no concern to the Division Bench of the Delhi High Court. Anticipating the catastrophic repercussions of such a change in policy, both the central and state governments in Delhi went on to appeal the Supreme Court, which stayed this High Court order and allowed the government's slum policy and allotment of land for relocation to continue, provided it clearly specified 'that the allotment would be subject to the result of the petitions'.[30] Until 7 September 2010, when the Supreme Court finally set aside the High Court judgment[31], all schemes for allotment of land to slum dwellers in Delhi carried this proviso.[32]

The two judgments of the Delhi High Court discussed above – *Pitampura Sudhar Samiti* and *Okhla Factory Owners Association* – turned out to be the last real instances of reflection on moral and constitutional questions faced by the court vis-à-vis slum demolitions, for the next seven years.[33] What the courts delivered after this were orders, not judgments; that is, no reasoned justifications were forthcoming, just pure assertions of power. Henceforth, the court concentrated on creating a machinery for slum demolition and went on to, as we shall see, oversee the process itself. But already, in the *Okhla* judgment, the looseness of legal language and the glaring incoherence of public reason had moved law towards non-law. The judgment did not actually rely on legal principles, but was based on the premise that a policy which seemed impractical based on past experience can simply be declared unconstitutional. The reliance on legal norms and reasoning is minimal, and the decision appears to be no more than a pure assertion of sovereignty. Despite all this, such an ideological judgment was, strictly speaking, possible to envisage as part of a regular litigation challenging the legality of Delhi Government's slum rehabilitation policy. What would soon follow it, I argue, would just not have been possible in a non-PIL judiciary.

The emergence of PIL as a slum demolition machine

After the judgment on the legality of slum rehabilitation as a general policy in the Okhla case, the High Court scheduled a hearing in the same case, ostensibly to give further directions in respect of individual grievances made in the two petitions relating to Wazirpur and Okhla, two specific industrial areas of Delhi. This hearing, which took place on 3 March 2003, became the site of an awesome display of judicial power through the means of PIL, setting the pace for court-led slum demolitions in Delhi over the next five years, on a scale for which the only precedent was the Emergency. It marked a new phase in the courts' relation with slums in Delhi.

The important departure here was one of geography. Although the relevant petitions were specific to two areas – Wazirpur and Okhla – the court decided not to be limited by such constraints and took the petition's concerns regarding 'encroachments' to a new location altogether – to the banks of the river Yamuna, the site of what was then the largest slum in Delhi, Yamuna Pushta. There was no justification for this bizarre segue other than the judges' own whims. To read Justice Vijender Jain's order, it was as if the Supreme Court had never passed a stay order on the High Court judgment about the slum rehabilitation policy – the High Court carried on as if resettlement was no longer necessary before a slum was demolished. In this order of 3 March 2003, after gleefully recounting the statistics based on which the *Okhla* judgment had been given, Jain suddenly moved into unconnected terrain:

> What is required to be done in the present situation in this never ending drama of illegal encroachment in this capital city of our Republic?... Yamuna Bed and both the sides of the river have been encroached by unscrupulous persons with the connivance of the authorities. Yamuna Bed as well as its embankment has to be cleared from such encroachments... In view of the encroachment and construction of *jhuggies/pucca* structure in the Yamuna Bed and its embankment with no drainage facility, sewerage water and other filth are discharged in Yamuna water... We therefore direct all the authorities concerned... to forthwith remove all the unauthorized structures, *jhuggies*, places of worship and/or any other which are unauthorisedly put in Yamuna Bed and its embankment, within two months from today.[34]

The court here made its own accusations, came up with its own facts and ordered its own remedy, without feeling the need to hear anybody else. Additionally, it made an unsubstantiated correlation between slums near the river and pollution caused to it by them. In fact, research by a reputed non-profit organization called Hazards Centre found that the slums near the Yamuna contributed less than 1 per cent of the total sewage released into the river.[35] The PIL petition was just an excuse for the court to dwell on its own hobby horses.

In another key move that Justice Jain would repeatedly come to make in such PIL cases, he appointed an amicus curiae to assist the court in this case.[36] The petitioners may have had specific complaints for which they had come to court, but the court had its own concerns which it intended to go ahead and set right through the same petition. To do so, it needed to appoint its own lawyer, the amicus curiae.

Finally, although the target of the court's intervention was Delhi's largest slum cluster, 'Yamuna Pushta', it was never referred to by name in its order. This refusal, too, became part of the judicial style of these PILs as patented by Justice Jain. Perhaps the judge did not wish to dignify the 'encroachers' by giving a name to their settlement. His decision also added to the opacity of the proceedings, and over the one year or so that it took for this order to be implemented, no resident or representative organization of the Yamuna settlements was ever made a party to the case. But the implication of such a widely worded order against all encroachments on the river Yamuna could be quite radical, as would be evident in a few years.

Yamuna Pushta, meaning 'embankment on the river Yamuna' was actually a series of slum colonies on the banks of the river behind Old Delhi. The colonies had different names, such as Gautampuri-I, Gautampuri-II, Kanchanpuri, Indira Colony and Sanjay Amar Colony, and altogether housed about 1,50,000 people.[37]

When this case next came up for substantive hearing on 29 October 2003, it was heard by a different bench of the High Court. Though this new bench was keen to implement the Okhla order of removing the slums mentioned in the petition without any need for relocation, it also noted with some apparent surprise that

> [W]hile hearing the matter on 3.3.2003, it appears that the Division Bench also took the cognizance of encroachers on Yamuna. The petition pertains to encroachment in Wazirpur area. Therefore, Registry is directed to give a separate number to the petition as the Court has taken cognizance on its own motion and to place the copy of the order passed by the Division Bench on 3.3.2003.

Such departures from basic legal procedures in PILs still surprised other judges of the High Court, though with Justice Jain having taken the lead, such judicial improvization would not be exceptional for very long.

The new petition of which the court had taken cognizance was numbered Civil Writ Petition 689/2004 and was called *Court on its own Motion vs. Union of India*. With Senior Advocate Amarjit Singh Chandhiok as the amicus curiae, this newly numbered writ petition came up before a new bench on 28 January 2004. The order on 3 March 2003 which sparked off this new writ was about the removal of encroachments from Yamuna. Strangely enough, notice of this new case was accepted on behalf of the Central Government by the Tourism Ministry and not the Ministry of Urban Development, which is responsible for the lawful planned development of Delhi and ordinarily deals with such cases. This was because the Tourism Minister was Jagmohan, the architect of the infamous Emergency-era demolitions, who was now most keen to resume his reputation as 'demolition man'.[38]

By the time the next hearing came around, in February 2004, Jagmohan had quickly manufactured a grand plan to develop the Yamuna riverfront after the anticipated removal of these slum clusters. The plan was to develop a 100-acre strip of land on the banks of the river Yamuna, 'into a riverside promenade with parks and fountains which would be marketed as a major tourist attraction'.[39] This was circulated as a brochure before the court and was called, 'Yamuna River Front: Undoing a tragedy of governance and ushering in a new dawn', with nine pages of glossy uncaptioned photographs of the Pushta showing industrial activities like 'electro-plating units' being carried on there, as well as photographs of homes with TV sets asking if these were homes of the 'poor'.[40] The court was persuaded by Jagmohan's rhetoric. In particular, it was agitated by the photographs showing the presence of industries in the Pushta and ordered the immediate clearing of all legal hurdles for the demolition of Yamuna Pushta.[41] Between February and May 2004, the Yamuna Pushta slums were finally destroyed under court orders.[42] About 6,000 of the 35,000 families displaced were resettled by the government 25 miles away in Bawana, at the extreme Northern edge of the National Capital Territory of Delhi.[43] Even after the demolitions in Yamuna Pushta, the *suo motu* case regarding encroachments on the river Yamuna continued. The court kept ordering demolitions of other slums near the river. It also came up with a novel interpretation to speed up the process and pre-empt the need for a Slum Rehabilitation Policy in this case. 'It is required to be noted', said the Court:

> That the policy of DDA for relocation would not apply to the river bed. It is not an encroachment on land. It is a water body and it is required to be maintained as a water body by the DDA and all other authorities.[44]

A few months after this order, Justice Vijender Jain took charge of this case. Over the course of the year that he presided over it, he took it to another level with his innovations and determination to demolish as many slums as possible. Dissatisfied with the authorities' less than complete implementation of his original *suo motu* order on Yamuna encroachments (he would quote his original order in subsequent orders repeatedly), and 'in the absence of a comprehensive policy by the Government… to clear the Yamuna bed and its embankment.' On 16 November 2005, he decided to create a special judicial mechanism for this purpose. Jain ordered the constitution of a Monitoring Committee chaired by a retired High Court Judge, Usha Mehra, 'to remove such encroachment forthwith and to monitor such operations'. The Committee consisted of highly placed ex-officio members[45], the amicus Chandhiok and a retired Additional District Judge S. M. Aggarwal, who was appointed as Convenor. The Committee was to submit a monthly report 'with regard to action taken in terms of order passed' on 3 March 2003.

This Committee, which came to be known as the 'Yamuna – Removal of Encroachment Monitoring Committee', was initially set up for a period of one year, but its tenure was later extended indefinitely.[46] Its members were given office space in the swanky India Habitat Centre. The Monitoring Committee appointed soon after by the Supreme Court in the 'sealing case', discussed in Chapter 2, functioned from the adjoining office. Having already zeroed in on encroachments as the cause of pollution in the river Yamuna and without any further discussion on other possible causes of such pollution, on the next date of hearing on 8 December 2005, Justice Jain ordered:

> We direct the Committee to take up in right earnestness and on day-to-day basis the task of removing encroachments upto 300 meters from both sides of River Yamuna in the first instance. No encroachment either in the form of *jhuggi jhopri* clusters or in any other manner by any person or organization shall be permitted... We make it clear that the Committee will take up the task of removal of illegal encroachment on the basis of directions issued above and will not entertain any request for grant of any time for such removal on the pretext of relocation or any other alternative allotment... Illegal occupants of the river bed did not have the right to pollute the river and if there was a policy to relocate or rehabilitate them somewhere else, the eviction measure would not wait for such a policy to be implemented.

The court did not provide any basis for arriving at the figure of 300 metres, but it became a benchmark of sorts, with government authorities soon turning it into some kind of a sacrosanct limit.[47] The court had effectively set up the machinery for efficient implementation of its commands. This PIL came up regularly before the court for the next one year, and its orders discussed the monthly reports submitted by the Monitoring Committee to the court, which contained an account of the progress made by the various government agencies in removing encroachments from the river bed. The Committee made frequent inspection of the areas in question and reported to the court. This improvisation by the court ensured that all government agencies followed the directions of the court and it could micro-manage the whole affair. The court would direct a senior officer of the government to be present in the court to make sure it performed, or recall the order requiring him to be present in court if there was a good progress report from the Committee.[48] Any further legal obstacles were removed by the court on 29 March 2006, when it ordered 'all the courts subordinate to the Delhi High Court not to deal with any matter with regard to grant of stay against removal of illegal encroachers from the river embankment'. To further systematize the slum demolition campaign, the court asked the DDA to submit 'area-wise sketch plans showing clusters of *jhuggis* and other structures on various parts of Western embankment of the river Yamuna'. In the absence of any such plans, the Committee was asked to arrange for 'satellite mapping instrument and technology', so as 'to have the mapping of all the *jhuggi* clusters and other structures on the western embankment on Yamuna river'.

The Yamuna Monitoring Committee appointed by the court, in the first year of its existence, was successful in removing 11,280 *jhuggies* and *pucca* structures, including more than 130 *dhobi ghats*[49], from various places on both banks of the river Yamuna. This was hailed as 'tremendous work' by Justice Jain and the Committee's term was extended for another year. Most of the settlements were demolished within the first five months of the committee's establishment, the biggest of its actions being the removal of 4,000 *jhuggies* situated in East Delhi, near Geeta Colony on the eastern embankment of the river Yamuna. Justice Jain would later tell me in an interview that he was particularly proud of having cleared this area, as a massive clover-leaf flyover and grade-separator came up there later, which he thought was one of his achievements and resented the fact that he was not invited for its inauguration a few years later.[50] Indeed, throughout this period, all kinds of ambitious road projects adjoining the river were given the green signal.

After Justice Jain left the Delhi High Court in November 2006, this PIL took a completely different and unanticipated direction. The Commonwealth Games was to be held in Delhi in 2010, for which purpose a massive Games Village was planned right on the floodplains of the river Yamuna. As this would violate the blanket directions that the court had previously given in this case against *any and all* construction near the river, a different PIL filed against the Games Village was referred to the same Committee. The Convenor of the Committee, perhaps naively believing in the blanket mandate of the Committee to actually cover all illegal structures, and not just slums and such sub-standard constructions, actually interceded with the High Court against the Commonwealth Games Village. The High Court bench in 2008 found grave illegalities in the process of granting permissions for the Games Village and ordered a committee to examine this issue, without stopping its construction, which was going full steam ahead. But even this committee was declared unnecessary by the Supreme Court when it came up for appeal. The Supreme Court cleared the Games Village Project: the PIL against it, said the judges, had been filed too late in the day.

The *Yamuna* case is a perfect example of what had by then become a definite judicial trend: that of turning a PIL filed about a specific problem in a specific part of the city into what I call an omnibus PIL: a PIL that deals with a particular issue 'wherever it comes up in the city'. The city was the level at which the court was thinking of the problem. The device of the omnibus PIL was deployed in particularly spectacular fashion by the High Court from 2003 onwards, with Justice Vijender Jain being its arch exponent. The whole city was thus made subject to judicial intervention and correction through this process. What was relatively new about this increasingly common and extremely powerful form of PIL was that the specific aggrieved party was removed, and a roving enquiry into the whole city conducted by the court through the amicus. To rely, therefore, on the language of the petitions to understand the nature of these PILs, as many commentators continue to do, is not particularly useful as the petitioners had little if any role to play in these cases by this point.

The means by which the city was made legible for this new optics of the court was usually the Delhi Master Plan that provided for strict zoning laws. Through this new manoeuver, PIL became a means to target the 'illegal' residents of the city, who until then had been protected by their elected representatives. These 'illegal' citizens were not even made party to the proceedings. All problems were blamed on the conspicuous urban poor, who were seen as obstructing the neat solutions proposed to make the city come up to scratch as a 'global city': they would simply have to go as collateral damage.

That the poor were there in the first place was a function of what Partha Chatterjee has called 'political society'. These people had been accommodated, however precariously, by the everyday populist politics that depended on them for electoral support. These were the networks most drastically unravelled by this new phase of PIL. The omnibus PIL and its procedural improvizations enabled the court to monitor and micro-manage nearly every aspect of the city's governance and make the whole city the direct object of its reformative attention. We have seen in the course of this chapter the move made by RWAs and other mediating actors as PIL petitioners asking the court to intervene and set the city right by cleaning up the excesses of political society. By 2003, it was as if the court no longer needed any external crutch to do this. It went about doing it on its own. Indeed, the effectiveness and thoroughness with which the Delhi High Court could pursue slum demolitions through its new machinery far exceeded the abilities of individual RWAs.

***

Another example of a Justice-Jain-style omnibus PIL that significantly changed the city is the case referred to as *Hem Nalini Mehra vs. Government of NCT of Delhi*[51]. This was a PIL filed in 2002 by the residents of two group housing societies in East Delhi, complaining of the callousness of the government authorities in not carrying out the requisite sewer repair work and laying of an arterial road. The court managed to get the repairs done in a year's time. But once this was done, at the hearing on 31 October 2003, the court decided to expand the scope of the writ petition to road repair and road safety all over Delhi and made Pushkar Sood, the lawyer for the PIL petitioners, the amicus curiae in this omnibus PIL. Over the next three years, the court in this PIL set up a centralized database of fatal accidents and a mechanism for cancelling driving licences of people involved in such cases. It demolished slum clusters, removed street vendors and kiosks as encroachment on public roads and footpaths[52], closed down unregulated automobile repair shops, ordered the move of wholesale paper and chemical markets to peripheral areas, ordered new interstate bus terminals to be set up in two peripheral areas of the city, ordered the construction of 14 multi-level parking lots for the decongestion of traffic in Delhi, ordered the installation of bollards (concrete separators) on roads and supervised the construction of flyovers (going into the details of alignment in the case of a clover-leaf flyover near Akshardham temple), underpasses and traffic lights near them.

Another omnibus PIL championed by Justice Jain was the case of *Hemraj vs. Commissioner of Police*[53]. The PIL was originally filed in 1999 to curtail goods traffic on the roads in and around the Chattarpur temple in South Delhi. But soon after this complaint was dealt with, the PIL was expanded to deal with 'proper handling of traffic and related problems in the entire city of Delhi' and a committee with ex-officio members and two amicus curiae[54] appointed by the court, which came to be called 'the Hemraj Amicus Curiae Committee'. By the time it was folded up by a new bench in 2008, this PIL and its committee had been handling the issue of traffic congestion in the entire city for almost a decade. It did all that the *Hem Nalini Mehra* PIL did and more, and ordered its share of slum demolitions. The most well known among the slum settlements demolished in this case was Nangla Machi, comprising about 2,800 houses in Central Delhi[55]. Among other reasons, this settlement irked the court because 'the unauthorised occupants also have buffaloes and other animals which not only give way to unhygenic conditions but also create hindrance on the smooth flow of commuters on the ring road of Delhi which are in thousands'.[56] The High Court's final order to demolish this settlement on 5 April 2006 explained:

> It is clear that these persons have no legal right to occupy the land in question, they should be removed and if they are entitled for any relocation, then that entitlement will be seen by the authority concerned. However, the removal will not wait for the relocation.

At no point during these court proceedings were the slum dwellers of Nangla Machi given a chance to be heard in the case[57].

On May 17 2006, Justice Jain ordered a massive crackdown on cycle-rickshaws in Delhi in the *Hemraj* case. The order began with a tirade against the 'plying of cycle rickshaws on the main roads, narrow roads and congested roads' which the Court said, 'has become a horrible experience'. It then directed the MCD not to grant any licenses in future for plying cycle rickshaws on Delhi roads and also ordered it to prohibit cycle rickshaws from plying on all arterial roads in the city. This would hit the livelihood of hundreds of thousands in a city with an estimated 0.6 million cycle rickshaws[58]. The court's impatience with the continued proliferation of cycle rickshaws in Delhi clearly seemed to emerge from a feeling of lack or a sense of embarrassment about the inadequately modern nature of the cycle rickshaw. In the most bizarre intervention to make real its fantasy of a truly modern city, the court in this same omnibus PIL ordered a ban on the plying of cycle rickshaws in the Chandni Chowk area at the behest of a traders' association in the Walled City of Delhi[59]. Chandni Chowk is the commercial heart of the Walled City. Having banned cycle rickshaws between Red Fort Chowk and Fatehpuri Mosque in order to reduce congestion there so that the entire area 'is reglorified and people are able to do hassle free shopping in an atmosphere of quality environment', it ordered the introduction of CNG buses as an alternative. Since the order was given with respect to a much fetishized and touristed part of Delhi, which is so obviously suited to non-motorized vehicles like cycle rickshaws[60], its manifest absurdity attracted a lot of attention. The New York-based Institute for Transportation and Development Policy (ITDP) issued a statement that read:

> We believe that for the court to make policy regarding road use is beyond its competence and judicial mandate... because roads are a public good, ultimately the use and allocation of scarce road space should be determined by a legitimate democratic political process informed by in-depth technical understanding.[61]

The Kalyan Sanstha case: The slum demolition machine perfected

> Looking back now, it's hard to map out everything that happened after the 14 December 2005 Delhi High Court order that called for the demolition of all unauthorized constructions in Delhi. The todh-phodh, as the regulars at Bara Tooti called it, spread rapidly across the city as the Municipal Corporation's demolition teams fanned out into markets and residential colonies...
> –Aman Sethi, *A Free Man*,[62]

The next giant move in this logical progression of the Delhi High Court presiding over the remaking of the city was to combine all the PIL cases relating to 'unauthorised construction, misuse of properties and encroachments on public land' into one master case, eventually dealing with the entire city. The history of this case tells us something about the trajectory of PIL in Delhi.

In 1989, in the middle-class neighbourhood of West Patel Nagar, a post-Partition 'rehabilitation colony', there was a dispute between two neighbours living in adjacent plots of 200 square yards each, leading one of them, Sarla Sabharwal, to file a writ petition in the Delhi High Court alleging that her neighbour was constructing extra floors on his property, which would exceed the municipal building by-laws and, therefore, asking the court to order the MCD to take action against him. The respondent neighbour promptly countered the charge by submitting a list of 32 buildings in the same neighbourhood that were also violating municipal rules – either by building more floors than permitted, or by using the residential premises for commercial purposes, or by extending the building on land beyond that allotted to them, and thus encroaching on public land, i.e. on the road on both sides of the building. A bench headed by Justice Kirpal heard this writ. This was the same judge who 10 years later in the Supreme Court gave the 'encroacher as pickpocket' judgment. In 1990, the judges declared that this was a 'fit issue... in which public is interested' and decided to regard this case as a PIL. In 1991, the court disposed of the case with orders to the MCD vis-à-vis 27 buildings in the area that were found to contain legal violations, to either 'regularize' illegalities which were compoundable and demolish those which were not compoundable. This order, and indeed the whole PIL, was restricted to middle-class houses in Patel Nagar and Rajinder Nagar areas of Karol Bagh zone of the MCD in West Delhi.

Twelve years later, the husband of the petitioner in the earlier writ filed a PIL in the Delhi High Court in the name of a 'social welfare organization' called 'Kalyan Sanstha',[63] which had never been heard of before or after, and of which he said he was the president. The petition alleged that the punitive actions for the West Delhi neighbourhoods ordered by the High Court in the earlier petition filed by his wife had not been implemented by the MCD, and the unauthorized constructions there had gone from bad to worse. The case plodded along for its first two years. On 30 November 2005, it suddenly acquired a completely different valence, when it got listed before a bench headed by Justice Vijender Jain.

Jain decided to deploy this case to start a demolition drive in Delhi. He summoned official figures of unauthorized construction for all of Delhi: there were a total of 18,299 recorded cases of unauthorized construction in the city over a period of five years. 'To check the mushrooming of unauthorized construction', he wanted these demolished forthwith 'in right earnest'. On 14 December, the court issued a clarification:

> We are making it clear that MCD has to launch a drive throughout Delhi in terms of our directions passed in this matter. There are other writ petitions… which relate to other areas. A copy of this order shall be placed on all the files so that the MCD shall start its working in right earnest. We are further making it clear that if there is any other area or locality in which there are buildings which do not conform to the parameters of building by-laws… the same shall be covered by order passed.

The demolition drive was on. From this date onwards, all other cases pending in the Delhi High Court relating to 'Unauthorized construction, Misuse of Properties and encroachments on Public Land' were to be heard under this omnibus PIL of *Kalyan Sanstha Social Welfare Organization vs. Union of India & Ors* (Civil Writ Petition 4582/2003). The MCD panicked at the enormity at the task before it and stated in a sworn affidavit that out of the approximately 4 million properties in Delhi, 3 million are 'in violation of law', i.e. 70–80 per cent of buildings constructed in Delhi are unauthorized. The court was livid and called this 'an attempt to create fear psychosis in the mind of honest citizens' and made the government 'delete' the statement saying it was not based on any exact survey.

After 18 January 2006, when its order noted that the 'demolition drive has been undertaken in Delhi but it has been far from satisfactory', the court started thinking of alternatives. Before it, was the example of the 'sealing case' in the Supreme Court, which had taken a new dimension in February 2006, as we saw in Chapter 2[64]. Observing that '[i]t seems that the MCD lacks the desire to check the rampant corruption and unauthorized construction', the High Court took the first step towards forging its own tools to oversee the implementation machinery of the demolition drive on 23 March. It appointed four lawyers of the Delhi High Court as 'Court Commissioners' for four of the twelve municipal zones of the city. The Court Commissioners were supposed to act as the 'eyes and ears of the court' and were directed 'to keep a vigil in these zones and take periodical inspections and wherever unauthorized construction is going on, they may note the number of the property and immediately inform the Commissioner of MCD.' The court also authorized the Court Commissioners 'to inspect the premises at the localities in their respective zones and to see whether in a residential area any commercial activity is being carried out' and if so, to inform the Commissioner of Police 'for immediate action'. The Commissioner of the MCD was to accordingly file an 'action taken report' before the court stating that the unauthorized construction/ misuse reported by the Court Commissioner has been removed. The names of these Court Commissioners along with their telephone numbers and addresses were published in the newspapers on the orders of the court 'so that any citizen or resident welfare association if they want to contact the Court Commissioners can contact them and the Court Commissioners can take cognizance of such complaints'. An apparatus was thus set up whereby the RWAs need no longer approach the Court to lodge complaints but could just go to its agents, the Court Commissioners, who would inform the MCD and/or the police, who would then file an 'Action Taken Report' before the Court.

When the first 'public notice' regarding the 'Appointment of Court Commissioners' appeared in the newspapers on 5 April 2006, there was interestingly no mention of 'illegal encroachments on public land'. It was limited to 'unauthorized constructions' and 'commercialization of residential premises'. This was soon to change. Like Justice Jain's other omnibus PILs, this too, the largest of them, would soon principally target slums. Such a choice was particularly glaring in this case, as the whole history of the PIL was about rampant middle-class illegality and its peculiar manifestations, but as always, the slums were the easiest target. The cross-mediation that was observable in most instances of slum-demolition at this time – the court ordering demolition, the media egging it on and the RWAs acting as the local agents of the court – was perhaps at its most developed in this case.

But before that stage was reached, the court's apparatus was refined further. On 18 May 2006, selected lawyers were appointed as Court Commissioners for all the 12 municipal zones of Delhi. Finding it 'difficult to monitor day-to-day activities of this magnitude', the court appointed a Monitoring Committee consisting of two retired senior policemen and another ex-officio senior policeman still in service, 'to monitor all the directions which have been given in this writ petition by this Court and also to carry out, implement and execute the directions passed by this Court'. The whole apparatus was ready now. The court had acquired the means to find the illegalities in the city and set them right. The RWA as the PIL petitioner at the demand end and the MCD at the supply end were just nodes for the court to do the right thing and clean the city up.

The Monitoring Committee was officially advertised in the newspapers as 'constituted by Hon'ble High Court, Delhi, regarding Unauthorised Construction, Misuse of Properties & Encroachment on Public land'.[65] The Monitoring Committee started submitting monthly reports to the court, on the basis of which the court passed orders. 'Illegal encroachments on public land' soon became the focus and 'public land' was increasingly understood in terms of its real estate value. This perspective is evident from the court's order dated 25 August 2006, when the Monitoring Committee was still in its early days:

> The report of the Monitoring Committee has been placed before us. It has been stated in the report that because of the relentless efforts of the Court Commissioners, encroachment on public land measuring more than 7,96,200 square yards having market value of more than Rs.500 crores[66] on the basis of a very conservative estimate have been retrieved by the MCD/ DDA from the encroachers and unauthorized occupants. The Monitoring Committee has advised to the Commissioner, MCD and the Vice Chairman DDA to get the cases of criminal trespass registered under the IPC against those individual.

The court would periodically give itself and its agents these self-congratulatory pats on the back, and the media would join the celebratory chorus. On 22 March 2007, the Hindustan Times carried a full page story to celebrate the first anniversary of the appointments of the first four Court Commissioners and quoted a figure from a Monitoring Committee report: 'In a joint effort under the guidance of the court-appointed Monitoring Committee, the commissioners have helped the government reclaim public land worth around ₹7,000 crore from the encroachers over the past one year.' The Monitoring Committee members are quoted as saying in a status report, 'The commissioners have done a wonderful job... The MCD and the DDA are, therefore, richer by thousands of crores.'

Much of the time during the court hearings went in the sparring between the court-appointed authorities and the governmental authorities. The Monitoring Committee would place its report, present its achievements and point out persistent obstacles to demolition in various areas. The court would pull up the respective governmental authority. The state would appear as the wrongdoer on the other side of the law. Both sides would be trying to speak for the public. The state would be seen as speaking for 'political society' and, therefore, characterized by the court and its agents as enmeshed in the toleration of illegality. Meanwhile, the court and its officials would represent themselves as speaking for civil society. The lawyers for the parties affected would barely get time to have their concerns heard. In this free-for-all, the high-profile lawyers ordinarily representing some cases of 'unauthorized construction' and other elite illegalities would be the only ones who had any chance of getting relief. Cases of subaltern illegalities cast as 'encroachments on public land' would have little or no chance even to be heard. In the rare situations when they did appear because at some pro bono lawyer's initiative, the court would provide new and remarkable legal arguments to ensure they enjoyed no legal protection.

By mid-2006, the court was finding it difficult to control the size of the case. Its orders became increasingly opaque and difficult to decipher. The orders would often read as some variation of the following, 'The xx Report of the Monitoring Committee is filed. xx acres of public land is encroached in xx area. Action taken report to be filed by the Municipal authorities on xx date.' Perhaps the court was being euphemistic, but since the relevant Report itself was not in the public domain, it was impossible to know from the order itself what action was actually to be taken. There was no possibility of availing data from the Monitoring Committee regarding its proceedings and recommendations, even if one was directly affected[67]. Police officers had been appointed to man the Committee and they ran it with as little transparency as any police department.

The attention of this case had by then been successfully turned to Justice Jain's old area of interest – slum demolitions. On 12 October 2006, the court noted some new insights regarding slums in Delhi:

> The Monitoring Committee has also pointed out that J. J. clusters have undergone sea change inasmuch as three to four storey buildings have come up in place of *Jhuggies* and several industrial and commercial establishments are running therefrom. Time has come for the authorities in Delhi to formulate a policy so as not only to stop these unauthorized trade activities being run from these *Jhuggi Jhopri* clusters but also in view of the fact that the occupants who are themselves unauthorized cannot be permitted to raise unauthorized, unplanned and hazardous structures thereby making Delhi a complete slum.

In a truly remarkable sleight-of-hand that could only have come from a deeply held prejudice (in the most literal sense of that word), the court had deemed a slum to no longer be a slum because it had grown vertically – but the proliferation of these very 'non-slums' was blamed for making the city look like a slum!

The emergence of upward mobility (pun unintended) in Delhi slums was used as a bogey to aid their demolition. By this time, the Delhi Laws (Special Provisions) Act, 2006 had come into force, with its moratorium on court-ordered sealing and demolitions. But the *Kalyan Sanstha* bench led by Justice Jain found ingenious ways to continue its exercise. On 16 November 2006, it did a bizarre reading of the new Act, stating that 'the intention of the Parliament is clearly discernible', it held that the moratorium could not be extended to unauthorized *pucca*[68] structures built on government land. There were very few slums in the harsh environs of Delhi that did not have features that could be considered *pucca.* Like Jagmohan had used photographs of slum houses with television sets to delegitimize them as not being poor enough, Justice Jain's court, too, found that the slums were not wretched enough and, therefore, did not deserve the sympathy of the law. The Monitoring Committee soon sent out a circular to the municipal authorities that:

> Those of the *Jhuggi Jhopri* clusters which have undergone a change in character and have been replaced by 2/3 storey tenements come under this ruling and can no longer be entitled to the moratorium. They are, therefore, liable to be demolished as has already been done in a few places in Delhi.[69]

This was Justice Jain's last order in this case before he was transferred to Chandigarh High Court as its Chief Justice[70]. The new judge who arrived to head the *Kalyan Sanstha* bench, Chief Justice M. K. Sharma, continued the case in the same vein. The enormity of the scale of this case soon meant it got listed every week, eventually acquiring a fixed two-hour time slot on Wednesday afternoons between 2 p.m. and 4 p.m. Having subsumed all other cases against encroachment on public land and unauthorized colonies in Delhi as per the orders of the court, it had become a mammoth case, with literally hundreds of Civil Miscellaneous Petitions (CMPs) being made part of it. Every person or organization affected by the case would have to file a CM to be heard by the court. The scope of the case was so large that people (or 'parties') affected in each hearing would be in the hundreds. But, it was impossible for everybody to be heard, as two hours a week was not enough for the scale of the case. It became difficult to physically enter these courtrooms even for lawyers appearing in the case. The *Kalyan Sanstha* hearings were held in courtrooms of enormous size – rooms which had proper seating for more than a 100 people – and there still would not be even standing room. Luckily for all concerned, these were centrally air-conditioned courtrooms. The journalists who ordinarily sat in the fourth or fifth row of upholstered chairs 'behind' the lawyers would in this case actually sit 'in front of' the lawyers, often right below the judges, next to the court-clerk – as if to underline how major a role they played in acting as cheerleaders for this case. One journalist would later tell me how judges would often look at them when making particularly volatile remarks like 'Catch the big fish', 'Close down the municipal corporation', or 'We don't care about (municipal) councillors'. These provocative pronouncements were made to be picked up by the media. And sure enough, they would often be reported as big headlines on the front pages of major newspapers the next day.

Under Vijender Jain, the possibilities of PIL were explored to the fullest, most gargantuan scale. As Pushkar Sood, one of the Court Commissioners in this case, said admiringly to me in an interview, 'Vijender Jain's was the golden period of PIL'.

Epilogue

In 2008, the Delhi High Court got a new Chief Justice, A. P. Shah. Shah was renowned as a left-liberal judge, and with the powers that accrued to his position, he started cleaning the Augean stables. As the Chief Justice, he could completely reset the tone of the Delhi High Court on PIL. As legal scholar Nick Robinson observes:

> The power to set benches is also given to High Court Chief Justices. Like their counterpart in the Supreme Court, they have a strong say in controlling their court's agenda. For example, in most High Courts, it's the Chief Justice's bench that first hears public interest litigation (PIL). Consequently,

High Courts gain a reputation either as sympathetic or unsympathetic to PILs based largely on the Chief Justice alone.[71]

Most of Justice Vijender Jain's omnibus PILs, which had remained active under Chief Justice M. K. Sharma, were finally terminated during Chief Justice Shah's benevolent reign. *Hemraj, Hem Nalini Mehra,* the Yamuna encroachments case – all were disposed of by the High Court during this period. *Kalyan Sanstha* was not fully disposed of under Shah, but was defanged with the disbanding of the Monitoring Committee and the Court Commissioners in 2008. It was finally disposed of in 2011.

In the omnibus PIL system, these cases were never meant to be closed. They were to be kept perpetually pending so that the court could govern the city on a continual basis – whether it be unauthorized constructions, traffic congestion or road safety. Justice Shah's PIL bench made a major departure from the earlier trend by passing orders closing these cases, like in *Hemraj,* where the court stated:

> It appears to this Court that the continued monitoring of the implementation of the earlier directions issued by this Court in these petitions is no longer necessary...Several directions have already been issued in these matters and it is needless to reiterate them.

Some of Justice Jain's most egregious decisions, like the ban on cycle rickshaws, were reviewed and set aside[72]. The constituency which had had a field day during Justice Jain's and Justice Sharma's time was despondent at this turn of events. As a journalist who covered the High Court 'beat' for an English newspaper told me, 'After this bench, [I have had] nothing newsworthy in last three weeks. Shah makes no off the cuff remarks. When PILs like *Hemraj* of 10-15 years vintage were disposed by him, even the lawyers were shocked.'[73] Another journalist compared the new judges on the PIL bench to eunuchs[74]. Such language reeking of machismo in which PIL-watchers speak of PIL judges tells its own story.

There were other important developments. Some of the excesses committed during Justice Jain's time finally came to light and could be legally recognized. The sinister possibilities of *Kalyan Sanstha's* Monitoring Committee were exposed in a writ filed by displaced street vendors in a market in south Delhi[75]. In this case, it was proved that an oral order was passed by the Monitoring Committee in 2006 and communicated telephonically to the concerned MCD official for removing 'unauthorized encroachers' in Ramji Lal Market, without any order in writing being given. This would pre-empt any legal action against the evictions, as no paper trail would exist at all. Such kind of arbitrary functioning of the Monitoring Committee had been speculated upon earlier, but it was now confirmed by the

High Court itself that the court-appointed Committee had been issuing oral orders for evicting and demolishing 'unauthorized encroachers'. The only reason it was found out was because the coordinator of the Monitoring Committee had written to the MCD official reminding him about the earlier telephonic communication and asking him for an Action Taken Report regarding the encroachments.

Justice Shah retired in February 2010. Soon the old PILs his bench had ordered to be closed were attempted to be revived. For instance, there was a PIL that had been filed by the Jangpura RWA in 2006 for 'the removal of unauthorized constructions and encroachments', which had led to demolition of slums in the Jangpura area in South-central Delhi in 2006–07. In July 2008, the RWA had filed a new application before the High Court, asking for the demolition of all remaining structures, including a mosque, used by the slum dwellers who were said to be Bangladeshis. This application was listed before Justice Shah's bench, who instead of ordering any further demolition, disposed of the PIL itself with this order:

> Most of the unauthorised structures have been removed and there is a boundary wall constructed to ensure that no further encroachments take place. It is stated by the counsel for the Respondents [MCD] that any further grievance that the Petitioner may have, including those made in the present application, will be promptly looked into and appropriate action will be taken thereon. In view of this statement, this Court does not consider it necessary to continue to monitor the progress of the implementation of its directions.

In October 2010, with Justice Shah gone, this old PIL was revived through the backdoor with a contempt case filed by the Jangpura RWA, alleging that the above order by Shah in 2008 had ordered the MCD to take action against encroachments in the area and they had not done so. The High Court, without issuing any notice to the affected parties, immediately ordered the MCD to take action against the encroachments and file a 'compliance affidavit'. Accordingly, on 12 January 2011, the MCD demolished the mosque called Noor Masjid in Jangpura[76].

Conclusion

In an interview conducted in January 2010, Justice Vijender Jain modestly explained to me that a new dimension to judicial authority had emerged in the period between 2003 and 2006, during his heyday. Just how right he was would be evident by now. Judicial charisma has been an important genre in the historiography of common law and the phenomena of heroic/diabolical judges have long been central to its institutional histories. Judicial power, however, is elevated to a whole different level thanks to the enormous powers that PIL vests in a judge, making such a narrative even more apposite. While judges have predilections like the rest of us, the rules of adjudication and court procedure act as constraints they have to work within. PIL removes any such limitation. In non-PIL individual cases, judges can decide between affected parties based on their opinions but that can only go only so far and can hardly translate into the kind of demolition drive that we see here. Because it is an entirely malleable jurisdiction, PIL enables a judge like Vijender Jain to act programmatically and go to whatever extent he might want to.

My principal aim here has been to display how effective the non-procedural and arbitrary nature of PIL makes it to systematically bulldoze its way through the slums, literally in this case. In the PIL cases I have discussed, the court can initiate a case on any public issue on its own, appoint its own lawyer, introduce its own machinery to investigate the issue and then order its own solutions to the issue at the level of the entire state. My interest here is to demonstrate how the court can effectively take over urban governance through PIL, rather than merely expose the ideologically slanted nature of such judicial urban governance. The latter is clear enough and it's easy to look at judicial discourse and expose their biases, which are writ large in their pronouncements. The real issue is the unprecedented efficacy of PIL in pursuing such an agenda, thanks to its fundamentally protean nature. As a weapon of civil society, PIL prima facie appears to be a mere legal tool and, therefore, a classic example of associational activity. But it is really a mirror image of the populist contemporary politics it assails without any of the protections that populist political mobilization regularly requires in a liberal democracy like India. Just as the practices of illegality rampant among India's white-collared denizens make its civil society uncontainable within any conventional notions of civic behaviour, its favourite weapon, PIL, too, has only a thin veneer of legality. The judicial populism of PIL allows for a radical instability that continually pushes the limits of what a court can do.

Endnotes

1 Interview, March 2009.

2 I will use the term 'slum' here, as it is colloquially understood and used even by courts, to refer to a type of settlement locally known as 'Jhuggi Jhopdi clusters' or more often, 'JJ Clusters'. Interestingly, the term 'slum' is not popularly deployed in Delhi for a settlement that has the legal status of a slum area under the 'Slum Areas' (Improvement and Clearance) Act 1956. The latter legally notified 'slum areas' are on privately owned land and enjoy certain statutory rights. On the other hand, JJ clusters are on 'public land', i.e. land owned by government agencies. For the vicissitudes of the term slum in legal and illegal discourses, see Ramanathan

(2005). Throughout this chapter, I will use the term 'slum' to refer to 'JJ clusters'. The term 'slum', of course, comes with a train of over-determined meanings and presupposes distance. But precisely such meanings and distance influenced the way the protagonists of this paper, the appellate judges of Delhi, viewed these settlements. I would prefer to use the term 'slum' in quotation marks throughout this paper, but since this would be too clumsy, I urge the reader to assume quotation marks whenever this term is used here.

3 Dupont, 2015, p. 4.

4 'Shah Commission's Findings – V: The Wrecking of Delhi,' *Economic and Political Weekly*, 24 June 1978, p. 1019–21. See also Tarlo 2003.

5 Ghertner, An Analysis of New Legal Discourse behind Delhi's Slum Demolitions; Ghertner, Rule by aesthetics.

6 Another argument, made by Gautam Bhan, suggests that claims based on poverty and vulnerability have a declining efficacy in the court during this period, suggesting shifts in judicial attitudes analogous to the shifts that Ghertner maps. Bhan, 'The disappearance of poverty'.

7 Dupont, 'Slum Demolitions in Delhi since the 1990s', p. 80.

8 Dupont and Ramanathan, The Courts and the Squatter Settlements in Delhi.

9 Ramanathan, 'Illegality and Exclusion 2004', p. 10.

10 Way back in 1993, when he was a judge in the Delhi High Court, Justice Kirpal had bemoaned the very existence of the relocation policy in Delhi in another PIL: 'It appears that the public exchequer has to be burdened with crores of rupees for providing alternative accommodation to *jhuggi* dwellers who are trespassers on public land'. He had also directed that where resettlement was done, the resettled should not be given the land on a lease-hold basis, as was the practice, but on licence – 'with no right in the licensee to transfer or part with possession of the land in question' – the idea being to deprive the resettled of property rights. *Lawyers' Cooperative Group Housing Society vs. Union of India*, CWP No 267 of 1993, Delhi High Court.

11 'Per capita waste generation per day in Delhi is 420 g for those in the high income group, 240 g for those in the middle income group, 150 g for those in the lower middle income group, and only 80 g for those in the JJ clusters.' Rajamani, Public Interest Environmental Litigation in India, p. 302.

12 Rajamani, Public Interest Environmental Litigation in India, p. 303. She also said that Supreme Court judges 'tend to focus first on cleaning up Delhi where they live and only then on other cities'.

13 On the increasing redundancy of the petitioner in PIL cases, see Chapter 1.

14 *Almitra H. Patel vs. Union of India*, Civil Writ Petition 888/1996, 15 February 2000. Urban planner Gita Dewan Verma records the response of a city editor in The Times of India welcoming this order, 'Delhi needs a Thanksgiving Day. To thank the Supreme Court…,' *Verma*, p. 20. Emphasis added by the author.

15 Ramanathan, Illegality and the Urban Poor, p. 3195.

16 Ghertner, An Analysis of New Legal Discourse behind Delhi's Slum Demolitions, p. 57.

17 *Mahesh R. Desai and Ors. Vs. Ahmedabad Municipal Corporation* on 26 September 1984, AIR 1986 Guj 154.

18 In some of these cases, the court did grant a stay order on eviction for short periods at the behest of the slum dwellers, but even this became increasingly rare.

19 *Prabodh Verma vs. State of UP*, AIR 1985 SC 167. For a more recent restatement of this position by the Supreme Court, see Suresh vs. Yeotmal Dist. Central Co-Op. Bank, (2008) 12 SCC 558.

20 Ghertner, An Analysis of New Legal Discourse behind Delhi's Slum Demolitions.

21 Chayes, The Role of the Judge in Public Law Litigation.

22 Krishnaswamy, The Supreme Court on 2G.

23 Civil Writ Petition No 4215 of 1995 in the Delhi High Court.

24 Civil Writ Petition Nos. 4125/95 and 531/90 decided on 27 September 2002.

25 Krishnaswamy, The Supreme Court on 2G.

26 For an excellent discussion of this judgment, see Ghertner, An Analysis of New Legal Discourse behind Delhi's Slum Demolitions.

27 Ghertner, An Analysis of New Legal Discourse behind Delhi's Slum Demolitions.

28 108 (2002) DLT 517. The other petition which it was combined with was also filed by a factory owners' association, *Wazirpur Bartan Nirmata Sangh vs. Union of India* (UOI), CWP 2112 of 2002.

29 Mehta, Can a Jurisprudence of Exasperation Sustain the Court's Authority?

30 SLP Civil No. 3166-3167/2003, Order Dated March 2003.

31 *Union Of India vs. Okhla Factory Owners' Asson. & Ors,* Civil Appeal No. 1688/2007 (Judgment delivered 7 September 2010); Special Leave Petition No. 3166-3167/2003. Faced with a hostile Bench in the Supreme Court, the original petitioners in the case actually withdrew their petitions at such a belated stage after almost a decade of adjudication.

32 Even after the judgment, the DUSIB website displays its policy dated 3 February 2010 for rehabilitation/relocation and allotment of flats to slum dwellers, which carries this as eligibility condition no. (xi): 'The allotment of flat will be subject to the result of pending decision and outcome of the SLP (Civil No. 3166-3167/2003) in the Hon'ble Supreme Court of India and all other similar cases relating to Slums relocation pending in the various courts.' http://delhishelterboard.in/main/?page_id=128 (Accessed on 12 June 2015). Such a condition hung like the sword of Damocles over the allottees for more than seven years.

33 This phase could be bookended by the Division Bench decision in *Sudama Singh vs. Government of Delhi*, delivered by Justices A. P. Shah and S. Muralidhar on 11 February 2010.

34 Order dated 3 March 2003 passed in W.P(C) No.2112/2002.

35 Dunu. *Pollution, Pushta, and Prejudices.*

36 The amicus curiae in this case was Mr. Amarjit Singh Chandhiok, Senior Advocate.

37 Bhan, You Can't Bank by This River.

38 'Demolition man cometh to jazz up Yamuna bank', *Times of India*, 10 January 2004.

39 Menon-Sen, Better to have Died than to Live like This, p. 1969.

40 Verma, 'Yamuna and Pushta: Tragedy of Governance'.

41 Interestingly, a month later, the same bench of Chief Justice B. C. Patel and Justice B. D. Ahmed reserved its judgment on two separate PILs urging the court to decide the status of South Delhi's 'poshest' unauthorized colony, Sainik Farms. However, the Chief Justice retired 16 months later without passing any judgment in the case. The case had to be heard all over again and was pending till 2011 when it was disposed of, without taking any action against Sainik Farms. 'Judgment reserved on status Sainik Farms', *The Hindu*, 20 March 2004: http://www.thehindu.com/2004/03/20/stories/2004032005960400.htm

42 For an account of the demolitions, see 'India Shining: A Report On Demolition and Resettlement of Yamuna Pushta Bastis', People's Union for Democratic Rights, Delhi: May 2004.

43 For an account of this resettlement process, see Menon-Sen and Bhan, *Swept off the Map*. In light of the history of previous large-scale forced demolitions and resettlement in Delhi, it is not insignificant that about 70 per cent of the population evicted from Yamuna Pushta was Muslim. See Menon-Sen, Better to have Died than to Live like This.

44 Order dated 3 May 2005 by Chief Justice B. C. Patel and Justice Sanjay Kishan Kaul.

45 These included, according to Jain's order, 'Mr. V N. Singh, a former Commissioner of Police, Vice-Chairman, DDA, Commissioner, MCD, Chief Engineer, UP State Irrigation Department, who has got his office at Okhla Barrage'.

46 Dutta, *The Unquiet River*, p. 55.

47 Dutta, *The Unquiet River*, p. 59

48 Dutta, *The Unquiet River*, p. 56

49 Paved or stepped portions of river banks used for washing clothes by members of the *dhobi* (washerman) caste.

50 Interview conducted in January 2010.

51 W. P.(C) No. 5239 of 2002.

52 The court ordered, 'There is no right of *tehbazari* [street-vending] on footpaths, roads or places which are meant for use by the people for walking/pedestrians on account of vehicular traffic.'

53 W. P.(C) No. 3419 of 1999.

54 These were Vijay Panjwani and Amarjit Singh Chandhiok. The latter was also the amicus in the Yamuna case.

55 The Hindu, 'MCD starts demolition work at slum cluster', 31 August 2006. http://www.thehindu.com/todays-paper/tp-national/tp-newdelhi/mcd-starts-demolition-work-at-slum-cluster/article3098134.ece (accessed on 10 June 2015).

56 WP (C) No.3419/1999, Order dated 14 December 2005.

57 See the appeal filed against the High Court order in the Supreme Court. http://nangla.freeflux.net/blog/archive/2006/05/10/synopsis-of-slp-filed-in-the-supreme-

court.html#post_content_extended (accessed on 10 June 2015). The appeal was summarily dismissed.

58 The number of cycle rickshaw licences had been capped at 99,000, but there were hundreds of thousands of unlicenced cycle rickshaws in Delhi, according to the MCD.

59 The association was called Chandni Chowk Sarv Vyapar Mandal.

60 The court, as usual, did not see any need to curtail private motor vehicles in this heavily congested area.

61 https://www.itdp.org/wp-content/uploads/2014/07/Position-of-ITDP-US-on-the-Recent-Delhi-High-Court-Decision.pdf (accessed on 15 June 2015).

62 Sethi, *A Free Man*, p. 166–67. 'Todh-phodh' is a colloquial Hindi phrase that might be loosely (and somewhat inadequately) translated as 'breaking and destroying'.

63 Civil Writ Petition 4582/2003.

64 Mehra, Protesting Publics in Indian Cities.

65 The Monitoring Committee members were allotted a monthly salary of ₹50,000, and the Court Commissioners, all practicing advocates in the Delhi High Court, were given monthly salaries of ₹45000 each by orders of the court.

66 Rupees 5 billion. Approximately $0.9 billion at today's rate.

67 Crucially, the 'right to information' did not apply to it.

68 A structure whose walls and roof at least are made of 'pucca' materials such as oven-burnt bricks, stone, stone-blocks, cement, concrete, jack-board (cement plastered reed), tiles and timber and corrugated iron or asbestos sheets for the roof. *Compendium of Environment Statistics,* Government of India (2000).

69 Letter from the Monitoring Committee to Secretary, Ministry of Urban Development, 27 December 2006.

70 Four years after Justice Jain's last *Kalyan Sanstha* order, a series of taped conversations between the corporate lobbyist Niira Radia and various well-known politicians, bureaucrats, industrialists and media persons were leaked to the press. The Radia tapes became one of the biggest political scandal in contemporary India. One of the lesser-known conversations leaked in these tapes is between Radia and a prominent bureaucrat named Sunil Arora in which he informs Radia that a Delhi High Court judge, Justice Vijender Jain, was paid off 90 million rupees at his residence in a sealing case related to real estate by a middleman. The favourable judgment, (Arora goes on), was written one month before it was delivered in court; the middleman was even given an advance copy. Arora also referred to Jain as Justice Y.K. Sabharwal's man – '*Sabharwal ka khaas aadmi*'. None of these allegations have yet been acted upon legally. Justice Jain was appointed chairman of the Human Rights Commission of the North Indian state of Haryana in October 2012. This was the man who led the campaign against illegalities in Delhi. 'This Litigant Told Me He Paid Vijender Jain 9 Cr,' *http://www.outlookindia.com/article.aspx?269667*

71 Robinson, Leading the Court.

72 Manushi Sangthan vs. Govt of Delhi, WP(C) 4572/2007, Judgment dated 10 February 2010.

73 Interview conducted by me, November 2008.

74 Interview conducted by me, November 2008.

75 *RamjiSabzi Market Welfare Association (Regd.) vs. MCD*, W.P.(C) 18709/2006, Order dated 10 December 2008.

76 Gayer and Mahajan, Delhi's Noor Masjid, pp. 12–15.

4

Good Judges, Bad Judges

Critical Discourses on Public Interest Litigation in India

> The average intelligent Indian thinks of PIL as the modern equivalent of the bell which the better kind of king is reputed to have strung outside his palace for the desperate citizen to tug at and get an instant hearing and instant justice. The average intelligent Indian also thinks that all the limitations of judicial power that he or she is otherwise familiar with will vanish when the Courts sit to hear PILs, namely that they become benign despots who can set every wrong right by passing a condign order.
>
> –K. Balagopal[1]

The Supreme Court, in a 2010 judgment, provided its own history of PIL, broadly dividing public interest litigation in India into three phases.

> Phase-I: It deals with cases of this Court where directions and orders were passed primarily to protect fundamental rights under Article 21 of the marginalized groups and sections of the society who because of extreme poverty, illiteracy and ignorance cannot approach this court or the High Courts.
> Phase-II: It deals with the cases relating to protection, preservation of ecology, environment, forests, marine life, wildlife, mountains, rivers, historical monuments, etc.etc.
> Phase-III: It deals with the directions issued by the Courts in maintaining the probity, transparency and integrity in governance.[2]

From 'poverty' to 'environment' to 'governance': this is the trajectory of PIL that the Indian Supreme Court itself confesses to. Sudipta Kaviraj has written as to how the decline of institutional spaces with Mrs Gandhi's more personalized politics made possible a new irresponsibility of ideology with baffling shifts of emphasis, the most spectacular of these being that 'fertility and not poverty became the major obstacle to Indian development' during the Emergency[3]. PIL, too, with its lack of institutional grounding and close identification with specific judges, has been prone to these sorts of wild fluctuations in ideology. The most celebrated of these has been the change of focus from poverty in its first phase in the early 1980s to 'bourgeois environmentalism' from the mid-1990s. It is the inherent instability of populism in both instances that allowed such a fundamental shift in priorities to take place.

This change in priorities in PIL cases has not gone unlamented. There has been a significant literature criticizing it, especially the dislodging of the poor from the position of PIL's foremost discursive constituency. From the early 2000s, partly as a result of the kind of court actions in PILs that we saw in the previous two chapters, there has been strong criticism of the court's approach to PIL. Two principal strands can be discerned in this debate – one led by the left-liberal and activist constituency that is disappointed by what they perceive as the decline and fall of 1980s-era PIL, and the other led by critical self-reflection from the Bench itself. This second strand is represented by a few incumbent judges, the most vociferous being Justice Markandey Katju in the Supreme Court.

The consequentialist critique of PIL

The argument of the first strand is best summed up by Upendra Baxi, who pithily characterizes post-liberalization PIL as the 'Structural Adjustment of Judicial Activism'.[4] He calls the new version of PIL 'judicial counter-revolution proceeding via the structural adjustment of judicial role, function, and power.'[5] Prashant Bhushan, possibly India's most well-known PIL lawyer, argues that the shifts in political economy since the 1990s led to changes in the nature of PIL:

> The court has in fact bought the ideology underlying the economic reforms – an ideology which venerates the virtues of the free market and undermines the role of the state in providing education, jobs, and the basic amenities of life to its citizens.[6]

A more subtle version of the same argument is made by the legal scholar Usha Ramanathan when she points out that by the end of the 1990s, 'the original constituency of PIL – the poor and the vulnerable to whom constitutional and legal rights had to be reached' did not 'have the court on their side'.[7] In this vein, there has been some recent work by economist Varun Gauri providing a quantitative analysis of PIL beneficiaries. Gauri writes:

> Win rates for fundamental rights claims are now significantly higher when the claimant is from an advantaged social group than when he or she is from a marginalized group. That constitutes a social reversal both from the original objective of public interest litigation and from the relative win rates in the 1980s.[8]

In its basic terms, this argument is nostalgic about the founding PIL era of the late 1970s and 1980s, which was spearheaded by 'progressive' judges – Justices Krishna Iyer, P. S. Bhagwati, Chinnappa Reddy and D. A. Desai (Baxi likes to call them 'the four musketeers'[9]). But now, in post-liberalization times, the argument goes, 'regressive' judges like Justices Kirpal, Sabharwal and Jain have led PIL in the opposite direction. Aditya Nigam, too, has drawn a similarly sharp distinction between what he calls 'PIL Mark 1' (1980s PIL) and 'PIL Mark 2' (post-liberalization PIL, which he labels 'The Brass Band of Neo-Liberalism.[10] This strand of argument tends to completely overlook the remarkable continuity between these two phases of PIL in terms of the processual instability at its heart. It insistently focuses on the discontinuities in PIL's career dwelling on the stark changes in its priorities in terms of political economy, while never really addressing the fundamental question: why is the PIL court so effective as the agent of 'neo-liberalism' in India?

This ideological approach to thinking about PIL is best summed up, as legal scholar Rajeev Dhavan had done in another context, as 'consequentialist' – 'the consequences of judicial decisions speak for themselves… From such a consequentialist analysis flows the further charge that the judiciary is essentially class-based.'[11] These accounts typically read the history of the Indian judiciary in 'progressive/regressive' terms. Such a perspective had a field day in the pre-Emergency era, when the Supreme Court was portrayed as having stood by the right to property and, therefore, deemed to be regressive and anti-land reform. It was this discourse that was so successfully mobilized by Indira Gandhi and Mohan Kumaramangalam in the early 1970s in their call for 'committed' judges who were ideologically suitable. It was also the basis of the supersession of judges, as we saw in the first chapter. The enduring legacy of Kumaramangalam is that the dominant critique of PIL today continues to mimic the terms of his discourse.

Not surprisingly, the most clearly articulated version of such a consequentialist approach to 'judicial activism' comes from Justice P. N. Bhagwati, the architect of PIL in India, in an article in 1985 where he reflected on this issue at some length.[12] It is important to rehearse Bhagwati's argument in some detail, because it has since become *the* hegemonic position on judicial politics in India. His point of departure in this article is that 'judges do make law' and that 'judicial activism is a necessary and inevitable part of the judicial process.'[13] The question would be 'what kind of judicial activism, how much of it' and 'to what willed results'. Based on these criteria, Bhagwati argues that judicial activism can take three forms. The first of these he calls 'technical activism', which declares judicial freedom to deploy various techniques and choices. It 'is merely concerned with keeping juristic techniques open-ended.'[14] The second is what Bhagwati refers to as 'juristic activism'. It 'is concerned… with the creation of new concepts irrespective of the purposes which they serve.'[15] It is not concerned with the social consequences of these concepts. Whether they 'help to preserve the status quo' or to 'impede equitable distribution' is irrelevant.

Bhagwati found both of these forms of judicial activism limited. What he was concerned about was the 'purpose for which such activism is practiced'. He was interested, he wrote, in 'the *instrumental* use of judicial activism'.[16] Legal scholars Craig and Deshpande have called his style an example of teleological reasoning.[17] For Bhagwati, judicial activism could 'be evaluated only in terms of its social objective'. He was, therefore, a votary of a third kind, which he called 'social activism' – juristic activism for achieving social justice. In a clear enunciation of the 'committed judiciary' principle, he explained what it meant. Judges in India, he wrote, 'have to justify their decision-making within the framework of constitutional values' aimed at the 'substantiviation of social justice'.[18] In this, they were 'motivated' by the 'Directive Principles of State Policy' of the Indian Constitution, which held out 'social justice as the central feature of the new constitutional order'. These principles 'inspired some of the justices to become social activists'. 'Judge led' and 'judge induced, PIL was the means they chose to achieve this. PIL has since been closely identified with 'social activist' judges. All the procedural limitations of common law adjudication—standing, adversarial procedure, fact-finding and judicial remedies were departed from in the precedent-setting landmark PIL cases of the early 1980s. And academic analyses as well as political rhetoric, I would argue, have since been skewed by an unquestioning adherence to this narrow consequentialist approach.

Bhagwati's theory of PIL, so pithily formulated in his article, has been hugely influential. It successfully set out the discursive boundaries within which PIL has since been evaluated: 'only in terms of its social objective'.[19] The terms set by it, inviting us to this era of PIL-led 'social activism' have largely been accepted: concentrate on evaluating the just-ness of outcomes, while condoning any level of improvization of judicial process. It is a formulation that has led most literature on PIL to concentrate on the outcomes alone. If the results were largely for the good, the questionable nature of PIL procedure was to be glossed over. The problem with PIL only arose for such analysis when the results were no longer to the liking of its erstwhile advocates. Because the judicial outcomes no longer seem to favour the classes one is sympathetic to, PIL suddenly becomes questionable. There is a certain 'God that failed' quality to such criticism of PIL.

In a recent book espousing many such views, the term 'conservative' is repeatedly used critically to describe the post-liberalization phase of PIL.[20] The fundamental problem with such a characterization is that there was nothing remotely conservative about the radical processual innovations introduced by PIL cases in this period. PIL was primarily a revolution in the procedure begun by Bhagwati in pre-liberalization India and taken to its logical culmination by judges like Vijender Jain in the changed circumstances of the twenty-first century. The latter were simply instrumentalizing the immense radical potential of PIL and the carte blanche it offered to appellate judges to pursue political causes they deemed fit. Once a frankly instrumental role is accepted for PIL courts, with its decisions moored only by concepts as capacious as 'social justice', whose meanings necessarily vary with the zeitgeist, it should be no surprise that the issues taken up by a new generation of PIL judges for their social activism are of a very different sort from the original votaries of PIL.

In the previous chapters, while I have drawn attention to the disastrous outcomes of certain PIL cases, my emphasis has been on how such outcomes result from the inherent unfairness of PIL procedure. The objection, however, may be that one can easily conceive 'good' outcomes also resulting from a process of adjudication which is similarly unjust: consider the typical *suo motu* PIL, where a court takes up a policy issue appoints its favourite lawyer as amicus curiae, suggests solutions based on half-baked evidence collected by its own random appointees, issues legislative guidelines binding as law and, then, appoints personnel to monitor the implementation of these policies. This rather familiar PIL process, so unremarkable as to seem like the contemporary norm, can certainly result in 'good' outcomes, and it sometimes does. So enduring is Bhagwati's criterion for PIL's evaluation, that any criticism of PIL per se is constantly confronted by the question: what about these good PILs, which have successfully offered such grand solutions to the country's problems? The analysts of PIL then reach for their Benthamite hedonistic calculus, measuring the pain of the people who have suffered from PIL against the pleasure of those who have gained from it. And after careful calculations, they declare that the despotism of PIL judges is still acceptable because it is, on balance, benevolent. My aim here is to move the debate on PIL away from an analysis based on such a facile calculus. The problem with PIL is not just that it increasingly leads to unjust outcomes because of the changed ideological climate, but that it can so easily do so because of its diminution of judicial process. My attempt in this section is to formulate an anti–anti PIL critique, aimed at moving this critique away from outcomes to process.

The implications of the hegemony enjoyed by Bhagwati's narrowly consequentialist framework of evaluating India's judicial process were even wider. One of the key attributes of the modern judicial process is that it results in a written order or judgment that has to be logically consistent. This impinges on the very definition of juristic activity in the words of Max Weber: 'the jurist, assuming the empirical validity of the legal propositions, examines each of them and tries to determine its logically correct meaning in such a way that all of them can be combined in a system which is logically coherent, i.e., free from internal contradictions.'[21] But as per Bhagwati, juristic activism was of secondary import compared to social activism, so the analysis of a judgment was to be conducted primarily in terms of its social impact, not so much the structure and soundness of legal arguments within it. Now that judges were supposed to think of themselves as social activists and not *mere* jurists, a certain looseness of legal language entered Indian appellate judgments, with Bhagwati himself leading the way.

The result was nothing less than a self-conscious departure from the very fundamental principles of modern law, characterized by 'logically formal rationality', according to Weber. By rationality here, he meant 'following some criteria of decision which is applicable to all like cases', and by formality, 'employing criteria of decision intrinsic to the legal system'.[22] While there is no conscious departure from rationality, what Bhagwati's consequentialist model does is move the Indian judicial process from principles of formally rational law to its opposite – substantively rational law. As Trubek's helpful guide through Weber's corpus on law informs us, substantive rationality:

> ...is in some sense governed by rules – that is why, it is 'rational' – but these are the principles of some body of thought *outside* the law itself, such as religion, ethical philosophy, or ideology. This type of law will be constantly tempted to reach specific results, dictated by the value premises of this external set of principles, which are neither general nor predictable.[23]

As Weber described the form of substantive legal rationality, 'the aim is rather to find a type of law which is most appropriate to the expediential and ethical goals of the authorities in question.'[24] This is precisely what Bhagwati's PIL model had transformed judicial process to – pure ideology.

As Bhagwati's model became increasingly hegemonic, commitment to principles of law in Indian judicial discourse mattered less and less, what mattered was commitment to an ideology. Careful judicial prose no longer had any premium attached to it. What replaced it were shoddily written judgments making the right political noises, generally holding forth on social problems, attempting to imitate the bizarre bombast of judges like Bhagwati, though hardly anybody could possibly match him in pomposity. The discourse had shifted to such an extent that when H. M. Seervai criticized Bhagwati's judgment in *EP Royappa vs. State of Tamil Nadu*[25] for making the elementary logical error of the fallacy of the undistributed middle, this did not have the serious repercussions it should have had.[26] To this day, *Royappa* is binding precedent and its dictum has been hugely influential, having added the 'arbitrariness' ground to the standard 'reasonable classification' test in order to examine violations of the Right to Equality. The fact that this dictum is also manifestly illogical makes no difference in the new scheme of things.

To take a more recent and equally egregious example, legal scholar Lavanya Rajamani has critically examined the Indian Supreme Court's famed 'environmental jurisprudence'.[27] She takes issue with the court's importation of the 'precautionary principle' into domestic law by blithely declaring it to be a part of customary international law in a much-cited case[28], when it is actually a highly contested concept. She found the court's reasoning 'riddled with logical leaps', its analysis 'intellectually sloppy' and its general mode that of 'transforming rhetoric into right'. Her broad conclusion is that public interest environmental jurisdiction is being extended in 'anarchic fashion.'[29] These gross instances of juristic incompetence by India's celebrated Supreme Court can be multiplied in many areas of law, but in the post-Emergency intellectual climate around law framed by what we might call Bhagwati's talisman, which infected legal academia too, criticism on such grounds is rarely voiced. Competitive radicalism had become the new currency in the academic sphere as well. Any criticism that demanded intellectual rigour from the judges would now be characterized as excessively legalistic and elitist.[30] All that mattered was fidelity to the ideological currents of the time. Old-fashioned concerns like the fairness of judicial process adopted or the logical application of legal principles in judgments were now of secondary importance.

The post-liberalization ideological critics of PIL, having earlier bought into its attenuated judicial process, naturally found themselves focusing their blinkered lens on the disastrous consequences alone of post-liberalization PIL, notably its grotesque class bias. This has also meant that they adopted a purely discursive strategy, with no serious critical focus on the materiality of PIL processes, which is where the problem lay all along. There is a chronic failure to recognize that PIL provides a whole new mechanism to concentrate policy-making power in the hands of judges and enables them to forge powerful tools to operationalize these new policies. Judges can raise an issue of public importance by themselves, suggest solutions, appoint people to collect evidence and even appoint personnel to monitor the implementation of these policies. Purely as an analogy, let us say for the sake of argument that a pro-management judiciary may have changed the very nature of labour jurisprudence in the last 15 years. But even if there were to be a stark trend in labour law that denudes labour of the legal protections it earlier enjoyed, such a trend would still not be comparable to what PIL has done in the same period. A pure conceptual development in the law can only go so far. It does not provide the apparatus to change the very nature of governance, to enforce their ideas via takeover of the whole arena. PIL has made this possible in the areas in which it has intervened. It provides the procedural infrastructure to create a field for its operation and transform it.

One of the few critics to foreground the extent of PIL's procedural departure is Usha Ramanathan, though for her, too, the problem primarily lies not in the extraordinary powers of the PIL court per se but in the change in ideological climate after liberalization. She criticizes a leading commentator on Indian judicial activism, S.P. Sathe, for looking at PIL 'as merely an aspect of judicial review'.[31] The newness of PIL, Ramanathan argues, is 'because of the extraordinary techniques of judicial intervention that the Supreme Court invented and adopted. It is also the casting aside by the court of restraints placed by the doctrine of 'separation of powers' that called for a degree of ingenuity, which marked this phase of judicial activism The departure from processual precision to substantive justice was accompanied by "juristic" activism.'[32] Indeed, PIL had gone far beyond judicial review, and to use the old tools to examine its 'achievements' would be severely limiting. More recently, Ramanathan has succinctly shown how the rise of the institution of the amicus curiae since the mid-1990s has meant 'the return to exclusive conversations between lawyers and the Bench with the additional dash of the power that the idea of "public interest" has brought with it.'[33]

The institutional critique of PIL

There has been a recent trend of legal scholars who diagnose the problem with PIL not just in its ideological transformation but in its judicial process as well. There is a realization that it is the process of PIL itself, which causes the outcomes that the ideological critics are singularly obsessed with, that needs to be at least partially reformed. In this vein, Krishnaswamy and Khosla have argued for the need to pay further attention to the judicial process in PIL, which this book tries to engage with seriously. There also seems to be a recognition that some clarity with regard to institutional norms regulating PIL procedure is necessary. This strand of criticism often relies on influential analyses of such litigation in other common law countries which would apparently bear comparison to PIL in India. While it is certainly a most useful exercise to contextualize and evaluate Indian PIL in a comparative manner, the difficulty is that such comparison ends up missing out on just how extreme the Indian experience of PIL really has been. Indeed, Krishnaswamy and Khosla take exception to India's PIL being seen as 'unique in the common law world'.[34] Similarly, Thiruvengadam has suggested that Abram

Chayes' influential theorization of 'Public Law Litigation' should be the reference point to think of the expanded role of a judge in PIL, as Clark Cunningham had also argued earlier.[35] However, Indian PIL has gone much further than even Chayes' heterodox model. Thiruvengadam himself argued that the dilution of *locus standi* already makes Indian PIL different from Chayes' model. In fact, for all the procedural departures that Chayes theorized, he could not have envisaged litigation without the very existence of the petitioner or the complete absence of any affected parties. Indian PIL allows for a process which is *sou motu*, or entirely judge initiated, as well as enables the court petitioner herself to be removed and replaced with an amicus curiae appointed by it, as we have seen repeatedly in previous chapters. We have also seen how Indian PIL allows the judge to rely on rather low standards of evidence, which as Krishnaswamy has elsewhere argued, goes completely against Chayes's suggestion of a higher burden of proof in such cases.[36] And Indian PIL cases can culminate in clearly legislative remedies as well as decisions instructing the Executive to undertake specific construction projects costing enormous amounts of money. These are way beyond the imagination of any judicial process almost anywhere outside South Asia. Another astute recent critic of PIL has been Lavanya Rajamani, who has relied on Lon Fuller's famous argument that a judicial forum is ill-equipped to handle 'polycentric disputes', i.e. disputes that 'involve many affected parties and a somewhat fluid state of affairs.'[37] She argues that intervention in such situations result in complex repercussions 'as not all affected parties are readily identifiable and therefore before the Court'.[38] This is undoubtedly an important point to ponder over in such litigation. However, in Indian PIL cases, the situation is much more extreme. Even the 'necessary parties' who are directly affected by a PIL case are either not even made a party as we repeatedly saw in the slum demolition PILs in Chapter 3, or are not heard even if they are allowed to intervene as we saw in the PIL relating to industrial closure in Chapter 2. However, this strand of criticism with its insightful procedural criticism of PIL offers a way forward if the pathologies of PIL are to be mitigated. Rajamani suggests that the court 'evolve a set of guidelines for restrained and responsible PIL', Thiruvengadam's suggestion is that the PIL judge should 'be encouraged to adopt a far more modest, facilitative role'[39], while Khosla and Krishnaswamy argue for the need to clarify the question of locus standi in PIL cases.

The other institutional critique of PIL has come from within the Supreme Court itself. The close identification of PIL with Justice Bhagwati in the early 1980s meant that the famous 'epistolary jurisdiction', by which letters written to the court would be treated as petitions, often had letters being personally addressed to Justice Bhagwati. He would then ensure that the PIL was heard by him. As Upendra Baxi wrote in the early 1980s, this imprinted the early PILs 'with the insignia of an individual justice, whereas what is needed in days to come is a collective imprimatur of the Court for the new litigation.'[40] An institutional response was attempted by the Bench of two judges (S. M. Fazal Ali and Venkataramiah J. J.) in the *Sudipt Mazumdar* case in 1983, when it formulated 10 questions regarding PIL and passed an order referring to a Constitutional Bench (of a minimum of five judges).[41] These questions included, among others:

> '1. Should this Court take notice of such letters addressed by individuals by post enclosing some paper cuttings and take action on them *suo motu* except where the complaint refers to deprivation of liberty of any individual?'
>
> 6. Can this Court take action on letters addressed to it where the facts disclosed are not sufficient to take action? Should these letters be treated differently from other regular petitions filed into this Court in this regard and should the District Magistrate or the District Judge be asked to enquire and make a report to this Court to ascertain whether there is any case for further action?
>
> '10. Would such informality not lead to greater identification of the Court with the cause than it would be when a case involving the same type of cause is filed in the normal way?'

After having kept this case pending for a long time, a Constitution Bench around 2000 decided that there was no need to order any such guidelines. Three decades after the 1983 order, these questions have still not been taken up and decided by any Bench of the Supreme Court. The ad hoc approach continues, and no attempt at tidying up PIL principles was ever successfully made. There have been a few judicial initiatives since then to lay down such principles, but all have met the fate of *Sudipt Mazumdar.*[42] It is still worthwhile, in my opinion, to examine these attempts and the institutional inertia they were met with.

In a concurring judgment to Justice Bhagwati's in the *Bandhua Mukti Morcha* case of 1984, Justice Pathak tried to formulate an institutional response so that PIL could 'command broad acceptance'. He clarified that:

> All communications and petitions invoking the jurisdiction of the Court must be addressed to the entire Court, that is to say, the Chief Justice and his companion Judges. No such communication of petition can properly be addressed to a particular Judge… Communications and petitions addressed to a particular Judge are improper and violate the institutional personality of the Court.

Feeling the need to place limits on the flexibility of procedure that can be adopted in a PIL, J. Pathak laid down certain basic norms:

> Whatever the procedure adopted by the court it must be procedure known to judicial tenets and characteristic of a judicial proceeding… The Court must ever remind itself that one of the indicia identifying it as a Court is the nature and character of the procedure adopted by it in determining a controversy. It is in that sense limited in the evolution of procedures pursued by it in the process of an adjudication and in the grant and execution of the relief.

His has been a lone voice in the wilderness.

In 1988, the Supreme Court did introduce a new streamlined procedure to deal with letter petitions: any letter petition received would first be screened by a new PIL cell and would then be placed before a judge nominated for this purpose by the Chief Justice. This was meant to make sure that letters, even if addressed to specific judges, would henceforth deal with in an institutional manner. But though their symbolic charge remains undiminished, letter petitions have come to form a negligible percentage of the PILs actually dealt with by the Supreme Court.[43]

In one of the few academic writings to have expressed the need for an institutional approach to PIL, S. K. Agrawala proposed in 1985 that

> The Court is not equipped in terms of the infrastructure to apply the non-adversarial procedure. If adversarial procedure is not to be applicable in PIL matters, the parties must know as to what the components of the alternative procedure(s) are. The laying down of guidelines for the non-adversarial procedure is, therefore, equally important.[44]

Particularly important are his suggestions regarding the approach to questions of fact in PIL cases:

> If the court has to manage the collection of facts, data and evidence on its own, it seems to be obviously desirable that a permanent, trained and experienced fact-finding machinery is set up under the control and supervision of the Supreme Court.[45]

In a prescient suggestion that anticipated Justice Vijender Jain's court commissioners in *Kalyan Sanstha*, Agrawala pointed out the problems that would emerge with Justice Bhagwati's blithe disregard for procedure:

> A judge who appoints commissioners would be inclined to appoint those, whom or about whom he knows personally. It is human nature. Such

> commissioners are likely to be at least as biased as the judges who have been enthusiastic about PIL litigation. Bias even for a good cause, is bias all the same. Secondly, they may not be adequately trained for the job that may be entrusted to them... Fact finding, investigation and reporting are not something that everybody and anybody can be entrusted with.[46]

In August 2009, when I interviewed a court commissioner appointed in *Kalyan Sanstha*, he drew a direct connection between his appointment in this case and the 1985 precedent laid down by Justice Bhagwati in *Bandhua Mukti Morcha*, that rules of civil procedure, which are normally made applicable in a modified form to all Supreme Court cases through the Supreme Court Rules[47] need not apply to PIL cases. Therefore, cross-examination of evidence collected by commissioners would not be necessary. This would lead to fundamental departures from certain principles of adjudication, as Muralidhar and Desai argued in 2000:

> The reports given by court-appointed commissioners raise problems regarding their evidentiary value. No court can found its decision on facts unless they are proved according to law. This implies the right of an adversary to test them by cross-examination or at least counter affidavits.[48]

Justice Pathak in *Bandhua Mukti Morcha* had tried to introduce this minimum idea of natural justice so that when evidence was collected by court-appointed commissioners in a PIL, at least a chance to hear the other side and contradict it be given to the affected party. But Justice Bhagwati did not want to encumber PIL with any such procedural safeguards. His radical ideas had now come home to roost.

During the proceedings of one of the applications filed in *Kalyan Sanstha*, I watched as the lawyer for a slum ordered to be demolished by the court, tried to make the factual point that these were *kaccha* houses which would be saved by the Delhi Special Provisions Act, as discussed in the previous chapter. Chief Justice MK Sharma sniggered at him, 'But this is a question of fact. We can't go into a factual question in writ jurisdiction.' In general, all the alleged facts (on the basis of which the commissioners were pushing the demolition apparatus into action) were deemed incontestable, thanks to the supposedly non-adversarial nature of PIL. The comment, 'this is not an adversarial proceeding' would be used repeatedly by the Bench to effectively deflect any inconvenient questions of fact. This was the exact phrase that Justice Bhagwati had used more than a dozen times in the *Morcha* judgment, that most celebrated of PIL cases.

After the 1980s, hardly any attempts were made to create clear procedural rules for PIL. In 1997, Chief Justice Verma, who had initiated the process that would culminate in the apotheosis of the amicus curiae in *Vineet Narain,* announced the setting up of a committee under a Supreme Court judge to draft a separate chapter on Public Interest Litigation to be introduced in the Supreme Court Rules, 'which would contain general rules for guidance to maintain uniformity'.[49] But Chief Justice Verma soon retired and nothing came of it.

In 2007, soon after the retirement of Chief Justice Sabharwal, just as the processes I have described in the previous chapters were reaching their peak, there was a severe attack on PIL from the Supreme Court Bench itself – by a maverick judge called Markandey Katju. Katju used to great effect a strategy commonly deployed by the Indian Supreme Court judges: to repeatedly cite one's own previous judgments as precedent. Katju passed at least four such judgments between 2007 and 2009. The first, given in May 2007, and the last, given in 2009, are particularly interesting because they were both delivered as part of a two-judge Bench, and the other respective incumbent judges gave their own answers to the questions Katju posed of PIL. But the most effectively destabilizing was the one time (in December 2007) when Katju found the other judge, A. K. Mathur, on the Bench, agreeing with him, because it immediately carried the force of law as binding precedent.[50]

Justice Katju's 2007 judgment in this singular instance, *Aravali Golf Club* tapped into the theory of separation of powers. He argued:

> In the name of judicial activism Judges cannot cross their limits and try to take over functions which belong to another organ of the State...Judges must know their limits and must not try to run the Government. They must have modesty and humility, and not behave like Emperors.

Katju quoted a lecture by Justice Verma to ridicule many PILs the Delhi High Court was in the news for:

> Judiciary has intervened to question a mysterious car racing down the Tughlaq Road in Delhi, allotment of a particular bungalow to a Judge, specific bungalows for the Judges' pool, monkeys capering in colonies, stray cattle on the streets, clearing public conveniences, levying congestion charges at peak hours at airports with heavy traffic, etc. under the threat of use of contempt power to enforce compliance of its orders.

Katju added to this list:

> The orders passed by the High Court of Delhi in recent times dealt with subjects ranging from age and other criteria for nursery admissions,

> unauthorized schools, criteria for free seats in schools, supply of drinking water in schools, number of free beds in hospitals on public land, use and misuse of ambulances, requirements for establishing a world class burns ward in the hospital, the kind of air Delhites breathe, begging in public, the use of sub-ways, the nature of buses we board, the legality of constructions in Delhi, identifying the buildings to be demolished, the size of speed-breakers on Delhi roads, auto-rickshaw over-charging, growing frequency of road accidents and enhancing of road fines etc. In our opinion these were matters pertaining exclusively to the executive or legislative domain.

None of this was incorrect, of course, but to point out from the Bench that these matters were not fit subjects for judicial intervention was by now immensely counter-intuitive, and Katju's intemperate style made it seem especially unpalatable.

Katju's opinions created enormous controversy in the media as well in legal and academic circles. The response was mostly acerbic. Rajeev Dhavan accused him of 'judicial terrorism'.[51] Interestingly, this was the same term that Upendra Baxi had used way back in 1982 to attack Justice Tulzapurkar's early attack on PIL, where he had mentioned his opposition to the forum-shopping that Justice Bhagwati's monopoly of PIL made possible.[52] Tulzapurkar had then said that the court should not 'in the name of alleviating the grave public injury... arrogate to itself the role of an administrator or an overseer looking after the management and day to day working of all non-functioning or malfunctioning public bodies or institutions.'[53]

Dhavan went on to oppose any attempt to reopen the questions posed in *Sudipt Mazumdar*, declaring that '[a]n assessment of PIL itself will open a Pandora's box, which is neither necessary nor desirable'. T. R. Andhyarujina, one of the few senior advocates of the Supreme Court somewhat critical of PIL, suggested in a newspaper editorial that:

> A larger bench of the Supreme Court should lay down authoritative criteria of the permissible and impermissible judicial interventions... To distil judicial power by rigid rules of conduct is not advisable but it may at least guide the future course of the action of courts in the vast and amorphous jurisdiction assumed by them in the name of judicial activism.[54]

The Chief Justice of India, K. G. Balakrishnan, immediately went into damage control mode in his judicial as well as extra-judicial capacities. He 'quelled dissenting voices by declaring that public interest litigation cases (PILs) will continue despite the order.'[55] He also immediately separated the two judges so that Katju would no longer find a willing partner for his heretical judgments. But the big question had again arisen before the Chief Justice: should a Constitutional Bench be set up to decide the principles of PIL that Katju was questioning? Again, the answer was no. A three-judge Bench was set up, but soon even that went into cold storage. It met the same fate as *Sudipt Mazumdar.* The reason for this steadfast refusal to systematize the PIL jurisdiction is perhaps best explained by Pratap Bhanu Mehta, 'The legitimacy and power that India's judiciary does enjoy most likely flow not from a clear and consistent constitutional vision, but rather from its opposite.'[56]

The reasoning of the two judges mentioned earlier, who disagreed with Katju while being on the same Bench as him – Justice S. B. Sinha in *State of UP vs. Jeet S Bisht*, and Justice A. K. Ganguly in *University of Kerala vs. Council, Principals, Colleges, Kerala & Others* – is important to rehearse here, because the tropes it deploys are consistently used to repel any criticism of PIL. Both judgments reject the idea that there is any strict 'separation of powers' in the Indian Constitution. Another strategy common to both judgments is that a key weapon they use to deflect Katju's attack on PIL is the international recognition it has received. This is not uncommon: Indian Supreme Court judges like to pat themselves on the back, routinely citing articles by foreign academics hailing the ingenuity of PIL. Justice Sinha began his discussion with the statement: 'Indian Supreme Court has achieved world-wide acclaim in fashioning new rights under Part III of the Constitution and also using Directive Principles as interpretive devices for giving a contemporaneous meaning to Part III.' He went on to quote an Oxford professor, Sandra Fredman's article in a British public law journal, which saw 'inspiration in the wide-ranging work of Indian Supreme Court for European Court of Justice'.[57]

Justice Ganguly, too, relied on two British luminaries, one writing expressly on PIL. Ganguly justified the judicial legislations made by the Supreme Court in PIL cases by noting 'that this attempted legislation by this Court has been applauded internationally'. He referred to a Cambridge Law Journal article[58] which celebrated India's departure from the idea of separation of powers:

> It is possible for a court deliberately to depart from the triadic structure in order to combat the resource deficiencies of litigants. An interesting example of this can be found in India where the Supreme Court has attempted to meet the institutional challenges posed by a combination of a weak legislation and a poor citizenry. The Supreme Court has relaxed the formal restrictions on applications to the court. An application can be made by a letter, or even a postcard, addressed to the court... These measures must be commended as a significant attempt to adapt the court to the needs of the unempowered citizenship....[59]

Another strategy that both the judges used was to subtly point out how all the lawyers concerned in these two specific cases, indeed most members of the bar, were in favour of PIL. This is seemingly correct and remarkable because it was certainly not true in the early 1980s. As Upendra Baxi noted then, the bar's reaction swung 'from indifference to indignation at what it regards as freak litigation.'[60] While the initial response to PIL from the bar, or at least its elite members, was one of hostility, two decades down, almost all the leading members of the Supreme Court Bar are leading exponents of PIL. This would be evident if one looks at the official online bios of the judges of the Delhi High Court and Supreme Court, most of whom are appellate lawyers who have been elevated to the Bench. Almost all prominently display their PIL cases as badges of honour. Pride of place is given to the cases they handled as amicus curiae. With the enormous symbolic capital that it commands, PIL has emerged as a currency for upward mobility in legal circles.

Perhaps the most disingenuous trope repeatedly used to defend PIL from these attacks was that of 'misuse'. Katju's attack on PIL was seen as throwing out the baby with the bathwater. Even the ideological critics of post-liberalization PIL were critical of this. After all, the argument went, it was not PIL per se that was the problem, it was the 'misuse of PIL'. This trope is a persistent one in Indian legal debates generally. It is not the law which is the problem, it is its misuse. Indian security statutes might give the police blanket powers to arrest and detain suspects indefinitely without bail, and confessions made to police officers be made admissible as evidence. But if such powers lead to endemic practices of torture, it is called 'misuse'. The PIL jurisdiction gave blanket powers to judges to act as per their ideological beliefs in order to help the poor and promote distributive justice. But this was not seen as a problem. Institutional checks were not needed, went the argument, what were needed were good judges. The right kind of PIL was still possible if we had the right kind of judges. So, different PIL commentators and dramatis personae were hopeful of their respective personifications of good judges. Upendra Baxi would be nostalgic about his 'four musketeers' from the 1980s. A successful PIL litigant from 1990s Shiv Sagar Tiwari would long for the days of Justice Kuldip Singh whom he described as a 'dabangg judge' – an uber masculine, fearless judge – while the rest were feckless 'eunuchs' according to him. And a *Kalyan Sanstha* commissioner would wistfully talk of the days of Justice Vijender Jain as the golden period of PIL. None of these PIL-*wallahs* had any problems with the kind of enormous powers PIL bestowed on judges. The idea of good judges' and 'bad judges' was part and parcel of the PIL game that they all wanted to play. As Colin Gonsalves, a leading PIL lawyer, told me in an interview in May 2009: '[The PIL] court has capacity to do good and do bad. I would rather the court has this capacity than not.' PIL was a Faustian bargain that its votaries have always been willing to make.

Epilogue

When his relatively serious attacks on PIL seemed to cut no ice, Justice Katju resorted to what can only be called devastating parody. He provided a most vivid portrayal of the amazingly protean possibilities of PIL in a two-judge Bench that he was heading in 2009. His actions were part immanent critique and part Brechtian satire that I had the privilege to witness.

A PIL had been filed in 2001 by a debarred Chennai lawyer about the poor condition of wetlands in India.[61] The various governments were asked to file replies but nothing much happened till 2009, when the case came before Katju. He decided that reviving all the wetlands in India was too small a matter to be dealt with in one case. He wanted to make the PIL into 'the water matter', where all the endemic water problems facing the country would come before him. The analogy drawn was to 'the forest matter', that has taken over the forest governance of the country, heard every week on Friday afternoons for two hours by a three-judge Bench of the Supreme Court (since 2010, heard by two such Benches).

Katju ordered:

> The present Writ Petition under Article 32 of the Constitition of India relates to conservation of wet lands which in our opinion would include ponds, tanks, canals, creeks, water channels, reservoirs, rivers, streams and lakes. Although, the writ petition as framed related to protection of wetlands in the country for preservation of the environment and maintaining the ecology, we have suo motu expanded its scope as mentioned below.

The court had its own diagnosis of the water problems facing the country:

> There is acute shortage of water in our country and one of the main reasons for that is that most of the water conservation bodies in our country such as ponds, tanks, small lakes etc. have been filled up in recent times by some greedy persons and such persons have constructed buildings, shops etc. on the same. Our ancestors were wise people who realized that because of droughts or some other reasons there may be shortage of water in future and hence they made the provision of a pond near every village, tanks in or near temples, etc.

And its own solutions, which Katju had already expressed himself in another judgment that he had passed earlier that year, in which he gratuitously held forth on water scarcity in India in an interstate water dispute.[62]

But this time, his words carried the force of law. Katju ordered:

> (the) Central Government to immediately constitute a body of eminent scientists in the field who should be requested to do scientific research in this area on a war footing to find out scientific ways and means of solving the water shortage problem in the country.[63]

It was also recommended that:

> The said body shall be given all the financial, technical and administrative help by the Central and State Governments for this purpose. The said body of scientists was requested to, inter alia, perform the following tasks:
> (i) to find out an inexpensive method or methods of converting saline water into fresh water.
> (ii) to find out an inexpensive and practical method of utilizing the water, which is in the form of ice, in the Himalayas.
> (iii) to find out a viable method of utilizing rain water.
> (iv) to utilize the flood water by harnessing the rivers so that the excess water in the floods, may instead of causing damage, be utilized for the people who are short of water, or be stored in reservoirs for use when there is drought.[64]

The Times of India reported this order with bemusement:

> A Bench headed by Justice Markandey Katju, who is known for his strict approach towards PILs and his conviction that administration cannot be run by the courts through such litigation, issued notice to the ministry of science and technology to tell the court about the follow-up action it has taken since his recommendations on February 6 in an inter-state water dispute case. The reaction of the Bench, also comprising Justice V Sudershan Reddy, may have surprised counsel Gopal Shankaranarayan, who appearing for petitioner M K Balakrishnan had been toiling for the past couple of years to convince the apex court for some urgent action to protect the disappearing wetlands vitally affecting the water table, flora and fauna. But, he would not complain for the Bench while expanding the scope of the PIL said that the prayers would include all methods needed to solve water shortage problems, including converting sea water into fresh water and water in snow cap peaks.[65]

Katju wanted this PIL to be heard by him every month. The case was heard seven times in 2009 while he was on the Bench. The Secretary, Ministry of Science and Technology, Union of India filed in August 2009 the first progress report of the 'Technology Mission: Winning, Augmentation and Renovation for Water (WAR for Water)', formulated as a result of the orders in this case. The petitioner was enjoying his moment of reflected glory and had made copies of the report for all the members of the press.

After Katju retired, this case was not listed by the Supreme Court for years. Not much came out of it, but Katju had provided a textbook demonstration of the amazing powers that PIL gave a judge. Perhaps nothing brings home the dangers of PIL as much as the fact that it gave free rein to a judge as mercurial as Katju.

Endnotes

1 Balagopal, 'Beyond Violence and Non-violence'.

2 *State of Uttaranchal vs. Balwant Singh Chaufal & Ors* (18 January 2010), 2010 (1) SCALE 492.

3 Kaviraj, 'Indira Gandhi and Indian Politics'.

4 Baxi, 'The Structural Adjustment of Judicial Activism', pp. A-A145-A–A-145-X.

5 Ibid., pp. A-A145-A–A-145-X.

6 Bhushan, Supreme Court and PIL.

7 Ramanathan, 'Of Judicial Power'.

8 Gauri, 'Fundamental Rights and Public Interest Litigation in India'. Gauri finds that less than 1% of the cases instituted in the Supreme Court every year are PIL cases, and based on that argues, 'This suggests that PIL does not drain significant court resources from the administration of day-to-day justice, contrary to the claims of some critics; but it also suggests that the outsize reputation of the Supreme Court's PIL work belies its modest scale.' This is an over-interpretation because even though in absolute numbers, PIL cases are relatively few, many of these cases individually take more of court's time than many a jurisdiction. For instance, a whole afternoon session of a three-judge Bench has been devoted every week to the forest PIL case alone for more than a decade. Similarly, in a system where many PIL cases are never supposed to end but accrue fresh causes of action from time to time, as we saw with WP (C) 4677/1985 in Chapter 2, it is misleading to look at fresh filings alone.

9 Baxi, 'The Promise and Peril of Transcendental Jurisprudence'.

10 Aditya Nigam, 'Embedded Judiciary or, the Judicial State of Exception?', Suresh & Narrain (ed.), pp., 22-–38.

11 Dhavan, 'Judges and Indian Democracy'.

12 Bhagwati, 'Judicial Activism and Public Interest Litigation', p. 23.

13 Ibid. p. 563.

14 Ibid. p. 564.

15 Ibid. p. 565.

16 Emphasis mine.

17 Craig and Deshpande, 'Rights, Autonomy and Process', p. 363.

18 Ibid. p. 566.

19 This formulation has interesting similarities with the logic of Article 31C introduced at the height of the 'committed judiciary' discourse, briefly discussed in Chapter 1.

20 Suresh and Narrain. *The Shifting Scales of Justice.*

21 Rheinstein, *Max Weber on Law in Economy and Society*, p. 11.

22 Trubek, 'Max Weber on Law and the Rise of Capitalism'.

23 Ibid. p. 730. Emphasis is of the author.

24 Rheinsten, *Max Weber on Law in Economy and Society*, p. 225.

25 (1974) 4 SCC 3

26 Seervai, *Constitutional Law of India*, p. 448. See also Andhyarujina, 'The Evolution of Due Process of Law', pp. 197–98.

27 Rajamani, 'The Right to Environmental Protection in India', pp. 274–86.

28 *Vellore Citizens Forum vs. Union of India* (1996), 5 SCC 647.

29 Rajamani, 'The Right to Environmental Protection in India', p. 284.

30 Of course, even the above two important examples pale into insignificance before the Indian Supreme court's so-called 'right to life jurisprudence' under Article 21 which has been extrapolated to such an extent that it includes all kinds of socio-economic rights. The only right it seems to exclude is the literal mandate of Article 21, a negative right against any deprivation of life or personal liberty by the state in an illegal manner. Since the 1980s, which have been the heyday of PIL, the Indian Supreme Court has upheld the constitutionality of a whole alphabet soup of repressive laws violative of Article 21 simpliciter. While this article became a receptacle for all manners of positive rights, the simple civil right it was meant to embody does not get the importance it is due. Of course, the problem here is not with the court reading an unnamed socio-economic right into the existing provisions listed in the Fundamental Rights chapter. The difficulty arises because of its reckless refusal to do minimal hermeneutic labour to be able to invoke such rights in a robust way. But in the new scheme of things, such qualities of juristic activism no longer mattered.

31 Ramanathan, *Judicial Activism in India.*

32 Ibid. As Ramanathan argues, 'It wouldn't be distant from fact to suggest that the association of judges with causes has had a yet-to-be assessed impact on both the issues with which they have been identified, as also with the jurisdiction itself'.

33 Ramanathan, 'In the Name of the People', pp. 39–58.

34 Krishnaswamy and Khosla, 'Social Justice and the Indian Supreme Court', p. 113.

35 Thiruvengadam, 'Evaluating Contemporary Criticisms of 'Public Interest Litigation'. See Chayes, 'The Role of the Judge in Public Law Litigation'; Cunningham, 'Public Interest Litigation in Indian Supreme Court'.

36 See discussion in Chapter 3.

37 Fuller, 'The Forms and Limits of Adjudication'. For a similar argument in the context of UK, also see Harlow, 'Public Law and Popular Justice' Fuller's argument has also come in for heavy criticism. See for example, King, Jeff. "The pervasiveness of polycentricity.".

38 Lavanya. 'Public Interest Environmental Litigation in India, pp. 319.

39 Thiruvengadam, 'Swallowing a Bitter PIL', p. 131.

40 Baxi, 'Taking Suffering Seriously'.

41 According to Article 145(3) of the Constitution, the court is required to sit in a bench of at least five judges to decide any case 'involving a substantial question of law as to the interpretation' of the Constitution. Such five-judge or larger benches are traditionally known as constitutional benches. A recent study has shown that 'while the Court averaged about a 100 five-judge or larger benches a year in the 1960s, by the first decade of the 2000s, this had decreased to about nine a year. Viewed in this light, despite deciding about 5,000 regular hearing cases a year in the 2000s, the Indian Supreme Court arguably produces less jurisprudence involving substantial questions of constitutional law than a Court like the United States Supreme Court, which wrote just 72 judgments in 2009, but whose cases often involved such questions.' The Supreme Court of India has thus increasingly been functioning more like a final court of appeal and less as a Constitutional Court. The same study concludes, 'The Supreme Court's attention has been diverted by thousands of more mundane decisions at the expense of developing its constitutional jurisprudence. As of November 2010, there were 754 five-judge or larger matters pending to be heard for regular hearing in the Supreme Court.' See Nick Robinson et al, 'Interpreting the Constitution: Supreme Court Constitution Benches since Independence', *Economic and Political Weekly*, 26 February 2011.

42 See also *Sachidanand Pandey vs. State of West Bengal*, A.I.R 1987 S. C. 1109. 'Public Interest Litigation has now come to stay. But one is led to think that it poses a threat to courts and public alike. Such cases are now filed without any rhyme or reason. It is, therefore, necessary to lay down clear guidelines and to outline the correct parameters sfor entertainment of such petitions.'

43 Varun Gauri found that, 'of the tens of thousands of letters and handwritten petitions that the Supreme Court receives from ordinary people each year, only a handful are converted into cases.' Gauri, 'Fundamental Rights and Public Interest Litigation in India', p. 83.

44 Agrawala, *Public Interest Litigation in India*. This book, one of the earliest critiques of PIL (and in my opinion, still the best), is out of print. While PIL is probably the most over-studied and fetishized part of contemporary Indian legal history, a book that is arguably the best critique of it is difficult to find in India.

45 Agrawala, *Public Interest Litigation in India*, p. 24.

46 Ibid. pp. 26–27.

47 The Supreme Court Rules are the procedural laws that govern the working of the Supreme Court of India, and in effect function like any other statute, except that they are enacted by the Supreme Court itself.

48 Desai and Muralidhar, 'Public Interest Litigation: Potential and Problems'.

49 'R. C. Ghiya Memorial Lecture: The Constitutional Obligation of the Judiciary', delivered by J. S. Verma, Chief Justice of India (1997) 7 SCC (Jour) 1.

50 *Divisional Manager, Aravali Golf Club vs. Chander Hass*, 6 December 2007.

51 Dhavan, 'It is too Late in the Day to Put a Lid on PIL', p. 10.

52 Baxi, 'Judicial Terrorism'.

53 Tulzapurkar, Justice V. D. 'Judiciary: Attacks and Survival'.

54 Andhyarujina, 'Courting limits'.

55 Rajeev Dhavan, 'It is too late in the day to put a lid on PIL,' *Mail Today*. The Chief Justice's pronouncement came in the case of Prajwala vs Union of India, WP(C) 56/2004 when this PIL was referred to him by another bench for clarification after Katju's judgment.

56 Mehta, 'The Rise of Judicial Sovereignty', p. 76

57 *State of UP vs. Jeet S. Bisht*

58 Barber, Nicholas W. "Prelude to the Separation of Powers." *Cambridge Law Journal* 60.1 (2001): 59-88.

59 *University of Kerala vs. Council, Principals, Colleges, Kerala & Ors*

60 Baxi, 'Taking Suffering Seriously', p. 131.

61 WRIT PETITION (CIVIL) NO(s). 230 OF 2001.

62 State of Orissa vs. Government of India and Another, JT 2009 (2) SC 233.

63 WRIT PETITION (CIVIL) NO(s). 230 OF 2001, Order dated 26 March 2009.

64 Baxi, 'Taking Suffering Seriously'.

65 http://timesofindia.indiatimes.com/India/SC-notice-to-govt-on-water-crisis/articleshow/4320146.cms

Conclusion

The Procedural is Political

In Max Weber's classic exposition of modern law in 'Economy and Society', he describes the need for a logically formal rational legal system to exist in tandem with the rise of capitalism. This model of modern law is that of a society dominated by an autonomous rule system, or 'legalism', as legal sociologist David Trubek calls it. A legalistic society in this sense is of course an ideal type, and so is its Weberian opposite: *kadijustiz*. As Weber's translator Max Rheinstein explains it, the term kadijustiz was used by Weber as 'a term of art to describe the administration of justice which is oriented not at fixed rules of a formally rational law but at the ethical, religious, political, or otherwise expediential postulates of a substantively rational law.'[1]

The legal history of post-Emergency India shows a remarkable opposition to legalism and a concomitant embrace of 'kadijustiz' at all levels of the judiciary – or, as Dr Rajeev Dhavan has called its Indian analogue, 'panchayati justice'. Being 'legalistic' has decisively emerged as a negative attribute for judicial performance in post-Emergency India. In this book, I have focused on the rise of this culture of legal informalism at the highest levels of the Indian judiciary and its impact, through an examination of PIL. But the institutional impact of such legal informalism is not limited to the PIL jurisdiction alone. It has infected every part of the legal system.

One of the most spectacular instances of 'panchayati justice' in recent years, which finally led to some critical debate on this phenomenon, was the verdict given by the Lucknow Bench of the Allahabad High Court in September 2010, in what is perhaps the most controversial legal case in contemporary India: the civil suit to decide the Ram Janmabhoomi–Babri Mosque dispute. The legal dispute was to settle title to the disputed property between three principal parties: the Hindu idol 'Shri Ram Lalla Virajman', another Hindu religious organization 'Nirmohi Akhara', and the Sunni Central Wakf Board. As a private property dispute filed in a civil court, such a case is governed by strict rules of procedure, and the court can only give forms of relief that are legally prayed for. However, the verdict given, after the suit had been pending for decades, was to divide the property equally among all three parties. What was especially strange was that the court dismissed the Wakf Board's suit as time barred for having been filed after the limitation period had expired, but still went on to award it relief. Particularly insidious was the looseness with which the judgment referred to the parties by their religion. But, for our purposes, what is of interest is the debate this verdict led to.

For once, 'panchayati justice' emerged as a term of criticism in India public discourse. Eminent senior advocate P. P. Rao said about the judgment:

> It is difficult to appreciate how the property can be divided by the court while dismissing the suits. This is nothing but a panchayati type of justice. If the court accepts that the Waqf Board is entitled to one-third of the land, it can't dismiss the suit. If the court dismisses the suits, it can't give only a portion of the land. The court has gone beyond the prayers in the suits. When no one had asked for division of the land, how can the court divide the land into three portions?[2]

Dhavan weighed in:

> Never in legal history has a title suit been converted into a partition suit in this way... This is panchayati justice which takes away the legal rights of Muslims and converts the moral sentimental entitlements of Hindus into legal rights.[3]

Retired Chief Justice of India, A. H. Ahmadi said

> I am not sure on what basis the Sunni Waqf suit has been timebarred. But if the title is not theirs, how can one-third be a masjid now, and if the title is theirs, how can two-thirds be divided? There certainly can be a compromise but that should have happened after the verdict. The verdict should not appear like a decision of a panchayat foisted forcibly on all parties.[4]

The contrary view, celebrating the judgment, showed its impatience with technicalities. I quote here three powerful senior advocates of the Supreme Court. Harish Salve said, 'It has used the judicial discretion available to a court. There is no legal principle preventing judges to exercise statesmanship as long as it is within the framework of the law.'[5] K. K. Venugopal declared, 'It is a statesmanship-like judgment and it is good for the country.'[6] And Mukul Rohatgi offered the following comment:

> I think it is a political kind of solution. It has given something to everybody. This seems to be the just possible solution in respecting the sentiments of all parties. We should be progressive on these issues and accept the judgment.[7]

Opinions on either side could be neatly contrasted. The former view could be seen as narrowly legalistic, critical of the court for overreaching itself, while the latter strand of opinion appreciates the court's political statesmanship, even if extra-legal, against the background of the need for communal peace. The latter argument might be summed in aphoristic terms as – it might be bad law, but it's good politics. Such teleological reasoning carries the day in post-Emergency Indian legal culture. The underlying assumption behind such an approach seems to be that the political is purely external to law, not immanent within it. The votaries of panchayati justice seem to believe that there is no political content to the legal form itself, that it can be evaluated purely by the decision it leads to. The normative basis of this legal form and the sedimented history it contains within itself is rarely paid any attention in such an analysis. But is it a valid assumption that this history has no political content which might need to be preserved, or at least dealt with less flippantly? Is there no way to understand law except on the basis of criteria external to it? Is the only way to evaluate legal developments in terms of their consequences? Does the utter collapse of court procedure – the systematic exclusion of necessary parties to a certain dispute, for instance – not affect the political evaluation of the decision arrived by such a 'court'? The consequentalism vs deontology binary might not be the most useful way to think about these questions. But I would argue that there is, at the very least, a need to think in terms of institutional consequences rather than narrow immediate results. An attempt has been made in this book to assess the enduring political repercussions of what I have argued has been a reckless overhauling of Indian legal institutions in the last few decades.

India since the 1970s has seen a general trend towards informalization in many areas of law. The apotheosis of legal informalism or panchayati justice in post-Emergency India has been achieved in spite of the fact that the biggest legal scandal of this period, the Bhopal settlement, was an astonishing example of judicial bad faith passing for panchayati justice. Then too, let us not forget, the Supreme Court said, 'Legal and procedural technicalities should yield to the paramount considerations of justice and humanity.' What came in the way of imposing legal liability in Bhopal, the court argued, was the suffering of the people. Upendra Baxi wrote in mourning after the settlement that it was if the poisonous methyl Isocyanate gas 'had entered the soul of Indian jurisprudence'.[8] Unfortunately, this 'Indian jurisprudence' survived the poison and lived on in an ever more mutant form. The lessons of Bhopal were not learnt. Let us not forget the principal perfidy of the Bhopal settlement. The victims were not even consulted before the court pronounced on their fate. They were considered 'irresponsible and uninformed'[9] and therefore given *a fait accompli*. Their grievance had been expropriated, first, by the Indian government and, then, by the Indian Supreme Court, which twice justified the settlement as if it could speak on behalf of the suffering victims. That such a court would soon get rid of the petitioner in PIL cases and arrogate powers as victim and adjudicator to itself can hardly be surprising. Veena Das ends her essay on Bhopal with a quote from Lyotard:

> It is in the nature of a victim not to be able to prove that one has been done a wrong. A plaintiff is someone who has incurred damages and who disposes of the means to prove it. One becomes a victim if one loses these means.[10]

PIL has become a giant machine to turn people who could be plaintiffs into victims.

The turn away from legality to panchayati justice is manifest in other spheres too. A classic example would be the Family Courts legally instituted in 1984 'with a view to promote conciliation in, and secure speedy settlement of disputes related to marriage and family affairs.'[11] The aim was to move away from the adversarial process towards mediation and conciliation. Such conciliation was interpreted as an impetus to reconciliation as the statute expected the judges to endeavour to preserve the 'institution of marriage and to promote the welfare of children'.[12] Anthropologist Srimati Basu sums up the result:

> Litigants are subjected to judges' directions and are expected to be best represented through the judge's mediation rather than their own. In fact, it could be argued that this format has vastly increased judges' unilateral powers in exchange for lawyers' and has fewer checks and balances.[13]

When the 'lok adalat' (literally 'people's court'), a kind of informal court for small causes, was first introduced nationally in 1987, it was to be 'guided by the principles of justice, equity, fair play and other *legal principles*'.[14] But even this vague phrase was seen as too rigid and an amendment in 2002 introduced the 'permanent lok adalat', which was to be 'guided by the principles of natural justice, objectivity, fair play, equity and *other principles of justice*, and shall not be bound by the Code of Civil Procedure, 1908 and the Indian Evidence Act, 1872.'[15] As Galanter and Krishnan argue:

> The shift of decisional standards from 'legal principles' to 'principles of justice' suggests a major enlargement of the presiding judge's discretion and a robust faith that the poor have more to gain from benign paternalism than from juristic or popular legality.[16]

The romance of indigenous justice that started enjoying currency in India since the Emergency era ideological attack on Anglo-Saxon legal institutions was later overlaid with the global cool of Alternative Dispute Resolution (ADR) in the post-liberalization era. Indian legal informalism continues to enjoy enormous ideological appeal, partly based on claims of autochthony, partly due to pragmatic considerations and more recently because it comes dressed up in the sleek global garb of ADR, making it seem 'cutting edge.'

Galanter and Krishnan record that when they presented their critical hypothesis on 'lok adalats' (they titled their paper 'debased informalism') to an audience of High Court and Supreme Court judges, they were accused of seeing things through a Western, even colonial lens. The judges' rather impatient response was to say that irrespective of how perfunctory such justice might be, lok adalats do improve the overall legal system: 'To ignore their contributions is to misunderstand... how justice functions in India'. Such an argument, that 'Indian conditions' require informalism, has been the basis of the valorization and justification of PIL right from its inception.

This normativization of substantive justice for Indian conditions has been advocated by Partha Chatterjee as well in his recent work on political society. Chatterjee asks, 'Is justice better served by the non-arbitrary procedures of the equal application of the law, or by the contextual and possibly arbitrary judgment that addresses the peculiarities of a particular case?'[17] This monograph is partly a response to that question, and an attempt to address, however partially, the related academic lack that Chatterjee underlines when he points out that 'the continuing social legitimacy of arbitrary power is an important and under-researched aspect of the practices of Indian democracy.'

So who decides what serves justice better? Chatterjee's own answer to this question is subtle but clear enough, 'Political society in India... affords the possibility of inviting the arbitrary power of government to mitigate the potentially tyrannical power of the law.'[18] He goes on to approvingly cite two historical accounts from colonial Bengal that criticized the British regime of non-arbitrary rule of law and argued that 'direct access to an impartial judge who was knowledgeable about and sensitive to the specific circumstances of a case was far more likely to serve the cause of justice'.[19] Chatterjee argues that this 'critique has continued to inform popular beliefs and practices about the judicial system of modern India.'[20]

According to Chatterjee, there are at least two discourses this 'widely shared popular critique of the modern normative idea of the non-arbitrary and equal application of the law' can draw its roots from. One should keep in mind that Chatterjee's project here is to lay out the colonial genealogy of an endemic tendency in modern political theory to diagnose an empirical deviation from the norm, and then carve out an exception to the norm itself. This tendency itself keeps evolving as we move from colonial to postcolonial regimes of power. While the first 'symmetrical' response of political theory since Bentham was of:

> Many conservative colonial officials of British India, that the impersonal procedures of rational law and bureaucracy were unsuited to backward societies used to customary rather than contractual obligations and that the exercise of personal but impartial authority was more appropriate.

This would lead to the declaration of a colonial exception. On the other hand, with the more contemporary 'sequential' approach of 'multiple modernities':

> We might be moved to suggest not the irrelevance of the norm of the impersonal and non-arbitrary application of the law but its critical re-evaluation in the light of emergent practices in many postcolonial countries that seek to punctuate or supplement it by appealing to the personal and contextual circumstances.

From this, Chatterjee goes on to speculate:

> That the enormous powers of judicial review of legislation and active surveillance of executive acts assumed by the Indian law courts – powers unknown in any other liberal constitutional system in the world – is a response to this popular critique of procedural non-arbitrariness.

Chatterjee's project includes an attempt:

> To redefine the normative standards of modern politics in the light of the considerable accumulation of new practices that may at present be described only in the language of exceptions but in fact contain the core of a richer, more diverse and inclusive, set of norms.[21]

In other words, 'emergent practices' or 'improvizations' are to lead to redefined norms – underlying this, I worry, is an attempt to derive an ought from an is. Chatterjee's confidence that such a new kind of Indian exceptionalism is somehow different from the 'colonial exception' seems to me difficult to sustain. The difference between these two colonial and postcolonial logics of carving out an exception to the global norm is not as stark as Chatterjee argues: the two do bleed into each other, in their common culturalist justification, for example.

Chatterjee's examples of such practices are in the realm of political society, where governmental authorities like municipal officials or the police carve out exceptions for marginal populations to inhabit spaces illegally or to get access to government largesse, in such a way that these temporary arrangements do not disturb the rule of law. The problem is that his argument moves from this world of administration to the world of law. To reiterate, Chatterjee argues that 'political society, operating under conditions of electoral democracy in India, affords the possibility of inviting the arbitrary power of government to mitigate the potentially tyrannical power of the law.' The reverse, too, can happen once his argument is carried through to law: the possibility now arises of inviting the arbitrary power of law to mitigate the potentially tyrannical power of the government. And this is exactly what PIL does, as we saw in Chapters 2 and 3. It invokes the arbitrary new populist powers of the law courts to mitigate the populist powers of political society. PIL might have arisen as a populist partner to Mrs Gandhi's politics, but the huge powers such populism lent it have enabled it to emerge as a bulwark against political society in the twenty-first century. It is important perhaps to keep in mind the specificity of this new mutant beast of judicial populism, which works very differently from any democratic theory of judicial review and is profoundly antagonistic to the populism of political society.

Chatterjee has written elsewhere that 'populism is the only morally legitimate form of democratic politics today....present day critics of populism must, to make their case, necessarily demand the restriction or modification of democracy.'[22] In the last decade or so, the Indian appellate judiciary has emerged as the most powerful institutional critic of the practices of populism in Indian politics. Concomitantly, it has also spearheaded, as Chatterjee and Katznelson have called it, a 'counter-democratic' tendency, 'justified by the alleged failures of the system of electoral representation to provide good government, caused, it is said, by the surrender of politicians to short-sighted populism.'[23]

One might be unsurprised by this and argue that after all is it not judiciary's constitutional function to be distrustful of the government. It is important to clarify, therefore, that the judicial function in a constitutional republic is not necessarily counter-democratic. On the contrary, John Hart Ely has provided a highly influential theory of constitutional adjudication, according to which the courts' role is precisely meant to preserve and reinforce democracy.

It is worthwhile to discuss in some detail what such a judicial function would entail, according to Ely. Judicial review, he says, is required to respond to systemic malfunctioning of the government. However, such a malfunction cannot be alleged just because it generates outcomes that the judiciary disagrees with. Thus, the 'quality of governance' cannot be such a ground.[24] Such a malfunction can only be said to occur when the democratic process is undeserving of trust. These are situations when the process of political representation itself is not working, to rectify which, the judiciary should perform a 'representation reinforcing' role, as Ely calls it. He identifies two broad situations when the process of representation can be said to require stringent judicial review: first, when the government in power 'clogs off the channels of political change to ensure that they will stay in'; and second, when a minority is being denied the protection afforded by a representative system and the government is acting as an accessory to majority tyranny. Ely gives three areas in which the first situation comes into play and where the courts should be heavily involved in 'clearing the channels of political change': (1) When the rights to free speech, publication and political association are violated, which are all 'critical to the functioning of an open and effective democratic process'.[25] (2) When the right to vote is undermined. (3) When there is excessive delegation of the legislative function to unelected administrators.

Interestingly, these three areas where the courts can play a crucial role in protecting democratic institutions are precisely where the Indian appellate judiciary has been remarkably timid[26]. As Pratap Bhanu Mehta evaluated the courts' role in restoring integrity to the democratic process:

> A student of the Indian scene need only recall the judiciary's 'no show' during the state of emergency and hands-off approach to preventive detention since then. Less dramatically but still seriously, the courts in ruling after ruling have been diluting the impact of two democratizing amendments (numbers 73 and 74) by insisting that unelected bureaucrats have more power than local elected officials.[27]

Ely's analysis of the second situation of systematic malfunctioning, according to which 'discrete and insular minorities' are entitled to 'heightened judicial solicitude' has been so widely accepted that the judiciary is increasingly viewed as a counter-majoritarian institution. On this issue, however, the Indian Supreme Court recently provided a most egregious example of abdication of any such responsibility. In the infamous judgment of *Suresh Kumar Koushal vs. Naz Foundation*, by which the Supreme Court upheld the constitutional validity of S. 377 of the Indian Penal code criminalising sexual intercourse 'against the order of nature,', the court derisively described the LGBT community as 'a miniscule fraction of the country's population'. That the supposedly small number of any community should at all be a negative factor in the court's determination of their rights shows how far the Indian appellate judiciary is from performing its classic institutional role in a democratic polity. The important aspect to note here is that such shocking judicial rhetoric is completely consistent with the court's post-emergency populist avatar, as legal scholar Tarunabh Khaitan has suggested. He argues that for such a court, its legitimacy no longer rests on constitutional mandate. 'Unsurprisingly, standing up for unpopular minorities becomes a very difficult task for such an institution,' he suggests.'[28] Indeed, its judgment upholding S. 377 is in continuum with its consistently cavalier approach to civil liberties throughout the post-emergency period which saw the rise of PIL. It has been a longstanding trend as the Indian Supreme Court has repeatedly upheld a whole alphabet soup of repressive statutes which violate basic civil and political rights. For a populist judiciary, a counter-democratic role comes much more naturally than its classic democratic function of reinforcing representation.

The larger question, however, that we are left with is this: can there be any normative critique possible of the Indian political present, without succumbing to a negative comparison with a global norm? Should we valorize the present and in fact deem it normative, just because the new forms of postcolonial politics depart from the global norm? Do the 'emergent practices' have to be celebrated just because they are different and happening in India? Postcolonial political theory has to have a critical relationship with postcolonial political practice. What the language of such critique should be, is a difficult question. It certainly cannot be the lack of its approximation to a global norm. For instance, it would be churlish to criticize the Indian Supreme Court simply based on an adverse comparison with the US Supreme Court. But I would be wary of the contrary tendency to impart normativity to the practice and popularity of PIL, for example, just because it departs from Anglo–Saxon jurisprudence. As Michel Foucault argued, popular justice, once reified into a court-like institution, becomes its deformation.[29]

Endnotes

1 Rheinstein (ed.), '*Max Weber on law in Economy and Society*', p. 213.

2 Venkatesan and Sunderarajan, 'Panchayati Justice that Takes away Legal Rights of Muslims'.

3 Rajeev Dhavan, 'A Clumsy Verdict of Doubtful Legality', *Mail Today*, October 4, 2010, http://epaper.mailtoday.in/4102010/epaperpdf/4102010-md-hr-12.pdf.

4 Chisti, 'On Muslim Street, the Jury is Out'.

5 Venkatesan and Sunderarajan, 'Panchayati Justice that Takes away Legal Rights of Muslims'.

6 Venkatesan and Sunderarajan, 'Panchayati Justice that Takes away Legal Rights of Muslims'.

7 Venkatesan and Sunderarajan, 'Panchayati Justice that Takes away Legal Rights of Muslims'.

8 Baxi, 'The Bhopal Victims in the Labyrinth of the Law'.

9 Das, 'Suffering, Legitimacy and Healing', p. 162.

10 Das, 'Suffering, Legitimacy and Healing', p. 174

11 Family Courts Act 1984.

12 Venkatesan and Sunderarajan, 'Panchayati Justice that Takes away Legal Rights of Muslims', Section 4(4)(a).

13 Basu, 'Judges of Normality', pp 469–92 at 489.

14 Section 20 (4), Legal Services Authorities Act, 1987.

15 Section 22D, Legal Services Authorities Act (Amended 2002).

16 Marc Galanter and Jayanth Krishnan, 'Bread for the Poor', p. 789.

17 Chatterjee, '*Lineages of Political Society*', p. 16.

18 Chatterjee, '*Lineages of Political Society*', p. 16.

19 Chatterjee, '*Lineages of Political Society*', p. 16.

20 Chatterjee, '*Lineages of Political Society*', p. 16.

21 Chatterjee, '*Lineages of Political Society*', p. 16, p.22

22 Chatterjee, 'Classes, Capital and Indian Democracy', pp. 89–93 at 92.

23 Chatterjee and Katznelson, *Anxieties of Democracy*, p. 16. This is broadly on the lines of a phenomenon Ran Hirschl sees as a global trend and calls 'juristocracy' – 'part of a broader process, whereby political and economic elites, while they profess support for democracy, attempt to insulate policymaking from the vicissitudes of democratic politics.' Hirschl, 'The Political Origins of the New Constitutionalism', p. 73.

24 Chatterjee and Katznelson, *Anxieties of Democracy*, p. 16; Hirschl, 'The Political Origins of the New Constitutionalism', p. 73..

25 Ely, '*Democracy and Distrust*', p. 105.

26 For an extended discussion on the Indian courts' approach to free of speech and expression, see Bhatia, Gautam. *Offend, Shock Or Disturb*. The judgment in *Shreya Singhal* in March 2015 striking down Section 66A of the Information Technology Act led to a hope for a change in the court's historically supine attitude towards this fundamental right, but this hope has since been belied in the *Devidas Tuljapurkar* and *Subramanium Swamy* judgments. On the right to vote, for a recent instance of a spectacularly brazen acceptance by the Indian Supreme court of restrictions on this right, see *Rajbala vs State of Haryana*, (2016) 1 SCC 463. It upheld the constitutionality of a legislation that laid down minimum educational qualifications to contest local elections, besides other criteria like functional toilets at home, which have a close relation to socio-economic class. This judgment closely relies on its earlier pronouncement in *Javed vs State of Haryana*, 2003 (8) SCC 369, in which the court had validated an analogous legislation. On delegated legislation, Indian courts have recognised and accepted vast powers of delegation since its reflections on this question in the case of *In Re Delhi Laws Act*, AIR 1951 SC 332, with a principled caveat that the essential features of legislative power may not be delegated away. This caveat is very seldom brought into play by the Courts. See Upendra Baxi, 'The Myth And Reality Of Indian Administrative Law'

27 Mehta, 'The Rise of Judicial Sovereignty,' p. 80

28 Khaitan, 'Koushal v Naz: Judges Vote to Recriminalise Homosexuality', pp. 672–80.

29 Foucault, 'On Popular Justice', pp. 1–36.

Bibliography

Agarwal, Ravi. 2010. 'Fight for a Forest', *Seminar 613*, September.

Agnes, Flavia. 1992. 'Protecting Women against Violence? Review of a Decade of Legislation, 1980–89.' *Economic and Political Weekly* 27(17): 19–33.

Agrawala, S.K. 1985. *Public Interest Litigation in India: A Critique.* New Delhi: The Indian Law Institute.

Ahuja, Sangeeta. 1997. *People, Law, and Justice: A Casebook of Public-interest Litigation.* New Delhi: Orient Longman.

Aman Trust. 2015. 'On the Road to Nowhere? Autorickshaws in Delhi: The System, Problems and Recommendations,' 12. New Delhi: AMAN Public Charitable Trust. Available at: http://www.amanpanchayat.org/Files/Reports/Auto%C2%AD-rickshaws_Delhi.pdf (accessed on 8 April 2016).

Andhyarujina, T. R. 2000. 'The Evolution of Due Process of Law.' In *Supreme but Not Infallible: Essays in Honour of the Supreme Court of India*, edited by B. N. Kirpal, Ashok H. Desai, Gopal Subramanium, Rajeev Dhavan and Raju Ramachandran, pp. 197–98 (New Delhi: Oxford University Press).

——— 2007. 'Courting Limits.' *Indian Express*, December 15. Available at: http://www.indianexpress.com/story-print/250392/ (accessed on 26 March 2013).

Arendt, Hannah. 1965. *On Revolution.* New York: Penguin.

Austin, Granville. 2003. *Working a Democratic Constitution: A History of the Indian Experience.* Oxford: Oxford University Press.

Balagopal, K. 2009. 'Beyond Violence and Non-violence.' Available at: http://kafila.org/2009/01/23/beyond-violence-and-non-violence-k-balgopal/ (accessed on 03 March 2013).

Banerjee, Anil Chandra. 1947. *The Constituent Assembly of India.* Calcutta: Mukherjee; Reprinted 1999. *Constituent Assembly Debates: Official Report.* New Delhi: Lok Sabha Secretariat.

Basu, Srimati. 2012. 'Judges of Normality: Mediating Marriage in the Family Courts of Kolkata, India,' *Signs* 37(2; Winter): 469–92, Unfinished Revolutions, a special issue edited by Phillip Rothwell.

Baviskar, Amita, Subir Sinha and Kavita Philip. 2006. 'Rethinking Indian Environmentalism Industrial Pollution in Delhi and Fisheries in Kerala.' In *Environmental Values in Four Countries*. Available at: http://www.

carnegiecouncil.org/education/006/forging_environmentalism/01/contents/part_1/5284.html (accessed on 19 February 2013).

Baviskar, Amita. 2002. 'The Politics of the City.' *Seminar*.

Baxi, Upendra. 1980. *The Indian Supreme Court and Politics*. Lucknow: Eastern Book Company.

——— 1983a. 'Judicial Terrorism: Some Thoughts on Justice Tulzapurkar's Pune Speech', 21 *Mainstream*, 1 January.

——— 1983b. 'On How Not to Judge the Judges: Towards an Evaluation of Judicial Role.' *Journal of the Indian Law Institute* 26: 211–37.

——— 1985. 'Taking Suffering Seriously: Social Action Litigation in the Supreme Court of India.' *Third World Legal Studies* 4(6): 107–32.

——— 1986. *Inconvenient Forum and Convenient Catastrophe: The Bhopal Case*. Bombay: N. M. Tripathi.———

——— 1993. 'Judicial Discourse: Dialectics of the Face and the Mask.' *Journal of the Indian Law Institute* 35: 1–12.

——— 1996. *On Judicial Activism, Legal Education and Research in a Globalising India*. New Delhi: Capital Foundation Society.

——— 1999. 'The Structural Adjustment of Judicial Activism.' In *Supreme Court on Public Interest Litigation*, edited by Jagga Kapur, Vol. I, A-A145-A–A-145-X. New Delhi: LIPS Publication.

——— 2001. "*The Myth And Reality Of Indian Administrative Law*," Introduction to IP Massey, *Administrative Law*, Lucknow: Eastern Book Company

——— 2007. 'The Promise and Peril of Transcendental Jurisprudence: Justice Krishna Iyer's Combat with the Production of Rightlessness in India.' In *Human Rights, Justice and Constitutional Empowerment*, edited by C. Raj Kumar and K. Chockalingam. New Delhi: Oxford University Press.

Bell, Ruth Greenspan, Kuldeep Mathur, Urvashi Narain and David Simpson. 2004. 'Clearing the Air: How Delhi Broke the Logjam on Air Quality Reforms.' *Environment* 46(3): 22–39.

Bhagwati, P. N. 'Judicial Activism and Public Interest Litigation.' *Columbia Journal of Transnational Law* 561.

Bhan, Gautam. 2006. 'You Can't Bank by This River.' *Outlook* 20 November. Available at: http://www.outlookindia.com/article.aspx?233141 (accessed on 4 March 2013).

——— 2014. 'The Impoverishment of Poverty: Reflections on Urban Citizenship and Inequality in Contemporary Delhi.' *Environment and Urbanization* 26(2): 547–60.

Bhatia, Gautam. *Offend, Shock Or Disturb: Free Speech Under the Indian Constitution*. Oxford University Press, 2016

Bhushan, Prashant. 2004. 'Supreme Court and PIL: Changing Perspectives under Liberalisation.' *Economic and Political Weekly* 39(18): 1–7 May.

——— 2009. 'Prashant Bhushan's Reply.' *Tehelka* 21 November 2009. Available at: www.tehelka.com/story_main43 .asp?filename=Pe211109bouquets_brickbats.asp. (accessed on 17 September 2010).

Bhuwania, Anuj. 2014. 'Courting the People the Rise of Public Interest Litigation in Post-Emergency India.' *Comparative Studies of South Asia, Africa and the Middle East* 34(2): 314–35.

Cassels, Jamie. 1989. 'Judicial Activism and Public Interest Litigation in India: Attempting the Impossible?' *The American Journal of Comparative Law* 37: 495–519.

Chakrabarty, Dipesh. 2007. 'In the Name of Politics: Democracy and the Power of the Multitude in India.' *Public Culture* 19(1): 35–57.

Chatterjee, Partha and Ira Katznelson, eds. 2012. *Anxieties of Democracy: Tocquevillean Reflections on India and the United States.* Delhi: Oxford University Press.

Chatterjee, Partha. 2004. *The Politics of the Governed.* Delhi: Permanent Black.

——— 2008. 'Classes, Capital and Indian Democracy.' *Economic and Political Weekly* 89–93.

——— 2013. *Lineages of Political Society: Studies in Postcolonial Democracy.* New York: Columbia University Press.

Chayes, Abram. 1975–76. 'The Role of the Judge in Public Law Litigation.' *Harvard Law Review* 89: 1281–316.

Chisti, Seema. 2010. 'On Muslim Street, the Jury is Out: A 'Panchayat Order' or a Legal Verdict?' *Indian Express* 1 October. Available at: http://expressindia.indianexpress.com/latest-news/on-muslim-street-the-jury-is-out-a-panchayat-order-or-a-legal-verdict/690889/ (accessed on 16 December 2010).

Chowdhury, Nupur. 2014. 'From Judicial Activism to Adventurism: The Godavarman Case in the Supreme Court of India.' *Asia Pacific Journal of Environmental Law* 17: 177.

Craig, Paul P. and S. L. Deshpande. 1989. 'Rights, Autonomy, and Process: Public Interest Litigation in India.' *Oxford Journal of Legal Studies* 9: 356–73.

Cunningham, Clark D. 1987. 'Public Interest Litigation in Indian Supreme Court: A Study in the Light of American Experience.' *Journal of the Indian Law Institute* 29: 494–523.

——— 2003. 'The World's Most Powerful Court: Finding the Roots of India's Public Interest Litigation Revolution in the Hussainara Khatoon Prisoners Case.' In *Liberty, Equality, and Justice: Struggles for a New Social Order*, edited by S. P. Sathe, 83–96. Lucknow: Eastern Book Company.

Dasgupta, Nandini. 1998. 'Tall Blunder.' *Down to Earth* 30 September. Available at: http://www.downtoearth.org.in/node/22419. (accessed on 19 March 2010).

Das, Veena. 1995. 'Suffering, Legitimacy, and Healing: The Bhopal Case.' In *Critical Events: An Anthropological Perspective on Contemporary India*, 137–74. New Delhi: Oxford University Press.

Dembowski, Hans. 2001. *Taking the State to Court: Public Interest Litigation and the Public Sphere in Metropolitan India.* USA: Oxford University Press.

Desai, Ashok H. and S. Muralidhar. 2001. 'Public Interest Litigation: Potential and Problems.' In *Supreme but Not Infallible: Essays in Honour of the Supreme Court of India,* edited by B.N. Kirpal,, B.N. Kirpal, Ashok H. Desai, Gopal Subramanium, Rajeev Dhavan and Raju Ramachandran, eds. New Delhi: Oxford University Press.

Dhanda, Amita and Upendra Baxi, eds. 1990. *Valiant Victims and Lethal Litigation: The Bhopal Case.* Bombay: N. M. Tripathi.

Dhavan, Rajeev. 1987. 'Means, Motives, and Opportunities: Reflecting on Legal Research in India.' *Modern Law Review* 50(6): 725–49.

——— 1992a. 'If I Contradict Myself, Well Then I Contradict Myself... Nehru, Law, and Social Change.' In *Nehru and the Constitution*, edited by Rajeev Dhavan and T. Paul, 45–62. Bombay: N. M. Tripathi.

——— 1992b. 'The Constitution as the Situs of Struggle: India's Constitution Forty Years on.' In *Constitutional Systems in Late Twentieth-Century Asia*, edited by L. W. Beer, 373–461. Seattle: University of Washington Press.

——— 1994a. 'Ambedkar's Prophecy: Poverty of Human Rights in India.' *Journal of the Indian Law Institute* 36: 8–36.

——— 1994b. 'Law as Struggle: Public Interest Law in India.' *36 Journal of Indian Law Institute* 302.

——— 2000. 'Judges and Indian Democracy: The Lesser Evil.' In *Transforming India: Social and Political Dynamics of Democracy*, edited by Francine R. Frankel, Zoya Hasan, Rajeev Bhargava and Balveer Arora, 314–52. Oxford: Oxford University Press.

——— 2007. 'Governance by Judiciary: Into the Next Millenium.' In *Indian Judiciary and Politics: The Changing Landscape*, edited by B. D. Dua, Mahendra Prasad Singh and Rekha Saxena, 73–103. New Delhi: Manohar.

——— 2010. 'A Clumsy Verdict of Doubtful Legality.' *Mail Today*, 4 October. Available at: http://epaper.mailtoday.in/4102010/epaperpdf/4102010-md-hr-12.pdf (accessed on 16 December 2010).

——— 2013. 'It is Too Late in the Day to Put a Lid on PIL.' *Mail Today*, 17 December 2007. Available at: http://www.rtiindia.org/forum/2277-judicial-activism.html (accessed 30 March 2013).

Divan, Shyam. 1995. 'Cleaning the Ganga.' *Economic and Political Weekly* 1 July: 1557–58.

——— 2002. 'A Mistake of Judgment.' *Down to Earth*, 30 April. Available at: www.downtoearth.org.in/node/14470. (accessed on 12 April 2012)

Divan, Shyam and Armin Rosencranz. 2002. Environmental Law and Policy in India. Oxford University Press, New Delhi.

Dupont, V. and U. Ramanathan. 2008. 'The Courts and the Squatter Settlements in Delhi – Or the Intervention of the Judiciary in Urban "Governance".' In *New Forms of Urban Governance in India. Shifts, Models, Networks and Contestations*, edited by I. Baud and J. de Wit, 312–43. New Delhi: Sage.

Dupont, Véronique. 2008. 'Slum Demolitions in Delhi since the 1990s: An Appraisal.' *Economic and Political Weekly* 79–87.

——— 2013. 'Which Place for the Homeless in Delhi? Scrutiny of a Mobilisation Campaign in the 2010 Commonwealth Games Context.' *South Asia Multidisciplinary Academic Journal* 8.

Dutta, Ritwick. 2009. *The Unquiet River: An Overview of Select Decisions of the Courts on the River Yamuna.* Delhi: Peace Institute Charitable Trust.

Ely, John Hart. 1980. *Democracy and Distrust: A Theory of Judicial Review.* Cambridge, MA: Harvard University Press. Danish Faruqui & Raghav Sud, 'Auto-rickshaws in Delhi: Murder by Regulation': CCS Working Paper No. 2, *http://ccsindia.org/ccsindia/policy/live/studies/wp0002.pdf (accessed on 23 January 2013)*

Fortun, Kim. 2009. *Advocacy after Bhopal: Environmentalism, Disaster, New Global Orders.* Chicago: University of Chicago Press.

Foucault, Michel. 1980. 'On Popular Justice: A Discussion with Maoists.' In *Power/Knowledge: Selected Interviews and Other Writings, 1972–1977*, edited by Colin Gordon, 1–36. New York: Pantheon.

——— 1978. *The History of Sexuality.* Trans. R. Hurley. Vol. 1. New York: Vintage.

Frank, Jerome. 1970. *Law and the Modern Mind.* New Jersey: Transaction Publishers.

Fuller, L. L. 1978. 'The Forms and Limits of Adjudication.' *Harvard Law Review* 92: 353, 395.

Galanter, Marc and Krishnan Jayanth K. 2003. 'Bread for the Poor: Access to Justice and the Rights of the Needy in India.' *Hastings Law Journal* 55 789–834.

——— 2003. 'Debased Informalism: Lok Adalats and Legal Rights in Modern India.' In *Beyond Common Knowledge: Empirical Approaches to the Rule of Law*, edited by Erik Gilbert Jensen and Thomas C. Heller, 104–16. Stanford, CA: Stanford University Press.

Galanter, Marc. 1968. 'Introduction: The Study of the Indian Legal Profession.' *Law and Society Review* 3: 201–17.

Gauri, Varun. 2011. 'Fundamental Rights and Public Interest Litigation in India: Overreaching or Underachieving?' *Indian Journal of Law and Economics* 1(1): 71–93.

Gayer, Laurent and Chakraverti Mahajan. 2011. 'Delhi's Noor Masjid: Tales of a Martyred Mosque.' *Economic and Political Weekly* xlvi(10): 12–15, 5 March.

Ghertner, D. A. 2008. 'An Analysis of New Legal Discourse behind Delhi's Slum Demolitions.' *Economic and Political Weekly* 43: 57–66.

——— 2011. 'Rule by Aesthetics: World-class City Making in Delhi.' In *Worlding Cities: Asian Experiments and the Art of Being Global*, edited by A. Roy and A. Ong. Oxford: Blackwell.

Gill, Kaveri. 2009. *Of Poverty and Plastic: Scavenging and Scrap Trading Entrepreneurs in India's Urban Informal Economy.* New Delhi: Oxford University Press.

Goffman, Erving. 1959. *The Presentation of Self in Everyday Life,* Garden City, NY: Anchor.

Harding, Simon. 2011. 'A Few Questions about a Few Thousand New Auto-rickshaws in Delhi.' Available at: http://kafila.org/2011/11/20/a-few-questions-about-a-few-thousand-new-auto-rickshaws-in-delhi-simon-harding/ (accessed on 3 February 2013).

Harlow, Carol. 2002. 'Public Law and Popular Justice.' 65 *Modern Law Review* 1.

Hidayatullah, Justice M. 1984. 'Highways and Bylanes of Justice.' 2 *SCC (Jour)* 1.

Hirschl, Ran. 2004. 'The Political Origins of the New Constitutionalism.' *Indiana Journal of Global Legal Studies* 11(1) Article 4: 73.

Jaffrelot, Christophe. 2000. 'The Hindu Nationalist Movement in Delhi: From "Locals" to Refugees—and towards Peripheral Groups?' In *Delhi: Urban Space and Human Destinies,* edited by Veronique Dupont, Emma Tarlo and Denis Vidal. Delhi: Manohar Publishers and Centre de Sciences Humaines.

Kaviraj, Sudipta. 1984. 'On the Crisis of Political Institutions in India.' *Contributions to Indian Sociology* 18(2): 223–43.

——— 1986. 'Indira Gandhi and Indian Politics.' *Economic and Political Weekly* 21: 1697–708.

——— 2009. 'The Post-colonial State: The Special Case of India.' *Critical Encounters: A Forum of Critical Thought from the Global South* (blog) 19 January. Available at: critical encounters.wordpress.com/2009/01/19/the-post -colonial-state-sudipta-kaviraj/.

——— 2011. 'Ideas of Freedom in Modern India.' In *The Enchantment of Democracy and India: Politics and Ideas,* 25–84. Ranikhet: Permanent Black.

Khaitan, Tarunabh. 2015. 'Koushal v Naz: Judges Vote to Recriminalise Homosexuality.' *Modern Law Review* 78(4): 672–80; July.

Khan, Maryam S. 2014 'Genesis and Evolution of Public Interest Litigation in the Supreme Court of Pakistan: Toward a Dynamic Theory of Judicialization.' *Temple International and Comparative Law Journal.* 28: 285–431.

Khetan, Ashish. 2011. 'Whose Amicus is Harish Salve?' *Tehelka* 8(10), 12 March. Available at: archive.tehelka.com/story_ main49.asp?filename=Ne120311WhoseAmicus.asp (accessed on 12 March 2012).

King, Jeff. "The pervasiveness of polycentricity." *Public Law* (2008): 101-124.

Krishnaswamy, Sudhir. 2013. 'The Supreme Court on 2G: Signal and Noise.' *Seminar* February.

——— 2011. *Democracy and Constitutionalism in India: A Study of the Basic Structure Doctrine.* Oxford: Oxford University Press.

Krishnaswamy, Sudhir and Madhav Khosla. 2014. 'Social Justice and the Indian Supreme Court.' In *The Sliding Scales of Justice: The Supreme Court in Neo-liberal India*, edited by Mayur Suresh and Siddharth Narrain, pp. 109–19. Hyderabad: Orient Blackswan.

Lokaneeta, Jinee. 2015. 'Debating the Indian Supreme Court: Equality, Liberty, and the Rule of Law.' *Law, Culture and the Humanities* 1–16.

Mahapatra, Dhananjay. 2009 'NGOs, Teesta Spiced Up Gujarat Riot Incidents: SIT.' *Times of India*, 14 April.

Mathur, Kuldeep. 2001. *Battling for Clean Environment: Supreme Court, Technocrats and Populist Politics in Delhi.* Available at: http://www.jnu.ac.in/cslg/workingPaper/CSLG%20WP%2003-01%20Kuldeep%20Mathur.pdf (accessed on 4 February 2013).

Mehra, Diya. 2012. 'Protesting Publics in Indian Cities: The 2006 Sealing Drive and Delhi's Traders.' *Economic and Political Weekly* 47(30): 79–88.

Mehta, Pratap Bhanu. 2002. 'The Inner Conflict of Constitutionalism: Judicial Review and the Basic Structure.' In *India's Living Constitution: Ideas, Practices, Contro-versies*, edited by Zoya Hasan, Eswaran Sridaharn and R. Sudarshan, , 179–206. Delhi: Permanent Black.

——— 2005. 'Can a Jurisprudence of Exasperation Sustain the Court's Authority?' *The Telegraph*, 17 October. Available at: http://www.telegraphindia.com/1051017/asp/opinion/story_5303862.asp (accessed on 1 *March 2013*).

——— 2007. 'The Rise of Judicial Sovereignty.' *Journal of Democracy* 18(2): 70–83

Mehta, Uday Singh. 2010. 'Constitutionalism.' In *The Oxford Companion to Politics in India*, edited by Niraja Gopal Jayal and Pratap Bhanu Mehta, 15–27. Oxford: Oxford University Press.

Menon, Nivedita. 2004. *Recovering Subversion: Feminist Politics beyond the Law.* Delhi: Permanent Black.

——— 2008. 'Citizenship and the Passive Revolution: Interpreting the First Amendment.' In *Politics and Ethics of the Indian Constitution*, edited by Rajeev Bhargava, 189–210. New Delhi: Oxford University Press.

Menon, Nivedita and Aditya Nigam. 2006. 'Lambs at the Law's Guillotine.' *Tehelka* 7 October.

Menon-Sen, Kalyani. 2006. 'Better to have Died than to Live like This: Women and Evictions in Delhi.' *Economic and Political Weekly* 20 May: 1969.

Menon-Sen, Kalyani and Gautam Bhan. 2007. *Swept off the Map: Surviving Eviction and Resettlement in Delhi.* New Delhi: Yoda Press.

Meschievitz, Catherine S. and Marc Galanter. 1982. 'In Search of Nyaya Panchayats: The Politics of a Moribund Institution.' In *The Politics of Informal Justice*, edited by Richard L. Abel, 47–77. New York: Academic Press.

Mohan, Dinesh and Dunu Roy. 2003. 'Operating on Three Wheels: Auto-rickshaw Drivers of Delhi.' *Economic and Political Weekly* 38(3): 177–80.

Moog, Robert. 2002. 'Judicial Activism in the Cause of Judicial Independence: The Indian Supreme Court in the 1990s.' *Judicature* 85: 268–76.

——— 2003. 'The Significance of Lower Courts in the Judicial Process.' In *The Oxford India Companion to Sociology and Social Anthropology,* 1392. New Delhi: Oxford University Press.

Muralidhar, S. 1998. 'India: Public Interest Litigation (Survey 1997–1998).' *Annual Survey of Indian Law (1997–98)*, No. 33–34. Available at: www.ielrc.org/content/a9802.pdf. (accessed on 18 August 2011).

Nigam, Aditya. 1997. 'Whose Delhi Is It Anyway? The Struggle against a Black Judgment', *Revolutionary Democracy*, III(1): April 1997.

——— 2001. 'Dislocating Delhi: A City in the 1990s.' *Sarai Reader 01: The Public Domain.*

——— 2014. '*Embedded Judiciary* or, the Judicial State of Exception?' In *The Shifting Scales of Justice: The Supreme Court in Neoliberal India*, edited by Mayur Suresh and Siddharth Narrain, 22–38. Delhi: Orient Black Swan.

Paudel, Shiva Prasad. 2012. 'Public Interest Litigation in Mountainous Ecosystem.' Available at: http://ceej.pk/cms/docs/SAEJ/4%20Thematic%20Session%202/5a%20Public%20Interest%20Litigation%20in%20Mountainous%20Conservation%20(Shiva%20Prasad%20Paudel).pdf. (accessed on 22 February 2013).

Prakash, R. 2001. 'Complete Justice under Article 142.' 7 *SCC (Jour)* 14. Available at: www.ebc- india.com/lawyer/articles/2001v7a3.htm. (Accessed on 11 August 2010).

Rajamani, Lavanya. 2007a. 'Public Interest Environmental Litigation in India: Exploring Issues of Access, Participation, Equity, Effectiveness and Sustainability.' *Journal of Environmental Law* 19(3): 293–321.

——— 2007b. 'The Right to Environmental Protection in India: Many a Slip between the Cup and the Lip?' *Review of European Community and International Environmental Law* 16(3): 274–86.

Ramanathan, Usha. 2002a. 'Of Judicial Power.' *Frontline* 19(6), 6–29 March. Available at: http://www.flonnet.com/fl1906/19060300.htm (accessed on 27 March 2013).

——— 2002b. *Judicial Activism in India: Transgressing Borders and Enforcing Limits,* review by S. P. Sathe. New Delhi: Oxford University Press, *Seminar* 512, April. Available at http://www.india-seminar.com/2002/512/512%20 books.htm.

——— 2004. 'Illegality and Exclusion: Law in the Lives of Slum Dwellers.' IELRC Working Paper, 2.

——— 2005. 'Demolition Drive.' *Economic and Political Weekly* 2908–12.

——— 2006. 'Illegality and the Urban Poor.' *Economic and Political Weekly* 41(29): 3193–97, 22–28 July.

——— 2008. 'Ostensible Poverty, Beggary and the Law.' *Economic and Political Weekly* 33–44.

——— 2014. 'In the Name of the People: The Expansion of Judicial Power', In *The Shifting Scales of Justice: The Supreme Court in Neoliberal India*, eds. Mayur Suresh and Siddharth Narrain (eds), New Delhi : Orient Blackswan, pp. 39–58.

Ranjan, Brajesh. 'Supreme Court of India and the Jurisprudence of Delay.' *SSRN 2830898* (2016).

Razzaque, Joan. 2009. *Public Interest Environmental Litigation in India, Pakistan and Bangladesh.* Austin: Wolters Kluwer.

Rheinstein, Max. ed. 1954. *Max Weber on Law in Economy and Society.* New York: Simon and Schuster.

Robinson, Nick. 2009. 'Expanding Judiciaries: India and the Rise of the Good Governance Court.' *Washington University Global Studies Law Review* 8: 1.

——— 'Hard to Reach.' *Frontline*, 30 January–12 February 2010. Available at: www.hindu.com/thehindu/thscrip /print.pl?file=20100212270304600.htm&date=fl 2703/&prd=fline&. (Accessed on 17 November 2010).

Robinson, Nick. 2015. 'Leading the Court.' 18 July 2010. Available at: http://casi.ssc.upenn.edu/iit/robinson (accessed on 15 June 2015).

Robinson, Nick, Robinson, Nick, Anjana Agarwal, Vrinda Bhandari, Ankit Goel, Karishma Kakkar, Reeba Muthalaly, Vivek Shivakumar, Meera Sreekumar, Surya Sreenivasan, and Shruti Viswanathan. 2011. 'Interpreting the Constitution: Indian Supreme Court Constitution Benches Since Independence.' *Economic & Political Weekly*. 46(9).

Rosencranz, Armin, Edward Boenig and Brinda Dutta. 2007. 'The *Godavarman* Case: The Indian Supreme Court's Breach of Constitutional Boundaries in Managing India's Forests.' *Environmental Law Reporter News and Analysis* 37(1): 10032–42.

Rosencranz, Armin and Michael Jackson. 2003. 'The Delhi Pollution Case: The Supreme Court of India and the Limits of Judicial Power.' *Columbia Journal of Environmental Law* (28): 15.

Roy, Arundhati. 'Scandal in the Palace.' *Outlook*, 1 October. Available at: http://www.outlookindia.com/article.aspx?235689 (accessed on 21 February 2013).

Roy, Dunu. 2004. *Pollution, Pushta, and Prejudices*. Delhi: Hazards Centre.

Rudolph, Lloyd I. and Susanne Hoeber Rudolph. 1987. *In Pursuit of Lakshmi: The Political Economy of the Indian State*. Delhi: Orient Longman.

——— 2008. 'Judicial Review versus Parliamentary Sovereignty: The Struggle over Stateness in India.' In *Explaining Indian Democracy: A Fifty-Year Perspective, 1956–2006*, 183–210. New Delhi: Oxford University Press.

Scheppele, Kim Lane. 2004. 'Constitutional Ethnography: An Introduction.' Law and Society Review 38: 89–148.

Scott, David. 2004. *Conscripts of Modernity: The Tragedy of Colonial Enlightenment*. Durham, NC: Duke University Press.

Seervai, H.M. 1994. 'Constitutional Law of India,' 4th ed. Vol. 1. Mumbai: NM Tripathi.

Sethi, Aman. 2012. *A Free Man*. 2012. New Delhi: Vintage/Random House India.

Sharan, Awadhendra. 2005. 'New Delhi: Fashioning an Urban Environment through Science and Law.' In *Sarai Reader 5: Bare Acts*. Monica Narula, Shuddhabrata Sengupta, Jeebesh Bagchi, Geert Lovink and Lawrence Liang, eds. pp. 69–77.

——— 2014. In the City, Out of Place: Nuisance, Pollution, and Dwelling in Delhi, C. 1850–2000. New Delhi: Oxford University Press.

Singh, Parmanand. 1981–82. 'Access to Justice: Public Interest Litigation and the Indian Supreme Court.' *Delhi Law Review* 10–11: 156–73.

Singh, Sandeep. 2006. 'Delhi: Demolitions and Sealings.' *Outlook* 20 September. Available at: http://www.outlookindia.com/article.aspx?232582. (accessed on 3rd February 2011).

Sudershan, V. 2000. 'In Defence of Judicial Activism.' *Frontline* 17(25): 9–22, December, Available at: http://www.frontline.in/static/html/fl1725/17250160.htm. (accessed on 12 December 2012).

Suresh, Mayur and Siddharth Narrain, eds. 2014. 'The Shifting Scales of Justice: The Supreme Court in Neoliberal India.' New Delhi: Orient Blackswan.

Tarlo, Emma. 2003. *Unsettled Memories: Narratives of India's Emergency.* Delhi: Permanent Black.

Thiruvengadam, K. Arun.2009. 'Evaluating Contemporary Criticisms of "Public Interest Litigation": A Progressive Conception of the Role of a Judge.' Paper presented at the 2009 Inaugural LASSNET Conference, New Delhi.

——— 2014. 'Swallowing a Bitter PIL? Brief reflections on Public Interest Litigation in India.' In *The Sliding Scales of Justice: The Supreme Court in Neo-liberal India*, edited by Mayur Suresh and Siddharth Narrain, 121–40. Orient Blackswan.

Thompson, E.P. 1975. *Whigs and Hunters: The Origin of the Black Act.* London: Allen Lane.

Trubek, David M. 1972. 'Max Weber on Law and the Rise of Capitalism.' *Wisconsin Law Review* 720.

Tulzapurkar, Justice V.D. 1983. 'Judiciary: Attacks and Survival.' *AIR Journal* 9–15.

Vandenhole, Wouter. 2002. 'Human Rights Law, Development, and Social Action Litigation in India.' *Asia Pacific Journal on Human Rights and the Law* 3(2): 136–210.

Venkatesan, J. and P. Sunderarajan. 2010. 'Panchayati Justice that Takes away Legal Rights of Muslims: Rajeev Dhavan.' *The Hindu*, Friday, 1 October. Available at: http://www.hindu.com/2010/10/01/stories/2010100163791500.htm (accessed on 19 December 2010).

Verma, Gita Dewan. 2002. *Slumming India: A Chronicle of Slums and their Saviours.* New Delhi: Penguin Books India.

——— (n.d.). 'Yamuna and Pushta: Tragedy of Governance', Available at http://www.architexturez.net/pst/99ffbe76-b412-4e33-a0a7-612bef8e6dfd (accessed on 10 March 2013).

Index